KITCHEN GLASSWARE

SIXTH EDITION

of the Depression Years

IDENTIFICATION & VALUES

GENE FLORENCE

COLLECTOR BOOKS
A Division of Schroeder Publishing Co., Inc.

The current values in this book should be used only as a guide. They are not intended to set prices, which vary from one section of the country to another. Auction prices as well as dealer prices vary greatly and are affected by condition and demand. Neither the author nor the publisher assumes responsibility for any losses which might be incurred as a result of consulting this guide.

Cover design: Beth Summers
Book layout: Holly C. Long

Searching For A Publisher?

We are always looking for people knowledgeable within their fields. If you feel that there is a real need for a book on your collectible subject and have a large comprehensive collection, contact Collector Books.

Collector Books

P.O. Box 3009

Paducah, KY 42002-3009

www.collectorbooks.com

Copyright © 2001 by Gene Florence
Values updated, 2003

Contents

About the Author

Gene Florence, born in Lexington, Kentucky, in 1944, graduated from the University of Kentucky where he held a double major in mathematics and English. He taught nine years in Kentucky at the junior high and high school levels before his glass collecting "hobby" became his full-time job.

Mr. Florence has been interested in "collecting" since childhood, beginning with baseball cards and progressing through comic books, coins, bottles, and finally, glassware. He first became interested in Depression Glass after buying a large set of pink Sharon dinnerware at a garage sale for $5.00.

By the time this book is published, he will have written over seventy books, at least sixty of them on glassware. Titles include the following: *Collector's Encyclopedia of Depression Glass*, in its fifteenth edition; *Collectible Glassware from the 40s, 50s, 60s* now in its sixth edition; *Elegant Glassware of the Depression Era*, now in its ninth edition; *Collector's Encyclopedia of Akro Agate; Glass Candlesticks of the Depression Era;* 2 volumes of *Pattern Identification;* 2 editions of *Anchor Hocking's Fire-King and More; Very Rare Glassware of the Depression Years,* (First through Sixth Series); *The Collector's Encyclopedia of Occupied Japan*, Volumes I through VI; and the *Pocket Guide to Depression Glass*, now in its twelfth edition. He also wrote six editions of an innovative *Standard Baseball Card Price Guide* and two volumes about Degenhart Collectibles.

If you know of any unlisted or unusual pieces of kitchen glassware like the examples shown in this book, you may write Mr. Florence at Box 22186, Lexington, KY 40522 or Box 64, Astatula, FL 34705. If you would like a reply, you must enclose a self-addressed, stamped envelope — and be patient. The volume of mail and e-mail from his web page (www.geneflorence.com) has begun to escalate alarmingly. He still answers mail when time permits, but much of the year is spent writing, traveling, and doing research.

Acknowledgments

A period of seven years to re-evaluate the field of kitchenware is arguably too long a time, but finding glassware not already covered in previous books was a decided chore.

Many people assisted with this book by lending glass for photography on various occasions. Here and there, pieces were slowly gathered for these pages. Photographers Richard Walker of New York and Charles Lynch of Kentucky took the pictures.

Thanks to the following for lending glass, sending pricing information or helping in photography: Dan and Geri Tucker, Terry and Celia McDuffee, Dick and Pat Spencer, Edna Barnes, Ron Holmes, Dan DePlanche, Zibby Walker, Jane White, and numerous collectors who have written me or shared information via the Internet or at shows. I want to especially acknowledge Lorrie Kitchen, who not only helped price but spent extra hours coordinating item prices that appear in more than one place in the book — no small chore! I am grateful to the editorial crew of Collector Books, Holly Long in particular, who helped put this book together. All of us have attempted to make this book the finest in its field.

Profound thanks are always due my family, Cathy, Marc, Chad, and Charles and Sibyl Gaines. They have weathered the myriad ordeals involved in writing books — the packing, travel, shows, and deadlines. Truly, I could never handle the sheer volume of work entailed in this business without their support.

I need, also, to acknowledge you, the reader/collector, whose financial support of my past books has made this one possible!

Foreword

In the seven years since I wrote the fifth *Kitchen Glassware of the Depression Years,* I have been asked repeatedly, "When is the next book coming out?" Assembling merchandise for a new book is more like collecting than you think. Availability of older kitchenware, or the lack thereof, has been the primary concern. Choice items for new pictures have been few and far between. We have added an additional 32 pages (with some new categories) in order to show as much new material as possible. This sixth book is a compilation of items from earlier books so that, now, over 5,000 pieces of kitchenware are included and priced!

Since I have observed that more collectors gather patterns or pieces made by a certain company, companies and patterns are the first listings in this book with colorations and items following. I'm aware this format causes some overlapping of pieces and information, but it seemed the most user-friendly system to help collectors to find items.

As with most collectibles, there are numerous pieces of kitchenware found over and over, and some equally hard-to-find items which show up infrequently. Exceptional pieces have been bought by fervent collectors and until those particular collections are resold, many rarely found items will not be offered to the market again at any price. It takes patience as well as cash to collect kitchenware. One of the joys is finding that specific piece that you have been pursuing for a long time. Many collectors have written or stopped by my booth at shows to express to me the genuine pleasure they have received from both collecting and learning about glass! So, enjoy! I hope you'll find all this effort was worthwhile!

Pricing

All prices in this book are retail prices for mint condition glassware. This book is intended to be only a guide to prices. A price range has been given for kitchenware items to allow for some wear and a little roughness that is normally not acceptable in collecting other forms of glass. The roughness or usage marks found on kitchenware is a turn-off to some few collectors who search for perfection. Remember, these were utilitarian items and most were in use for years; therefore, most kitchenware collectors will tolerate some evidence of use. This does not mean cracks, chips or chunks are acceptable. To the contrary, these greatly reduce the value of a piece. It simply means that kitchenware collectors are a little more tolerant about the condition of their glassware than are collectors of Depression dinnerware. They almost have to be because most of the kitchenware does not exist in absolutely mint condition! You might note that the price range has been expanded in several areas, but principally in reamer and measuring cup collecting.

I have received pricing ideas from several dealers and collectors and the range of those prices was staggering. The advent of Internet auctions has created some unheard of valuations that seem out of line with what is being asked at shows. Obviously, many of those Internet bidders have never been to a Depression Glass show to see this pricing. For the prices herein, I take the brunt of any pricing discord from collectors and dealers alike. However, I want you to know that the only rule in pricing is determined by two people, the buyer and the seller. You, ultimately, have to decide if the price is right for you.

I have seen both higher and lower prices for most items shown; however, the prices listed here are prices that collectors somewhere in the country have been willing to pay. These are "real" prices — not "hoped for" prices.

Colors

Any time the word "green" or "pink" occurs, it means a transparent (see-through) color. Other color items are described below.

Amethyst – a transparent, violet color.

Black Amethyst – color appears black but will show purple under a strong light.

Blue – "Chalaine," an opaque, sky blue made by McKee; "Cobalt," a transparent, dark blue; "Delphite," an opaque, medium blue made by Jeannette.

Clambroth – translucent off-white or translucent green.

Custard – an opaque beige.

Green – "Jade-ite," an opaque green made by Hocking; "Jadite," an opaque green made by Jeannette; "Skokie," an opaque green made by McKee.

White – milk white; milk glass; opal white (all these terms simply indicate a white color); "Vitrock," a white made by Hocking.

Yellow– vaseline, a transparent greenish-yellow; "Seville" yellow, an opaque yellow made by McKee.

PART 1 – COMPANIES & PATTERNS
Anchor Hocking

Page 7 Sapphire Blue Ovenware

Baker, 1 pt., round or square	6.00 – 8.00	Cup, 8 oz measuring, 3 spout	28.00 – 32.00
Baker, 1 qt.	10.00 – 12.00	Custard cup, 5 oz.	4.00 – 5.00
Baker, 1½ qt.	14.00 – 16.00	Custard cup, 6 oz., 2 styles	4.00 – 5.00
Baker, 2 qt.	14.00 – 16.00	Loaf pan, 9⅛" deep	25.00 – 30.00
Bowl, 5⅜", cereal or deep dish pie plate	20.00 – 22.00	Nurser, 4 oz.	18.00 – 20.00
		Nurser, 8 oz.	30.00 – 35.00
Bowl, 4⅜", individual pie plate	20.00 – 22.00	Pie plate, 8⅜"	8.00 – 10.00
Bowl, 16 oz. measuring, 2 spout	28.00 – 32.00	Pie plate, 9"	9.00 – 10.00
Cake pan (deep), 8¾"	40.00 – 45.00	Pie plate, 9⅝"	8.00 – 10.00
Casserole, 1 pt., knob handle cover	12.00 – 14.00	Pie plate, 10⅜", w/juice saver rim	110.00 – 125.00
Same, 1 qt.	16.00 – 18.00	Percolator top, 2⅛"	4.00 – 5.00
Same, 1½ qt.	20.00 – 22.00	Refrigerator jar & cover, 4½" x 5"	12.00 – 15.00
Same, 2 qt.	20.00 – 22.00	Same, 5⅛" x 9⅛"	30.00 – 32.50
Casserole, individual, 10 oz.	11.00 – 13.00	Roaster, 8¾"	50.00 – 55.00
Casserole, 1 qt., pie plate cover	16.00 – 18.00	Roaster, 10⅜"	70.00 – 80.00
Same, 1½ qt.	18.00 – 20.00	Table server, tab handles (hot plate)	20.00 – 22.00
Same, 2 qt.	22.00 – 25.00	Utility bowl, 6⅞"	16.00 – 18.00
Coffee mug, 7 oz., 2 styles	25.00 – 28.00	Utility bowl, 8⅜"	18.00 – 20.00
Cup, 8 oz., dry measure, no spout	850.00 – 900.00	Utility bowl, 10⅛"	20.00 – 22.00
Cup, 8 oz. measuring, 1 spout	25.00 – 28.00	Utility pan, 8⅛" x 12½"	90.00 – 100.00

Page 8

Row 1: #1 "Swedish Modern," "Turquoise Blue" 8⅜" mixing bowl, 3 qt.   55.00 – 60.00
    #2 Same, 7¼" 2 qt.   30.00 – 35.00
    #3 Same, 6", 1 qt.   30.00 – 35.00
    #4 Same, 5", 1 pt. (not shown)   25.00 – 30.00
Row 2: "Splash Proof," "Turquoise Blue,"
    #1 Mixing bowl, 8½", 3 qt.   22.00 – 24.00
    #2 Same, 7½", 2 qt.   22.00 – 24.00
    #3 Same, 6½", 1 qt.   18.00 – 20.00
Row 3: #1 "Splash Proof," "Fruit," 9½" mixing bowl, 4 qt.   65.00 – 75.00
    #2 Same, 8½", 3 qt.   65.00 – 75.00
    #3 Same, 7½", 2 qt.   65.00 – 75.00
    #4 Same, 6½", 1 qt. (not shown) 85.00 –95.00

Row 4: #1 "Ivory" 9⅛" deep loaf pan   12.00 – 15.00
    #2 Same, 6 oz. individual baker   4.00 – 5.00
    #3 Same, 9" cake pan   12.00 – 15.00
    #4 Same, 10½" x 6½" baking pan   16.00 – 18.00
Row 5: #1 Jade-ite juice saver pie plate, 10⅜"   325.00 – 350.00
    #2 Mug w/design on outside (no design $20.00 – 25.00) 100.00 – 125.00
    #3 Jade-ite mixing bowl, 8"   25.00 – 28.00
    Same, 9" (not shown)   28.00 – 30.00
    #4 Same, 7"   22.00 – 25.00
    Same, 6" (not shown)   25.00 – 28.00

Page 9

Row 1: #1 "Modern Tulip" 3 qt. mixing bowl   18.00 – 20.00
    #2 Same, 4 qt.   20.00 – 22.50
    #3 Same, 2 qt.   18.00 – 20.00
    #4 Same, 1 qt.   20.00 – 22.50
Row 2: #1,3 "Modern Tulip" salt and pepper pr.   40.00 – 45.00
    #2,5 "Modern Tulip" or Apples and Cherries grease jar   30.00 – 35.00
    #4 "Kitchen Aids" 2 qt., Spags mixing bowl   75.00 – 90.00
Row 3: #1 Basket weave 4" bowl   18.00 – 20.00

Row 3 (Continued):
    #2 Chanticleer 1 qt. mix bowl   12.50 – 15.00
    #3 Same, 2½ qt.   18.00 – 20.00
Row 4: #1 "Tulips" bowl, 9½"   27.50 – 30.00
    #2 Same, 8½"   25.00 – 27.50
    #3 Same, 7½"   20.00 – 22.50
Row 5: #1 Same, 6½"   20.00 – 22.50
    #2 Same, grease jar   25.00 – 30.00
    #3 Same, shaker   32.50 – 35.00
    #4 Batter bowl, "Fruits" (peaches, grapes, and pears)   200.00 – 225.00

Gay Fad Studios (a decorating company in Lancaster, Ohio) had a "Peach Blossom" pattern shown in their 1954 – 1955 catalog. It has been called "Dogwood" and "Apple Blossom" in the past. Peach blossoms have five petals; dogwood and apple blossoms, only four. "Peach Blossom" can be found on Federal and Hazel-Atlas glass. All lids are crystal unless otherwise noted.

Page 11

	Fruits	Peach Blossom
Baking dish, 11¾" , divided	30.00 – 35.00	——
Baking pan, 6½" x 10½"	30.00 – 35.00	25.00 – 30.00
Batter bowl, handled w/spout	200.00 – 225.00	——
Bowl, 5", cereal, straight side	12.50 – 15.00	——
Bowl, 5", chili	12.50 – 15.00	10.00 – 12.00
Casserole, 1 pt.	25.00 – 30.00	25.00 – 30.00
Casserole, 1 qt.	25.00 – 30.00	25.00 – 30.00
Casserole, 1 qt., tab handles, white lid	40.00 – 45.00	40.00 – 45.00
Casserole, 12 oz., French, handled	*10.00 – 12.00	15.00 – 20.00
Casserole, 1½ qt.	30.00 – 35.00	20.00 – 25.00
Casserole, 1½ qt., oval, au gratin lid	35.00 – 40.00	25.00 – 30.00
Casserole, 1½ qt., oval, au gratin white lid	——	40.00 – 45.00
Casserole, 2 qt.	30.00 – 35.00	25.00 – 30.00
Creamer, stacking	20.00 – 25.00	——
Custard, 5 oz.	8.00 – 10.00	6.00 – 8.00
Custard, 6 oz.	8.00 – 10.00	6.00 – 8.00
Grease jar	100.00 – 125.00	——
Loaf pan, 5" x 9", deep	25.00 – 30.00	10.00 – 25.00
Mixing bowl, 2 qt., w/gold leaf, FEDERAL	——	15.00 – 20.00
Mixing bowl, 3 qt., w/gold leaf, FEDERAL	—	15.00 – 20.00
Mixing bowl, Colonial Kitchen, 6"	12.50 – 15.00	14.00 – 16.00
Mixing bowl, Colonial Kitchen, 7³⁄₁₆"	14.00 – 16.00	16.00 – 18.00
Mixing bowl, Colonial Kitchen, 8¾"	16.00 – 18.00	18.00 – 20.00
Mixing bowl, Splash Proof, 1 qt.	85.00 – 95.00	——
Mixing bowl, Splash Proof, 2 qt.	65.00 – 75.00	——
Mixing bowl, Splash Proof, 3 qt.	65.00 – 75.00	——
Mixing bowl, Splash Proof, 4 qt.	65.00 – 75.00	——
Mixing bowl, tab handled, 1 qt.	60.00 – 65.00	——
Mixing bowl, tab handled, 1½ qt.	45.00 – 50.00	——
Mixing bowl, tab handled, 2½ qt.	50.00 – 55.00	——
Mug, 8 oz.	8.00 – 10.00	10.00 – 12.00
Mug, 8 oz., stacking	12.50 – 15.00	——
Pan, cake, 8" x 8", square	25.00 – 30.00	25.00 – 30.00
Refrigerator, 4" x 4", square	12.50 – 15.00	12.50 – 15.00
Refrigerator, 4" x 8", rectangular	15.00 – 18.00	15.00 – 18.00
Refrigerator, 4¼", round, "star burst" lid	——	20.00 – 25.00
Refrigerator, 4¼", x 9", oval, "star burst" lid	——	30.00 – 35.00
Relish, 13", 3-part, Lace Edge	75.00 – 80.00	——
Sugar, stacking	20.00 – 25.00	——

* Banana 60.00 – 65.00   Purple grape 12.50 – 15.00   Orange slice, green grape 15.00 – 18.00

Fry Glassware Co.

Page 13

Row 1:	#1	Reamer, fluted, jello mold, "Canary"	350.00 – 375.00
	#2	Meat loaf w/lid, rectangular, 9"	85.00 – 95.00
	#3	Reamer, straight side	375.00 – 395.00
Row 2:	#1	Grill plate, 8½", "Rose"	30.00 – 35.00
	#2	Same, "Azure" blue	45.00 – 55.00
	#3	Measure cup, 3 spout, "Pearl"	85.00 – 95.00
	#4	Bean pot w/lid, 1 pt.	95.00 – 110.00
Row 3:	#1	Grill plate, 10½", "Rose"	40.00 – 45.00
	#2	Measure cup, 1 spout	85.00 – 95.00
	#3	Grill plate, 10½", "Pearl" w/blue trim	45.00 – 50.00
Row 4:	#1	Same, w/orange enamel trim	45.00 – 50.00
	#2	Reamer, straight side, "Azure" blue	1,800.00 – 2,000.00

Row 4	(Continued):		
	#3	Same as #1, "Royal" blue	75.00 – 85.00
Row 5:	#1	Meat platter, 13", green, "Not Heat Resisting Glass"	125.00 – 135.00
	#2	Percolator top w/blue finial	40.00 – 45.00
	#3	Snack plate, 6" x 9", w/cup "Royal" blue	95.00 – 110.00
Row 6:	#1	Same as Row 5 #1, 17"	125.00 – 145.00
	#2	Percolator top w/green finial	35.00 – 40.00
	#3	Casserole, oval, 7", w/green trim	100.00 – 125.00

Page 14

Row 1:	#1	Domed roaster (1946-14) 14" x 10" x 7½"	200.00 – 225.00
Row 2:	#1	Same as #1 but in metal holder. Paper label reads: "This is a 'ROYALLOY' Steel Frame. Dry thoroughly after using and it will serve you well and long."	210.00 – 235.00

Row 3:		Sunnybrook Cookie Jar (Introduced at $0.57; original price $0.75)	
	#1	"Royal" blue	275.00 – 300.00
	#2	Green	225.00 – 250.00
	#3	"Rose"	225.00 – 250.00
	#4	Black	275.00 – 300.00

Page 15

Row 1:	#1	Bean pot w/lid, 1 qt. in holder	125.00 – 135.00
	#2	Cream soup, 5¼", ftd.	60.00 – 65.00
	#3	Casserole w/lid, 8" round, in holder	35.00 – 40.00
Row 2:	#1	Casserole, oval, 10" w/green finial	125.00 – 135.00
	#2	Sundae glass "MACO-MFG-CO, VAPOR-RITE, MAY-WOOD-ILL	55.00 – 60.00
	#3	Oval platter, 9" x 13"	40.00 – 45.00
Row 3:	#1	Casserole, 6" round	35.00 – 40.00
	#2	Baker, 6" round	30.00 – 35.00
	#3	Cocotte, 5" (for indiv. meat, chicken, oyster pies)	25.00 – 30.00
	#4	Same, 4"	25.00 – 30.00
	#5	Custard cup, 4½ oz.	20.00 – 25.00
Row 4:	#1	Snack plate, 6" x 9" w/cup	45.00 – 50.00

Row 4 (Continued):			
	#2	Mushroom baker/round shirred egg, 6"	135.00 – 145.00
	#3	Baker, oval, 6"	35.00 – 38.00
	#4	Apple baker or custard, 4¾"	35.00 – 38.00
Row 5:	#1	Butter pat (?) "Fry's Heat Resisting Glass"	10.00 – 12.00
	#2	Ramekin, 3"	15.00 – 18.00
	#3,4 & 7	Custard cup, 4 or 6 oz. (1927 or 1936), ea.	10.00 – 12.00
	#5,6	Custard cup, 6 oz., engraved (1927 or 1936), ea.	10.00 – 12.00
Row 6:	#1	Casserole, 7" round, engraved w/blue finial	125.00 – 135.00
	#2,3	Ramekin "Pearl" or "Lime glass," ea.	15.00 – 18.00
	#4	Oval server, 8 sided, engraved, 6½" x 9"/holder	65.00 – 75.00

The opalescent white color most people are familiar with was called "Pearl" by the factory. Decorated pieces are more desirable than the regular issues.

All colors are rarer than the "Pearl" with both blue shades ("Azure" {light} and "Royal" {cobalt}) the most in demand. Fry glass without an opalescent effect is called "lime glass." According to avid Fry collectors, ovenware condition is not as important as obtaining an important addition to a collection.

All dates or numbers listed are marked on the piece.

The antique business is a conduit to meeting many interesting collectors from all over the country. Most people in all collecting fields are more than willing to share glass and information. That is one of the more rewarding aspects of writing. I hope you gain knowledge to help your collecting from the long hours spent compiling this.

Row 5 on page 17 consists of a child's set that was sold for $2.50 in 1922. It was called "Little Mother's Kidibake Set" and now sells for $300.00.

Page 17

Row 1:	#1	Casserole w/lid, 7" square, in holder	85.00 – 95.00
	#2	Baker, pudding, 2⅛" x 6⅜"	35.00 – 40.00
	#3	Casserole w/lid, 8" oval, engraved in holder	45.00 – 55.00
Row 2:	#1	Brown betty, 9"	55.00 – 65.00
	#2	Casserole w/lid, 7" round, engraved side & lid	55.00 – 65.00
		Trivet, 8", under casserole	25.00 – 30.00
	#3	Shirred egg, 7½", round	30.00 – 35.00
Row 3:	#1	Vegetable dish, 2 part, 9¾"	42.00 – 48.00
	#2	Fish platter, 11", engraved	45.00 – 50.00
	#3	Pie plate, 9½", engraved, in holder	45.00 – 50.00
Row 4:	#1	Cake, 9" round	30.00 – 38.00
	#2	Cup and saucer, No. 1969	45.00 – 48.00
	#3	Pie plate, 10", in metal holder	40.00 – 45.00
Row 5: Child's toy set			
	#1	Pie plate, 5"	70.00 – 75.00
	#2	Casserole w/lid, 4½" round	85.00 – 95.00
	#3,4	Ramekin, 2½", ea.	25.00 – 30.00
	#5	Bread baker, 5"	85.00 – 95.00
Row 6:	#1	Fish platter, 17", engraved	75.00 – 85.00
	#2	Casserole w/lid, 7" round, embossed w/grapes	55.00 – 65.00

Hazel-Atlas Glass Co. ════════

Collectors were first attracted to "Crisscross" because of the blue color. Now there are advocates for all colors, including crystal. Crystal is often mixed with one of the other colors for a more varied appearance. Crystal prices have soared since the last book while the other colors have risen more slowly.

There are no new discoveries in this pattern, but the $5^1/_2$" round bowl shown on page 21 is the piece presently eluding everyone. I have found a green lid, but no bottom.

Pink tumblers are elusive as are all colored sugars and creamers. No one has found a sugar and creamer in blue — yet. Nor have there been blue tumblers found to go with the pitchers. Those of you who collect other patterns of Depression era glass know how frustrating it is to collect a pattern that has a pitcher with no tumblers or vice versa.

Cobalt blue mixing bowls are just not being found! Many collectors are settling for bowls with use marks to have them at all. This has caused the prices for mint condition bowls to rise to the point that other collectors are settling for buying only the smaller mixing bowls and forgetting the two larger sizes.

One thing that confuses new collectors is the difference in the pound butter and the refrigerator dish that is like the butter. The butter has a bottom that sticks out with tabs. The top of the refrigerator dish is flush with the edges of the bottom.

Page 19, 20, 21

	Blue	Crystal	Green	Pink
Bottle, water, 32 oz.	——	35.00 – 40.00	150.00 – 165.00	——
Bottle, water, 64 oz.	——	40.00 – 45.00	165.00 – 175.00	——
Bowl, mixing set (5)	400.00 – 450.00	100.00 – 120.00	185.00 – 200.00	185.00 – 210.00
Bowl, mixing, $6^5/_8$"	50.00 – 55.00	12.00 – 15.00	25.00 – 30.00	25.00 – 30.00
Bowl, mixing, $7^5/_8$"	65.00 – 70.00	15.00 – 18.00	30.00 – 35.00	30.00 – 35.00
Bowl, mixing, $8^3/_4$"	80.00 – 90.00	22.00 – 25.00	35.00 – 40.00	35.00 – 40.00
Bowl, mixing, $9^5/_8$"	85.00 – 95.00	25.00 – 28.00	40.00 – 45.00	40.00 – 45.00
Bowl, mixing, $10^5/_8$"	120.00 – 135.00	28.00 – 32.00	55.00 – 60.00	55.00 – 60.00
Butter, $1/_4$ lb.	135.00 – 145.00	25.00 – 28.00	60.00 – 65.00	60.00 – 65.00
Butter, 1 lb.	135.00 – 145.00	25.00 – 28.00	60.00 – 65.00	60.00 – 65.00
Creamer	——	25.00 – 30.00	60.00 – 65.00	60.00 – 65.00
Food mixer (baby face)	——	85.00 – 95.00	——	——
Pitcher, 54 oz.	1,200.00 – 1,500.00	150.00 – 175.00	——	——
Reamer, lemon	——	18.00 – 22.00	40.00 – 45.00	300.00 – 345.00
Reamer, orange	300.00 – 325.00	20.00 – 25.00	35.00 – 40.00	295.00 – 325.00
Refrigerator bowl, round $5^1/_2$" w/cover	300.00 – 325.00	35.00 – 40.00	185.00 – 195.00	185.00 – 195.00
Refrigerator bowl, w/cover				
4" x 4"	42.00 – 48.00	12.00 – 15.00	30.00 – 35.00	30.00 – 35.00
4" x 8"	115.00 – 125.00	20.00 – 25.00	65.00 – 75.00	65.00 – 75.00
8" x 8"	135.00 – 145.00	25.00 – 30.00	80.00 – 85.00	80.00 – 85.00
Refrigerator dish (like butter), $3^1/_2$" x $5^3/_4$"	135.00 – 145.00	25.00 – 30.00	70.00 – 75.00	——
Sugar	——	20.00 – 25.00	40.00 – 45.00	40.00 – 45.00
Sugar lid	——	40.00 – 45.00	75.00 – 85.00	75.00 – 85.00
Tumbler, 9 oz.	——	50.00 – 60.00	——	150.00 – 175.00

"Jennyware" is popular with collectors due, in part, to the many different items that can be acquired. A major problem in collecting "Jennyware" is the variations of color occurring in ultra-marine. The greenish shade of "Jennyware" has few collectors. Dealers usually avoid buying that shade for resale. The crystal rectangular 12½" box with lid below will fetch $45.00 – 50.00.

That decanter in the top row was made by Imperial and is not a part of the "Jennyware" set. Many collectors buy it as a "go-with" item. It sells for $50.00 – 60.00.

Page 23, 24

	Crystal	Pink	Ultramarine
Bowl, mixing set (3)	90.00 – 105.00	200.00 – 225.00	200.00 – 225.00
Bowl, 10½"	35.00 – 40.00	85.00 – 95.00	85.00 – 95.00
Bowl, 8¼"	30.00 – 35.00	65.00 – 70.00	65.00 – 70.00
Bowl, 6"	25.00 – 30.00	50.00 – 60.00	50.00 – 60.00
Butter dish, deep bottom	65.00 – 75.00	175.00 – 195.00	175.00 – 195.00
Butter dish, flat bottom	——	——	250.00 – 300.00
Coaster	——	10.00 – 12.00	——
Measuring cup set (4)	150.00 – 170.00	240.00 – 260.00	240.00 – 260.00
1 cup	40.00 – 45.00	70.00 – 75.00	70.00 – 75.00
½ cup	40.00 – 45.00	60.00 – 65.00	60.00 – 65.00
⅓ cup	35.00 – 40.00	60.00 – 65.00	60.00 – 65.00
¼ cup	35.00 – 40.00	50.00 – 55.00	50.00 – 55.00
Pitcher, 36 oz.	95.00 – 110.00	150.00 – 160.00	160.00 – 170.00
Reamer	85.00 – 100.00	125.00 – 135.00	125.00 – 135.00
Refrigerator dish, 70 oz., round	30.00 – 35.00	75.00 – 85.00	75.00 – 85.00
Refrigerator dish, 32 oz., round	25.00 – 30.00	65.00 – 75.00	65.00 – 75.00
Refrigerator dish, 16 oz., round	20.00 – 25.00	55.00 – 65.00	55.00 – 65.00
Refrigerator dish, 4½" x 4½"	20.00 – 22.00	30.00 – 35.00	30.00 – 35.00
Refrigerator dish, 4½" x 9"	25.00 – 30.00	45.00 – 55.00	45.00 – 55.00
Shaker, footed, ca.	20.00 – 25.00	30.00 – 35.00	30.00 – 35.00
Shaker, flat, ea.	20.00 – 25.00	35.00 – 45.00	——
Tumbler, 8 oz.	22.00 – 25.00	45.00 – 50.00	50.00 – 55.00

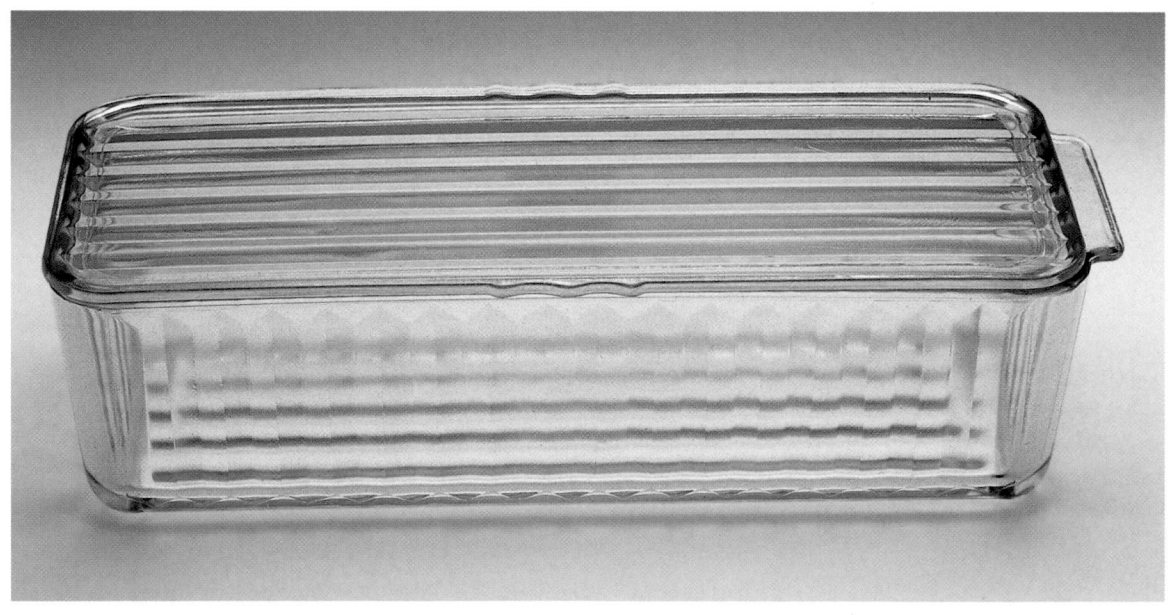

McKee Glass Company's products can be found labeled or marked with names other than the regularly seen McK. Bakeware is often marked Glasbake and stove ware is found under the auspicious Range-Tec. Both product lines competed with Anchor Hocking's Fire-King and Corning's Pyrex brands. More collectors are noticing Glasbake wares of late.

Row 1:

#1,2	Glasbake baking "chicken dish"	18.00 – 20.00
#3,	Range-Tec skillet	12.50 – 15.00

Row 2:

#1,2	Glasbake "apple" casserole w/cover	18.00 – 20.00
#3,	Glasbake white 2 qt. casserole in metal holder	20.00 – 25.00
#4,	Glasbake white w/red lettering 2 qt. measure pitcher	30.00 – 35.00

Row 3:

#1,2,4,5	Glasbake individual handled casserole wo/cover, ea.	6.00 – 8.00
#3,	Glasbake individual handled casserole w/cover, ea.	12.00 – 14.00

Notice the handle (black) on the first crystal teapot on Row 2, page 27. This handle is typical of the McKee Range-Tec line introduced in the early 1940s. These old tea kettles and coffee makers are becoming very much in vogue with present day collectors of kitchen items. Particularly desirable are the more colorful "ringed" items and the opaline or white kettles and boilers.

The "sweetheart" Safe Bake pie dish at the end of Row 4 is one of a set of five and is of more recent origin than anything else on the page. It is considered to be collectible, however, and comes in 10½" through 6½" sizes.

I can't imagine anyone actually wanting the "measles" casserole; but it was interesting enough to include as a conversation piece. That's carrying "dots" too far.

Page 27

Row 1:	#1	Double boiler, Cory	22.00 – 25.00
	#2	Coffee pot, silver rings, McKee	25.00 – 30.00
	#3	Coffee pot, pastel rings	35.00 – 40.00
Row 2:	#1	Teapot, McKee Range-tec	25.00 – 30.00
	#2	Teapot, pastel rings, Glasbake	35.00 – 40.00
	#3	5" x 4¼" dish, yellowish cast	12.00 – 15.00
	#4	Refrigerator dish, 4" x 4"	12.00 – 15.00
Row 3:	#1,2	Covered casseroles, ea.	12.00 – 15.00
	#3	3¾" deep pan, 7" x 12"	10.00 – 12.00
Row 4:	#1	Loaf pan, 3" x 5" x 10"	8.00 – 10.00
	#2	Casserole, heart shape	25.00 – 30.00
	#3	"Sweetheart" pie, Saben Glass Co. (1 of 5)	10.00 – 12.00
Row 5:	#1	Red Dot casserole, crystal	20.00 – 25.00
	#2	Red Dot custard, crystal	3.00 – 4.00
	#3,4	Measure cups, Glasbake, ea., crystal	45.00 – 65.00

Large roaster shown below, $65.00 – 70.00

Pyrex Glass Co.

The blue colored Pyrex shown at the bottom of page 29 comes in two distinct colorations, a "Delphite" shade, most often found in Canada, and a lighter "robin egg" blue shade found mostly in the northern United States.

The tab handled mixing bowls and casseroles pictured on pages 30 and 31 were called Cinderella bowls according to a 1957 *Ladies' Home Journal* advertisement. The blue and white print depicting a farmer, his mate, and a rooster was called "Butter-print" in that ad. The pieces decorated with flowering vines were called "Gooseberry."

Page 29 top

Row 1: #1   Bowl, 12", blue, square based 55.00 – 65.00
      #2   Refrigerator dish,
          4¼" x 6¾", red   135.00 – 150.00
Row 2: #1   Divided dish, blue   30.00 – 35.00
      #2   Measure cup, 16 oz., red   100.00 – 125.00
      #3   Pie plate, 10", blue   35.00 – 40.00

Creamer	12.00
Cup	5.00
Cup, demitasse	20.00
Plate, 6¼" bread and butter	3.50
Plate, 9¾" dinner	8.50
Plate, 11½" sandwich	12.00
Saucer	2.00
Saucer, demitasse	5.00
Sugar, open	10.00

Page 29 bottom

Bowl, 5¾" cereal	6.50
Bowl, 7¾" soup	9.50
Bowl, 9" vegetable	12.00

Page 30

Row 1: Gooseberry Cinderella mixing bowls
      #1,5   5¼"   4.00 – 6.00
      #2,6   6¾"   6.00 – 8.00
      #3,7   8¼"   8.00 – 10.00
      #4,8   9¾"   10.00 – 12.00
Row 2: #1   Butter-print mixing bowl, 6¾"   8.00 – 10.00
      #2   Refrigerator dish, 3½" x 4¾"   8.00 – 10.00
      #3   Refrigerator dish, 4¼" x 6¾"   10.00 – 12.00
      #4   Mixing bowl, 5¼"   6.00 – 8.00
      #5   American Heritage
          mixing bowl, 6½"   8.00 – 10.00
      #6   Same, 8½"   12.50 – 15.00

Row 3: #1   Butter-print Cinderella
          mixing bowl, 6¾"   8.00 – 10.00
      #2   Same, 8¼"   10.00 – 12.00
      #3   Same, 9¾"   12.00 – 14.00
      #4   Butter-print, 5½"   6.00 – 8.00
      #5   Butter-print Cinderella
          mixing bowl, 5¼"   4.00 – 6.00
      #6   Same, 4¼" x 6¾",
          refrigerator dish   12.50 – 15.00
      #7   Refrigerator dish, 4¼" x 6¾"   10.00 – 12.50

Page 31

Row 1: #1   Mixing bowls, 8½"   20.00 – 25.00
      #2   Same, 6½"   15.00 – 18.00
      #3   Same, 7½"   18.00 – 22.00
Row 2: These are most commonly found, but most desirable
      to collectors
      #1   Mixing bowl, yellow, 9½"   12.50 – 15.00
      #2   Same, blue, 6½"   8.00 – 10.00
      #3   Same, red, 7½"   10.00 – 12.50
      #4   Same, green, 8½"   10.00 – 12.50

Row 3: Cinderella casseroles
      #1-3   All with lid, ea.   15.00 – 20.00
Row 4: #1   Mixing bowl, 6½"   8.00 – 10.00
      #2   "Art Deco" casserole   50.00 – 60.00
      #3   "Clambroth" white oval
          casserole   100.00 – 125.00

Page 32

Row 1: Pyrex store display   90.00 – 100.00
Row 2: Pyrex boxed set of 8   40.00 – 45.00
Row 3: #1   Pyrex boxed set of 9   45.00 – 50.00
      #2   Casserole, Corning "Opening
          night at Lincoln Center," 1961
          (Scenes of NY buildings)   20.00 – 25.00

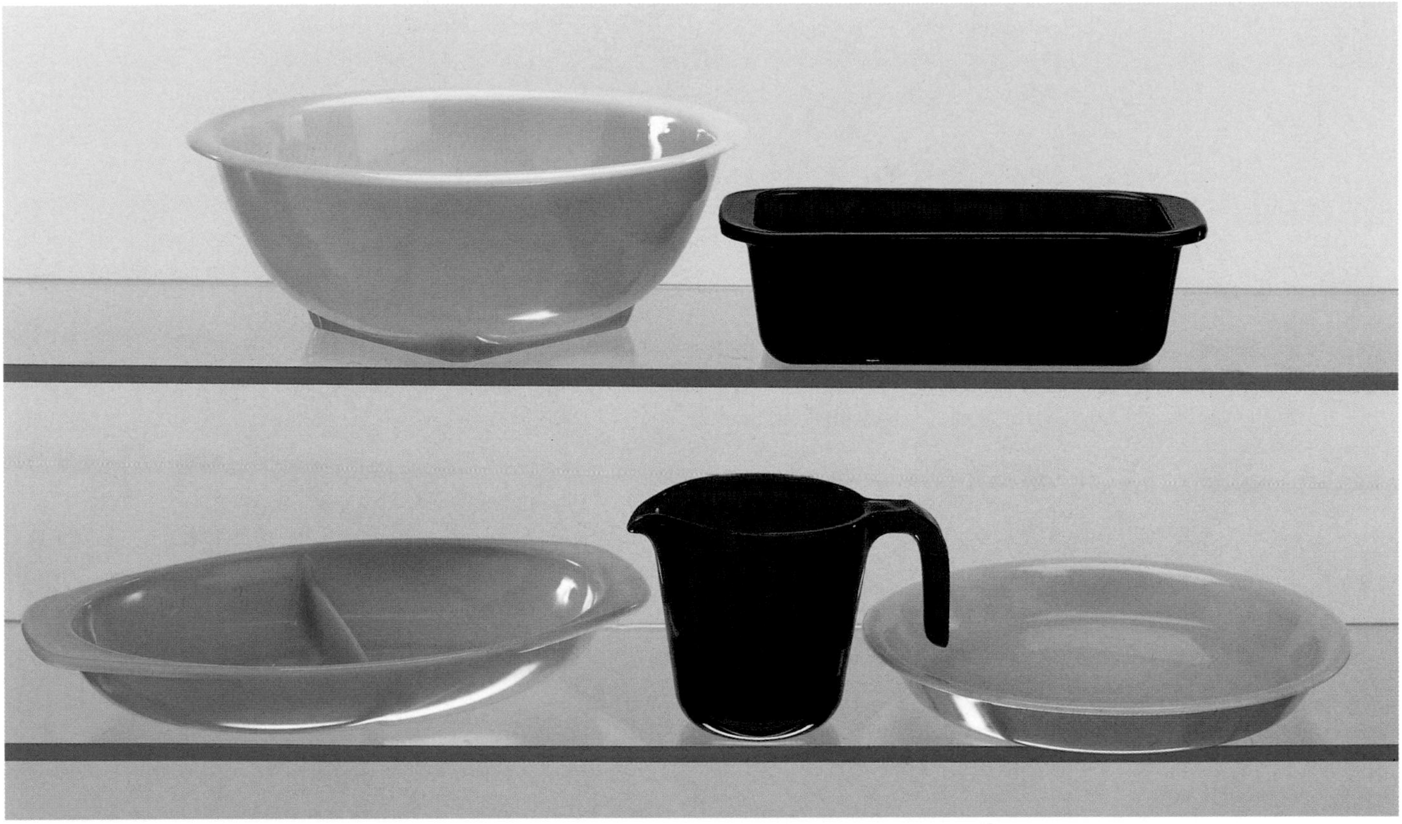

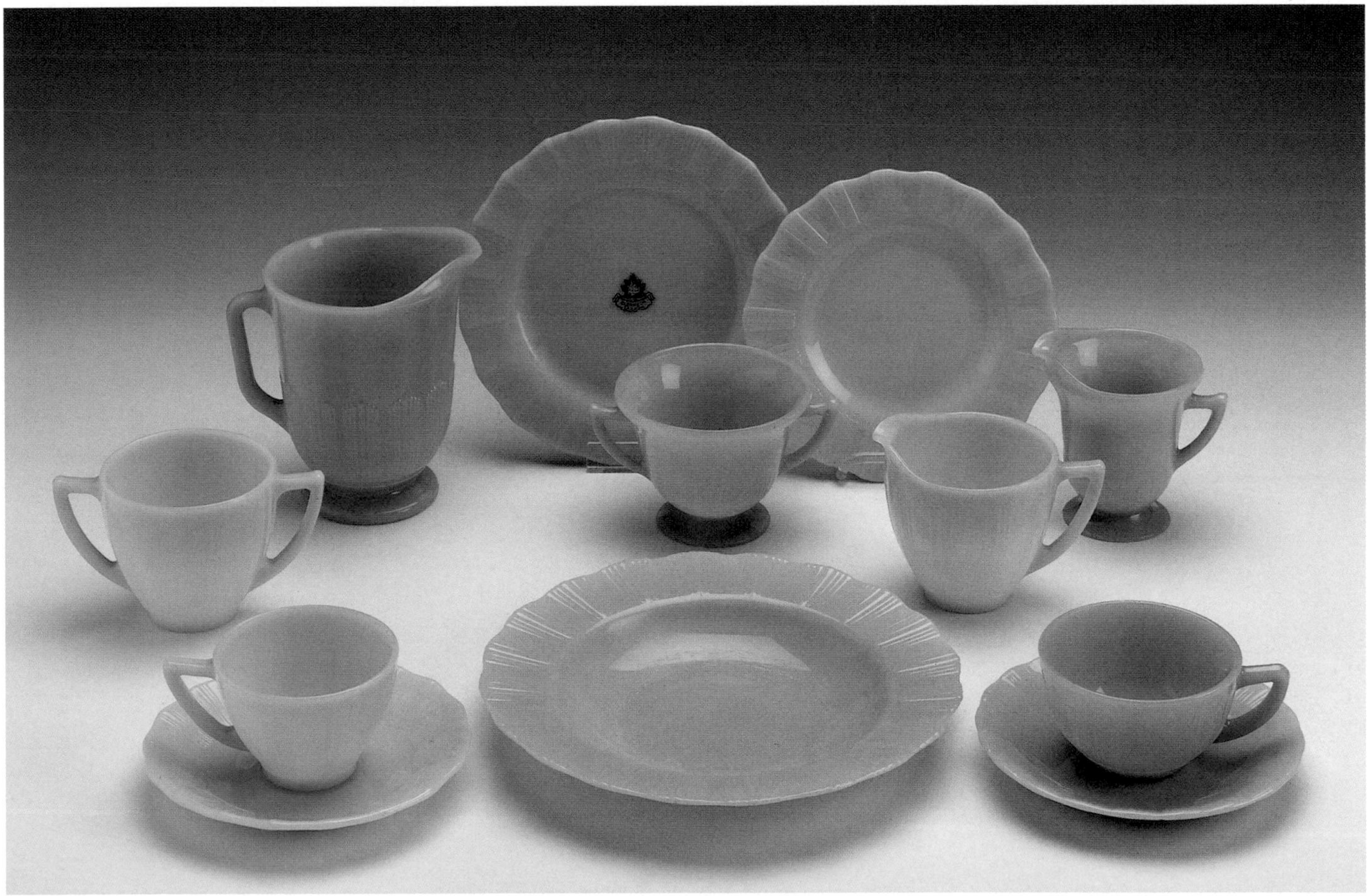

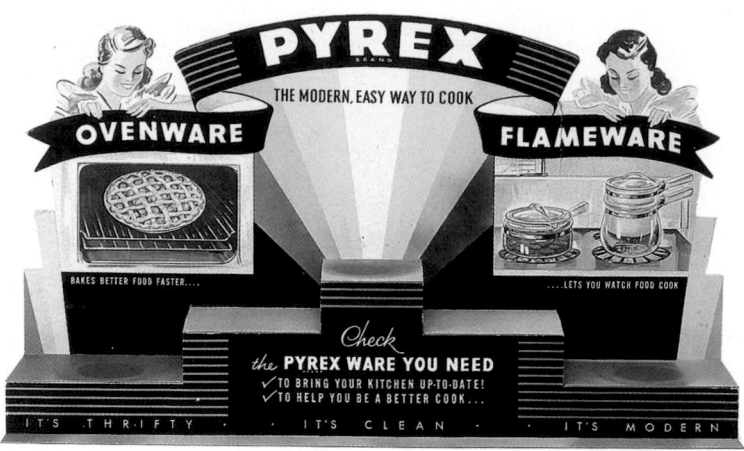

McKee issued this as a "Deluxe" line of kitchenware and sold items to merchants for the princely sums of four to twelve dollars per dozen! Collectors are searching high, low, long, and hard to find some of these dotted goodies for their kitchens. The dots, red being most popular, appear also in blue, green, black, and yellow according to data and are to be found on "white opal" or "French ivory" backgrounds. As you can tell from the picture, very little "Dots" is found in colors other than red; and the black, though attractive, is the least popular color with collectors at the moment. Perhaps black and white kitchen decor was a 1930s exclusive? Some collectors are buying blue dot pieces and incorporating them with their Delphite blue collections.

Page 34 McKee

	Red Dots on Custard	Black/Green/Blue Dots	Dots on White
Bowl, 9", scalloped edge	35.00 – 40.00	35.00 – 40.00	30.00 – 35.00
Bowl, 9" w/spout	45.00 – 55.00	35.00 – 40.00	45.00 – 55.00
Bowl, drippings	50.00 – 65.00	35.00 – 40.00	50.00 – 65.00
Bowl, egg beater w/lip	45.00 – 55.00	35.00 – 40.00	45.00 – 55.00
Butter dish	155.00 – 165.00	125.00 – 140.00	155.00 – 165.00
Canister, 48 oz., screw-on lid	225.00 – 275.00	150.00 – 165.00	225.00 – 275.00
Canister, 28 oz., screw-on lid	225.00 – 275.00	150.00 – 165.00	225.00 – 275.00
Canister & lid, round, 48 oz.	65.00 – 75.00	38.00 – 42.00	65.00 – 75.00
Canister & lid, round, 40 oz.	65.00 – 75.00	33.00 – 38.00	65.00 – 75.00
Canister & lid, round, 24 oz.	55.00 – 65.00	33.00 – 38.00	55.00 – 65.00
Canister & lid, round, 10 oz.	40.00 – 50.00	28.00 – 33.00	40.00 – 50.00
Mixing bowl, 9"	40.00 – 45.00	33.00 – 38.00	40.00 – 45.00
Mixing bowl, 8"	35.00 – 40.00	25.00 – 30.00	35.00 – 40.00
Mixing bowl, 7"	30.00 – 35.00	20.00 – 25.00	30.00 – 35.00
Mixing bowl, 6"	25.00 – 28.00	15.00 – 20.00	25.00 – 28.00
Pitcher, 2 cup	50.00 – 55.00	50.00 – 60.00	50.00 – 55.00
Refrigerator dish, 4" x 5"	35.00 – 38.00	25.00 – 28.00	35.00 – 38.00
Refrigerator dish, 5" x 8"	45.00 – 55.00	25.00 – 28.00	45.00 – 55.00
Shaker, salt or pepper, ea.	35.00 – 45.00	35.00 – 45.00	35.00 – 45.00
Shaker, flour or sugar, ea.	50.00 – 60.00	50.00 – 60.00	50.00 – 60.00

Page 35

Row 1: #1-3 McKee round canisters,
	48 oz.	65.00 – 75.00
	Same, 40 oz.	65.00 – 75.00
	Same, 24 oz.	55.00 – 65.00
#4	McKee, bowl, 9"	45.00 – 50.00
#5	McKee, 2 cup pitcher	50.00 – 55.00

Rows 2 – 4 ALL HAZEL-ATLAS

Row 2: #1 Covered round refrigerator
	bowl	35.00 – 40.00
#2	Stack set	50.00 – 60.00
#3	Pitcher, 2 cup	45.00 – 55.00
#4-6	Tumblers, 10 oz. ea.	8.00 – 10.00

Row 3: Mixing bowl, set (5) 130.00 – 152.00
| | 9" (shown in Row 4) | 35.00 – 40.00 |
| #1 | 8" | 30.00 – 35.00 |

Row 3 (Continued):
	7" (not shown)	25.00 – 30.00
#2	6"	22.00 – 25.00
#3,5,6	Shaker, salt, pepper or flour, ea.	40.00 – 50.00
	5" (shown in Row 4)	18.00 – 22.00
#4	Drippings bowl w/cover	60.00 – 70.00

Row 4: #1-3 Mixing bowls (priced in Row 3)
| #4 | Butter dish | 150.00 – 165.00 |

Row 5: #1,6 Hocking mixing bowls, 2 qt. 20.00 – 22.50
	9½", 4 qt.	27.50 – 30.00
	8½", 3 qt.	25.00 – 27.50
	6¾" (not shown)	20.00 – 22.50
#2,4	Shakers (black dots), ea.	30.00 – 35.00
#5,7	Shakers (red dot), ea.	40.00 – 45.00
#3	Grease jar	40.00 – 45.00

Dutch and Ships

Page 37

Rows 1-2: **Hazel-Atlas "Skating Dutch"**

Row 1:	#1	One piece stack set	35.00 – 40.00
	#2	Three piece stack set	65.00 – 75.00
	#3	Mixing bowl, 9"	30.00 – 35.00
	#4	Same, 8"	28.00 – 30.00
Row 2:	#1	Same, 7"	22.00 – 28.00
	#2	Same, 6"	22.00 – 28.00
	#3	Same, 5"	15.00 – 20.00
	#4	Cereal bowl, 5"	15.00 – 20.00
	#5	Salt and pepper pr.	50.00 – 55.00

Row 3:	#1	Dutch/tulips/windmills, 9" mixing bowl	30.00 – 35.00
	#2	Same, 8"	28.00 – 30.00
	#3	Same, 7"	22.00 – 28.00
	#4	Same, 6"	22.00 – 28.00
Row 4:	#1	Same, 5"	15.00 – 20.00
	#2	Fired-on Dutch set w/holder, 3"	100.00 – 120.00
	#3	Same set, 4"	120.00 – 140.00

Page 38 Miscellaneous

Row 1:	#1	Jadite, 9¾" bowl, w/windmills	125.00 – 135.00
	#2, 3	Hocking canister w/Dutch decal, ea.	18.00 – 22.00
	#4	Hocking provision jar w/Dutch decal	18.00 – 20.00
Row 2:	#1	Windmill "Drippings" (turned wrong)	40.00 – 45.00
	#2	Dutch boy shaker	12.50 – 15.00
	#3	Dutch boy and girl shakers	28.00
		w/holder	40.00 – 45.00
	#4	"Churn lady" pr. shakers	40.00 – 45.00

Row 2 (Continued):			
	#5-7	Tipp City Dutch shakers, ea.	15.00 – 18.00
Row 3:	#1	Black "Ships" beater bowl, 6½"	45.00 – 55.00
	#2	Same, 10 oz. canister	25.00 – 28.00
	#3	Same, 24 oz.	30.00 – 35.00
	#4	Same, 46 oz.	35.00 – 40.00
Row 4:	#1	Same, refrigerator dish, 5" x 8"	30.00 – 35.00
	#2	Same, 4" x 5"	25.00 – 30.00
	#3	Same, 6" mixing bowl	22.50 – 25.00

Page 39 Ships

Bowl, drippings, 8 oz.	50.00 – 55.00		Mixing bowl, 9"	40.00 – 45.00
Bowl, drippings, 16 oz.	50.00 – 55.00		Mixing bowl, 8"	35.00 – 40.00
Bowl, drippings, rectangular (4" x 5")	50.00 – 55.00		Mixing bowl, 7"	30.00 – 35.00
Bowl, egg beater w/spout, 4½"	50.00 – 55.00		Mixing bowl, 6"	25.00 – 28.00
Bowl, beater w/spout, 6½"	45.00 – 55.00		Pitcher, 2 cup	45.00 – 50.00
Butter dish	60.00 – 70.00		Pitcher, "go-with"	30.00 – 35.00
Canister & lid, round, 48 oz., 5"h	65.00 – 75.00		Refrigerator dish, 4" x 5"	35.00 – 40.00
Canister & lid, round, 46 oz., 4½"h	65.00 – 75.00		Refrigerator dish, 5" x 8"	45.00 – 55.00
Canister & lid, round, 24 oz., 3½"h	55.00 – 65.00		Shaker, salt or pepper, ea.	25.00 – 27.50
Canister & lid, round, 10 oz., 2½"h	40.00 – 50.00		Shaker, flour or sugar, ea.	35.00 – 38.00
Lamp shade (pictured below)	60.00 – 75.00		Tumbler (or Egg Cup)	25.00 – 35.00
Mixing bowl set (4)	95.00 – 105.00		Tumbler, "go-with"	10.00 – 12.00

PART 2 – COLORATIONS
Amber

Row 1:	#1	Imperial's #600 Chesterfield pitcher	120.00 – 125.00
	#2	Chesterfield mug #600	25.00 – 30.00
	#3	Imperial syrup	70.00 – 75.00
	#4	Sugar shaker	295.00 – 320.00
	#5	"Visible" mail box	125.00 – 135.00
Row 2:	#1	Cambridge oval covered casserole	50.00 – 55.00
	#2	Cambridge covered casserole with underliner	50.00 – 55.00
	#3	Cheese dish (possibly foreign)	75.00 – 85.00
Row 3:	#1	U.S. Glass 2 cup and reamer top	350.00 – 375.00
	#2	Cambridge 2-spout gravy boat	45.00 – 55.00
	#3	Cambridge footed cream sauce boat for asparagus platter	40.00 – 45.00
	#4	Westmoreland 2-piece reamer	200.00 – 225.00
	#5	Lemon reamer (foreign)	125.00 – 135.00
	#6	Oil bottle	35.00 – 40.00

Row 4:	#1	Paden City "Party Line," #191 ice bucket	40.00 – 45.00
	#2	Same, 14 oz. tumbler	12.00 – 15.00
	#3	Paden City egg cup	15.00 – 18.00
	#4	Paden City hotel sugar, cover	25.00 – 28.00
	#5	Paden City salt box	55.00 – 65.00
	#6	Cambridge oil bottle	55.00 – 65.00
	#7	Tobacco jar	45.00 – 50.00
Row 5:	#1	"Feathered" curtain tie backs, pr.	30.00 – 35.00
	#2	"Sandwich" round tie backs, pr.	27.50 – 35.00
	#3	"Plume" tie backs or small round, pr.	28.00 – 35.00
	#4	et. al. drawer pulls, ea. (large screws)	12.50 – 15.00
		Same w/small screws	12.50 – 15.00
	#5	Door knobs, set	100.00 – 125.00

Row 1:	#1	Embossed "Coffee" canister	135.00 – 150.00
	#2	Embossed "Tea" canister	125.00 – 135.00
	#3-6	Spice shakers, ea.	25.00 – 30.00
	#7	Salt box	185.00 – 195.00
	#8	Measuring cup	300.00 – 325.00
Row 2:	#1	Sugar canister	135.00 – 150.00
	#2	New Martinsville batter set	200.00 – 220.00
	#3	Cambridge etched grapes design ice bucket	50.00 – 55.00
	#4	Valencia reamer, unembossed	325.00 – 350.00
Row 3:	#1	Water bottle	65.00 – 75.00
	#2-5	U.S. Glass mixing bowl set (4)	110.00 – 130.00
		9" bowl	35.00 – 40.00

Row 3 (Continued):

		8" bowl	30.00 – 35.00
		7" bowl	25.00 – 30.00
		6" bowl	20.00 – 25.00
Row 4:	#1	Cake stand (fairly recent vintage)	25.00 – 28.00
	#2	Fry reamer	375.00 – 395.00
	#3	Butter dish (foreign)	65.00 – 75.00
	#4	Butter dish (similar to canisters above)	65.00 – 75.00
Row 5:	#1	Indiana Glass reamer	300.00 – 350.00
	#2	Fry meat platter	125.00 – 135.00
	#3	Knife, 8¼", "Stonex"	275.00 – 295.00
	#4	Knife rest	20.00 – 25.00
	#5	Apothecary measure, 1 oz.	30.00 – 35.00

Row 1:	#1	Cambridge 3400 cocktail shaker	135.00 – 150.00
	#2,4	Jars (recent vintage)	20.00 – 25.00
	#5	Tobacco jar	35.00 – 40.00
	#6	Sugar shaker	135.00 – 150.00
Row 2:	#1	Batter jug, Paden City #90	65.00 – 75.00
	#2	Tobacco jar	30.00 – 40.00
	#3	Sugar shaker, #90, Paden City	275.00 – 320.00
	#4	Sugar shaker	275.00 – 295.00
	#5	Sugar shaker	150.00 – 175.00
	#6	Syrup, Cambridge	55.00 – 65.00
Row 3:	#1	Reamer, Cambridge	500.00 – 550.00
	#2	Reamer, foreign	45.00 – 55.00
	#3	Reamer, top only	70.00 – 75.00
		Same, complete	200.00 – 225.00
	#4	Sugar shaker, Paden City	225.00 – 250.00

Row 3 (Continued):

	#5	Paden City, #191, molasses can	50.00 – 55.00
Row 4:	#1	Reamer, Westmoreland	325.00 – 350.00
	#2	Butter, ¼ lb., Federal	40.00 – 45.00
	#3	Federal measure cup, no handle	35.00 – 40.00
	#4	Butter, ¼ lb., Federal	40.00 – 45.00
	#5	Jelly jar	18.00 – 20.00
Row 5:		All Federal Glass Company	
	#1	Butter, 1 lb., #2353	40.00 – 45.00
	#2	Butter tub, #307	40.00 – 45.00
	#3	Measure cup, w/handle, #2534	35.00 – 40.00
	#4	Lemon reamer, tab handle, #2520	20.00 – 25.00
	#5	Reamer, tab handle	300.00 – 325.00

Colorations

Black

Black still carries a mystique all its own for collectors. Have you noticed how many modern kitchens are using black as a decorating color? Our home in Florida has a major black color scheme in the kitchen appliances. All five reamers shown on page 45 are prizes worthy of possessing, but they can annihilate the glass budget.

Page 44

Pitcher with black reamer top, 300.00 – 350.00; Tumbler, 15.00 – 20.00; String holder, 30.00 – 35.00

Page 45

Row 1:	#1	Cookie jar, L. E. Smith	100.00 – 125.00
	#2	Batter jug, Fenton #1639	175.00 – 195.00
	#3	Syrup, same	125.00 – 135.00
	#4	Reamer pitcher, Fenton	1,000.00 – 1,200.00
Row 2:	#1	Ice bucket, Fostoria #2543	60.00 – 65.00
	#2	Jar, import?	20.00 – 25.00
	#3	Sugar shaker	425.00 – 450.00
	#4	Saunders reamer	1,500.00 – 1,600.00
Row 3:	#1	McKee grapefruit reamer	1,000.00 – 1,200.00
	#2	Sunkist reamer	600.00 – 650.00
	#3-5	Shakers, ea.	45.00 – 65.00
	#6	Tray for shaker set	35.00 – 40.00

Row 4:	#1	Mixing bowl, 9⅜"	65.00 – 70.00
		Bowl, 8⅜" (not shown)	55.00 – 60.00
		Bowl, 7⅜" (not shown)	55.00 – 60.00
		Bowl, 6⅜" (not shown)	45.00 – 50.00
		Bowl, 5⅜" (not shown)	45.00 – 50.00
	#2	Bowl, 7⅜" McKee	40.00 – 45.00
	#3	Mug	30.00 – 35.00
	#4	Ladle, whipped cream, #1800, Westmoreland	35.00 – 40.00
Row 5:	#1	McKee, 2 spout	800.00 – 900.00
	#2	Reamer, Tricia	1,400.00 – 1,500.00
	#3	Tray	25.00 – 30.00
	#4	Shaker, Fenton hobnail #3602	25.00 – 30.00

Page 46

Row 1:	#1	Sellers sugar canister	140.00 – 150.00
	#2	Salt or pepper, ea.	30.00 – 35.00
	#3	McKee batter jug	150.00 – 160.00
	#4	Cocktail shaker, Paden #991	75.00 – 85.00
	#5	Syrup, covered, Fenton	125.00 – 135.00
Row 2:	#1	McKee, 4½" salt (harder to find than pepper)	25.00 – 30.00
		Same, pepper (weak lettering, 50% of prices)	25.00 – 30.00
		Same, flour or sugar	45.00 – 50.00
	#2	McKee, 3½" sugar (priced as above)	25.00 – 30.00
	#3	Covered ice bucket	100.00 – 110.00
	#4	McKee tumbler	18.00 – 20.00
	#5	Straw in tumbler	8.00 – 10.00
	#6	Paden City batter jug set	275.00 – 300.00

Row 3:			
	#1,5	Shakers, pr.	50.00 – 55.00
	#2	Shakers, pr.	60.00 – 65.00
	#3,6	Shakers, pr.	40.00 – 45.00
	#4	Shakers, ea.	30.00 – 35.00
Row 4:	#1	Butter dish w/crystal top (possibly foreign)	85.00 – 95.00
	#2	Egg cup	20.00 – 25.00
	#3	Drawer pull, double	25.00 – 28.00
	#4	Paden City, "Party Line" napkin holder	150.00 – 175.00
	#5	Nar-O-Fold Napkin Company Chicago, U.S.A.	150.00 – 175.00
Row 5:	#1	Punch ladle	125.00 – 150.00
	#2-5	Drawer pulls, ea.	18.00 – 25.00
	#3	Cambridge salad set	150.00 – 195.00

Chalaine blue is one of the more challenging colors to find in Depression kitchenware. It is often confused with Delphite blue by beginning collectors. I have always referred to Chalaine as "robin's egg" blue to help distinguish the color from Delphite.

Several of the costly rolling pins have surfaced lately. Besides the rolling pin, the measuring pitcher without a handle is the most elusive piece. Only a few of these have been found, and the price is notably high on these. Good strong lettering on the shakers and canisters is necessary; but be aware that there are "artists" who have been known to "doctor" this black lettering.

Peacock blue now seems to be as plentiful as Chalaine, but neither color is abundant. You should find Peacock blue canisters with serious searching. Labeling is not a problem with this color since the names are embossed in the glass.

Page 48 Chalaine Blue

Row 1:	#1-4	Canisters (press-on lids), ea.	475.00 – 500.00
	#5	Refrigerator dish, 4" x 5", ea. (shown stacked)	55.00 – 65.00
Row 2:	#1,2	Shakers, salt or pepper, ea.	125.00 – 135.00
	#3,4	Shakers, flour or sugar, ea.	150.00 – 160.00
	#5	Shaker, nutmeg	165.00 – 185.00
	#6	Sunkist reamer	200.00 – 225.00
Row 3:	#1	Butter dish, plain, no tabs	475.00 – 525.00
	#2	Butter dish, ribbed, tab handles	425.00 – 475.00

Row 3 (Continued):			
	#3	Ginger (?) jar	30.00 – 35.00
Row 4:	#1	Measure pitcher, 4 cup	500.00 – 550.00
	#2	Measure cup, 2 spout	800.00 – 900.00
	#3	Rolling pin, shaker top	1,800.00 – 2,000.00
Row 5:	#1	Refrigerator dish, 7¼" sq.	150.00 – 160.00
	#2	Toothbrush holder	35.00 – 40.00
	#3	Towel bar, 17"	55.00 – 65.00
	#4	Drawer pull, double	30.00 – 35.00
	#5	Drawer pull, single	15.00 – 20.00

Page 49 Chalaine Blue

Row 1:	#1	Pitcher, ftd.	150.00 – 200.00
	#2	Measure pitcher, 4 cup	1,500.00 – 1,600.00
	#3-5	Canisters, screw-on lids	475.00 – 500.00
Row 2:	#1	Canister, rnd, 48 oz., blue lid	95.00 – 110.00
	#2	Canister, rnd, 24 oz., blue lid	75.00 – 95.00
	#3	Canister, rnd, 10 oz., blue lid	55.00 – 65.00
Row 3:	#1	Beater bowl, w/spout, 4½" tall	80.00 – 90.00
	#2	Beater bowl, w/spout, 4" tall	80.00 – 90.00

Row 3 (Continued):			
	#3	Grapefruit reamer	900.00 – 950.00
	#4	Egg cup	25.00 – 28.00
Row 4:	#1	Mixing bowl, 9"	125.00 – 135.00
	#2	Bowl, 7½"	85.00 – 95.00
	#3	Bowl, 6"	85.00 – 95.00
Row 5:	#1, 2	Salt box (2 shades)	225.00 – 230.00
	#3	Shakers (2 shades), embossed print, ea.	225.00 – 230.00

Page 50 Peacock Blue

Row 1:	#1	Strawholder (probably 1950s)	135.00 – 150.00
	#2	L.E. Smith cookie jar	100.00 – 125.00
	#3	Paden City #191 decanter	60.00 – 70.00
	#4	Dispenser (for a liquid or syrup)	275.00 – 295.00
Row 2:	#1	Sugar, 5 lb. canister	325.00 – 350.00
	#2	Coffee, 40 oz. canister	275.00 – 325.00
	#3	Tea, 20 oz. canister	225.00 – 250.00
	#4-6	Shakers, 8 oz., ea.	50.00 – 60.00
	#7	Salt box	145.00 – 155.00
Row 3:	#1	Ice tub	40.00 – 45.00
	#2	Rolling pin	275.00 – 295.00

Row 3 (Continued):			
	#3	Mug	20.00 – 30.00
Row 4:	#1	Jar (paper label, sold by route merchants)	20.00 – 22.50
	#2-8	Tie backs, large pr.	35.00 – 45.00
		small pr.	30.00 – 40.00
Row 5:	#1	Towel rod	55.00 – 65.00
	#2	Double towel rod	75.00 – 95.00
	#3	Towel rod	50.00 – 55.00
Row 6:	#1, 2	Spoons, ea.	35.00 – 40.00
	#3, 4	Salad set, pr.	85.00 – 95.00
	#5, 6	Double drawer pulls, ea.	25.00 – 30.00
	#7-11	Single drawer pulls, ea.	18.00 – 25.00

Colorations

Colorations

A word of warning to those of you who may have found a cobalt blue rolling pin recently. An "old" cobalt blue rolling pin with a screw-on metal cap was never found. In fact, no rolling pins with screw-on metal lids have ever been found in a transparent color other than crystal. I mention that here because I still receive letters regularly about these "rare" finds. I'm sorry, but they are all **newly** made.

The mystique of the cobalt blue color continues. Some collectors recently have been willing to pay "whatever it takes" to finish up their collections. Unfortunately, that makes it difficult to fairly price some rarely found items that have sold recently. Just because a wealthy collector buys an item at a big price does not necessarily mean the next like item on the market will fetch a big price also. Cobalt blue canisters with exceptional lettering and undamaged lids are bringing phenomenal prices. There are a few canisters with worn lettering and chipped lids available, but collectors are willing to pay a premium for mint canisters. Know that lettering is sometimes being redone on worn canisters!

Items with an asterisk (*) in the book have been reproduced! See pages 266-270 for further information. On page 52, Row 2, #1 and #5 have both been reproduced and the price made a downward adjustment for a while. It was only temporary!

Page 52   All Hazel-Atlas except last row.

Row 1: #1-5 Canister w/lid (deduct
for worn lettering) 400.00 – 450.00

Row 2: #1 2-cup measure w/reamer
top 325.00 – 350.00

#2 Tab-handled orange reamer 295.00 – 325.00

#3 Tab-handled lemon reamer 325.00 – 345.00

#4 Milk pitcher 85.00 – 100.00

#5 1-cup measure, 3 spout *300.00 – 350.00

Row 3: #1 Stack refrigerator,
$4^1/2$" x 5", ea. 60.00 – 70.00

#2 Round refrigerator, $5^3/4$" 65.00 – 75.00

#3 Water bottle, 64 oz., 10" tall 60.00 – 75.00

#4 Hazel-Atlas bottle (possibly
medicinal) 20.00 – 25.00

Row 3 (Continued):

#5 Mixer, Vidrio Products 125.00 – 135.00

Row 4: #1 Butter dish 300.00 – 325.00

#2 Bowl, $5^3/4$", "Restwell" 30.00 – 35.00

#3 Bowl, 6" 30.00 – 35.00

#4 Tumbler, marked HA 18.00 – 20.00

Row 5: #1 Spoon stirrer 20.00 – 22.50

#2 Curtain tie back, ea. 20.00 – 22.50

#3 Drawer pull 22.50 – 25.00

#4, 5 Stirrers, ea. 3.00 – 5.00

#6-8 Spoons or forks, ea. 42.50 – 47.50

#9 Coaster 6.00 – 8.00

Page 53

Row 1: #1 Bowl, $6^5/8$" (add $5.00
w/metal) 30.00 – 35.00

#2 Bowl, $7^5/8$" (add $5.00
w/metal) 35.00 – 40.00

#3 Bowl, $8^1/2$" (add $5.00
w/metal) 45.00 – 50.00

Row 2: #1 Bowl, $10^5/8$" (all three
are Hazel-Atlas) 85.00 – 95.00

#2 Bowl, $11^5/8$" 110.00 – 125.00

#3 Bowl, $9^5/8$" (add $5.00
w/metal) 50.00 – 55.00

Row 3: #1,2 Shakers, pr. (possibly
bath powder) 35.00 – 40.00

#2 Cambridge mug 75.00 – 80.00

#3 L.E. Smith water dispenser 400.00 – 450.00

Row 4: #1 L.E. Smith bowl, $6^1/4$" 35.00 – 40.00

#2 Same, $7^1/4$" 40.00 – 45.00

#3 Same, $8^1/4$" 45.00 – 50.00

Row 5: #1,2 Fork and spoon, set 75.00 – 85.00

#3 Fry cake plate, 3 ftd. 125.00 – 140.00

#4 Mustard pot 35.00 – 40.00

Page 54

Row 1: #1 Barbell cocktail shaker 135.00 – 150.00

#2 Strawholder 225.00 – 250.00

#3 Cocktail shaker 75.00 – 85.00

#4 McKee batter jug 150.00 – 160.00

Row 2: #1 New Martinsville batter
set 350.00 – 400.00

#2, 3 Shakers w/blue tops 50.00 – 55.00

#4 Sugar shaker (older than
Depression era) 325.00 – 350.00

#5 Sugar shaker 900.00 – 1,000.00

Row 2 (Continued):

#6 Tumble-up 85.00 – 90.00

Row 3: #1 Paden City, #11,
batter jug, 30 oz. 90.00 – 95.00

#2 Same, #11, milk jug, 20 oz. 90.00 – 95.00

#3 Same, #11, syrup jug, 9 oz. 65.00 – 75.00

#4 Cambridge reamer 2,750.00 – 3,000.00

Row 4: #1 Cobalt rolling pin 450.00 – 500.00

#2 Cobalt handled rolling pin 300.00 – 350.00

Colorations

Page 55 Delphite Flour, 165.00 – 185.00; Pepper or salt, 125.00 – 140.00

Page 56 Delphite

Row 1:	#1	Canister, 40 oz., sugar	400.00 – 425.00
	#2	Same, coffee	400.00 – 425.00
	#3	Canister, 20 oz., tea	200.00 – 225.00
	#4	Shaker, 8 oz., paprika	135.00 – 145.00
	#5	Same, sugar	130.00 – 140.00
		Same, flour (not shown)	130.00 – 140.00
	#6	Matches holder	125.00 – 135.00
	#7	Bowl w/metal beater	80.00 – 95.00
Row 2:	#1	Bowl, 5½", horizontal rib	70.00 – 75.00
	#2	Measure, 1 cup	75.00 – 85.00
		Same, ½ cup	55.00 – 65.00
		Same, ⅓ cup	55.00 – 65.00
		Same, ¼ cup	45.00 – 50.00
		Set	230.00 – 265.00
	#3	Bowl, 7½", horizontal rib	75.00 – 85.00
	#4	Bowl, 9¾", horizontal rib	115.00 – 125.00
		Bowl set (#1, 3, 4)	260.00 – 285.00
Row 3:	#1	Reamer, large	1,350.00 – 1,500.00
	#2	Reamer, small	125.00 – 135.00
	#3	Shaker, pepper	45.00 – 50.00

Row 3 (Continued):

	#4	Drippings jar w/lettering	125.00 – 150.00
	#5	Shaker, salt	45.00 – 50.00
Row 4:	#1	2-cup pitcher sunflower bottom	110.00 – 125.00
	#2	Butter	425.00 – 475.00
	#3	Cup measure (spout professionally removed)	25.00 – 30.00
	#4	Shaker, square salt	120.00 – 135.00
	#5	Same, pepper	120.00 – 135.00
	#6	Same, flour	135.00 – 150.00
	#7	Same, sugar	135.00 – 150.00
Row 5:	#1-3	Canister, square, 29 oz., 5", ea.	275.00 – 295.00
	#4, 5	Mixing bowl set (4) vertical rib	325.00 – 360.00
		Bowl, 6", rare	100.00 – 110.00
		Bowl, 7"	65.00 – 75.00
		Bowl, 8"	65.00 – 75.00
		Bowl, 9"	95.00 – 100.00

Page 57 Delphite

Row 1:	#1	McKee measure pitcher, 4 cup	600.00 – 650.00
	#2	McKee measure pitcher, 2 cup	110.00 – 125.00
	#3	McKee 48 oz. round canister	175.00 – 185.00
	#4	McKee 10 oz. round canister	50.00 – 60.00
	#5	Vase	30.00 – 35.00
	#6	Ginger (?) jar	20.00 – 25.00
Row 2:	#1	McKee butter dish	425.00 – 475.00
	#2	McKee refrigerator dish, 4" x 5"	50.00 – 55.00
	#3,4	Shakers, ea.	125.00 – 150.00
	#5	Ashtray, possibly McKee or Pyrex	25.00 – 27.50
Row 3:	#1	Mixing bowl, 9"	110.00 – 125.00

Row 3 (Continued):

	#2	Mixing bowl, 7⅜"	60.00 – 75.00
	#3	Bowl w/spout, 4¼"	100.00 – 110.00
	#4	Bowl, 4⅜" (cocotte)	30.00 – 35.00
Row 4:	#1	L.E. Smith, 9¼" bowl	85.00 – 95.00
	#2	L.E. Smith, 7" bowl	65.00 – 75.00
	#3	Fry, cornflower blue reamer	1,800.00 – 2,000.00
	#4	Hocking, "Block Optic" butter dish	500.00 – 550.00
Row 5:	#1	Cheese dish (possibly foreign)	90.00 – 100.00
	#2	Scoop	50.00 – 60.00
	#3	Paden City bunny, cotton ball dispenser	150.00 – 175.00
	#4	Soap dish, "Home Soap Company"	22.50 – 25.00

"Clambroth" White & Crystal

The translucent, washed-out white color shown in the bottom three rows on page 59 is commonly called "Clambroth" (white) by collectors. Although this is a rarely found color (except for the rolling pin), there is not much collector demand for "Clambroth" white either. A remarkable exception to that statement is the oval Pyrex casserole pictured in the middle of Row 3. This casserole is embossed "Pyrex" on one end and "193-197" on the other. Very few of these have appeared so far. You can see additional pieces of "Clambroth" white in the reamer section.

Collectors of crystal kitchenware still have fair prices at their disposal when compared to prices of other popular colored wares. However, be warned that the acquisition of crystal is beginning to deplete even this supply. Many older items can be found at prices comparable to recently manufactured wares.

On page 61, Row 4 #1 is an item marked, "The Pot Watcher." My understanding is that this is placed in the bottom of a pan or pot, and when the liquid begins to boil, this glass piece begins to rattle around, announcing the boiling. Another collector wrote that placing this in the bottom would prevent the liquid from boiling over. (These are presently available in hardware stores.)

Page 59 "Clambroth" White & Crystal

Row 1:	#1	Canister, Owens-Illinois, frosted, 40 oz.	30.00 – 35.00
	#2, 3	Same, 20 oz.	25.00 – 30.00
	#4, 5	Cruet, frosted, chicken decal, ea.	15.00 – 18.00
Row 2:	#1	Rolling pin w/wooden handles	125.00 – 135.00
	#2	Sugar shaker, lid w/one hole	55.00 – 65.00
	#3, 4	Salt or pepper w/normal lid, ea.	22.00 – 25.00
Row 3:	#1	Canister, large	65.00 – 75.00
	#2	Pyrex oval casserole	100.00 – 125.00
	#3	Canister, medium	55.00 – 65.00
		wo/label subtract $5.00 on canisters	
Row 4:	#1	Tray, 10⅝", square	25.00 – 30.00
	#2	Server, 7⅜", round	20.00 – 25.00
	#3	Server, 9⅞", round	20.00 – 25.00

Page 60 Crystal

Row 1:	#1	Canister, large, w/"Taverne" scene	40.00 – 45.00
	#2	Canister, medium, same (rare size)	50.00 – 55.00
	#3, 4	Shaker, ovoid shape, Owens-Illinois, ea.	18.00 – 22.00
	#5	Canister, ovoid shape, Owens-Illinois	50.00 – 55.00
Row 2:	#1	Instant coffee, w/sterling top	30.00 – 35.00
	#2	"Bohner's Safety crushed fruit bowl" (pat. Feb 22, 1898)	25.00 – 30.00

Row 2 (Continued):			
	#3-7	Sneath spice shaker, ea.	25.00 – 30.00
Row 3:	#1	Fleur-de-lis flour canister	25.00 – 35.00
	#2-4	Canister, 20 oz., ea.	15.00 – 20.00
	#5	8 oz. Kroger Embassy peanut butter	8.00 – 10.00
	#6	Spee-Dee mixer	30.00 – 35.00
Row 4:	#1-6	Small canister, 16 oz., ea.	10.00 – 18.00
	#7	MOXIE (licensed only for serving)	25.00 – 30.00

Page 61 Crystal

Row 1:	#1	Canister, Dutch boy design	20.00 – 22.00
	#2	Canister, embossed coffee	30.00 – 35.00
	#3	Canister, emb. coffee, Zipper design	40.00 – 45.00
	#4	"Kwik Whip all purpose mixer"	10.00 – 18.00
	#5	"No Drip Server," Federal Tool Corp., 1 qt.	18.00 – 22.00
Row 2:	#1	Salt, large	25.00 – 35.00
	#2	Salt, small	22.50 – 35.00
	#3	Canister, embossed tea	30.00 – 35.00
	#4	Syrup, w/glass top (2 pc.)	35.00 – 40.00
	#5	Pint server (same as #5 in Row 1)	15.00 – 18.00
Row 3:	#1	Glasbake tea kettle, w/glass handle	35.00 – 40.00

Row 3 (Continued):			
	#2	Canister, raised dots design	35.00 – 40.00
	#3-5	Shaker, raised dots design, ea.	12.00 – 18.00
	#6	Glasbake tea kettle w/wood handle	25.00 – 30.00
Row 4:	#1	"The Pot Watcher"	8.00 – 10.00
	#2	McKee Range-Tec skillet	12.00 – 15.00
	#3-8	Six-piece set from box marked "Serve U Set" Medco No. 86"	
		Salt and pepper, pair	6.00 – 10.00
		Syrup	22.00 – 28.00
		Marmalade	18.00 – 22.00
		Ketchup	22.00 – 28.00
		Sugar	22.00 – 28.00

Crystal kitchenware lends itself to any kitchen decor and has the added attraction of see-through storage. Prices remain reasonable on most items. Unlike many of today's products that are made to be disposed of after one use, these housewares can be used over and over. The McKee water dispenser shown below has a separate center holder for the ice. I guess that idea never caught on, but it seems like a neat idea to me! The cooler below sells for $100.00 – 150.00. It is that insert for the ice that can seldom be found. Temperature changes and slippery hands must have done them damage over the years.

Page 63

Row 1:	#1	McKee Glasbake Scientific Measuring Cup	20.00 – 25.00
	#2-5	Hocking canister w/Dutch decal	18.00 – 22.00
	#6	Pint measure in tablespoons for coffee, tea & wine	18.00 – 20.00
Row 2:	#1,2	John Alden (salt) & Priscilla (pepper), pr.	20.00 – 25.00
	#3	Westmoreland baby reamer, w/decal	50.00 – 55.00
	#4	Horseradish jar	12.50 – 15.00
	#5	Salt box	22.50 – 25.00
	#6	Toast holder	50.00 – 65.00
	#7	Spoon holder (Pat. Feb. 11, 1913)	20.00 – 22.50
Row 3:	#1-8	Dutch shakers (12 oz.), ea. (Cocoa in 6th)	12.00 – 15.00
	#9-10	Dutch shakers (16 oz.)	15.00 – 18.00
Row 4:	#1	Flour canister, 128 oz.	40.00 – 45.00
	#2	Coffee dripolator	20.00 – 25.00
	#3	Measure spoon (markings for table, dessert, tea)	18.00 – 22.00
	#4	Sprinkler (leaning in back), cardboard wrapped instructions	30.00 – 35.00
	#5	Cambridge ashtray holder	30.00 – 35.00
	#6	Jiffy one-cup coffee maker w/filter	10.00 – 12.50

McKee water dispenser, 2 part, $100.00 – 150.00

Custard

The darker shade of Custard (shown in the bottom row on page 65), is referred to as "caramel" by collectors. This color may have been experimental or just a bad batch of Custard. Today, we do not have the luxury of obtaining that information. The canister on the far right is not a fired-on color, but a solid, caramel color like the other pieces. I mention that because I have seen a few fired-on pieces similar in color.

There are some avid collectors of the Custard colored ware, but its popularity with most collectors is still lackluster. Many pieces are commonly found, but some are elusive. Although the Sunkist custard reamer is abundant, custard grapefruit reamers are rare.

If you would like a challenge, try putting together a set of four (salt, pepper, flour, sugar) in any particular lettering design. Unless you are lucky enough to buy a complete set at one time, it will take a lot of searching to come up with a matching set.

Page 65

Row 1:	#1, 2	McKee canister, coffee or tea, ea.	150.00 – 165.00
	#3	Measure pitcher or batter jug, McKee, 4 cup	50.00 – 55.00
	#4	Bowl, 9"	35.00 – 40.00
Row 2:	#1	Bowl, 8"	30.00 – 35.00
		Bowl, 7" (not shown)	25.00 – 30.00
	#2	Bowl, 6"	20.00 – 25.00
	#3, 4	Shaker, Roman arch, flour, sugar	30.00 – 35.00
	#5, 6	Same, salt or pepper	20.00 – 25.00
Row 3:	#1-4	Salt or pepper shakers, ea.	18.00 – 20.00
	#5	Cinnamon shaker	95.00 – 100.00
	#6-9	Flour or sugar shaker, ea.	40.00 – 45.00
Row 4:	#1	Pepper shaker	20.00 – 25.00
	#2	Lady w/apron shaker	40.00 – 45.00
	#3	Custard or gelatin	8.00 – 10.00
	#4	Pitcher, 2 cup	30.00 – 35.00
	#5	Tumbler	12.00 – 15.00
	#6	Tom & Jerry mug (w/good lettering)	12.00 – 15.00
Row 5:	#1	Reamer, 6" embossed McK	35.00 – 40.00
	#2	Grapefruit reamer	600.00 – 650.00
	#3	Sunkist orange reamer, McKee	40.00 – 45.00
Row 6:	**All Caramel Color**		
	#1	Canister, 40 oz.	95.00 – 110.00
	#2	Grapefruit reamer	700.00 – 750.00
	#3	Sunkist reamer	375.00 – 395.00
	#4	Measure cup, 2 spout	550.00 – 650.00
	#5	Canister, 48 oz.	250.00 – 275.00

Colorations

Fired-On Colors

Page 67

Row 1:
#1, 2	Rooster decanter w/4 shots	40.00 – 50.00
#3	Sugar shaker (Gemco)	28.00 – 35.00
#4	Canister, blue	30.00 – 40.00
#5	Rooster canister, small	25.00 – 30.00
#6	Same, medium	30.00 – 35.00
#7	Same, large	45.00 – 50.00

Row 2:
#1	Measure, 2 cup	45.00 – 55.00
#2	Pyrex, refrigerator jar, 3½" x 4¾"	10.00 – 12.00
#3	Hazel-Atlas cup, green	55.00 – 65.00
#4	Same, red	55.00 – 65.00
#5, 6	Hocking ribbed shakers, blue, ea.	15.00 – 18.00

Row 3:
#1,2,4,5,7,8	Hocking, salt or pepper	20.00 – 25.00
#3,6,9,10	Flour or sugar	30.00 – 35.00

Row 4:
#1-3	Roman arch side panel, ea.	18.00 – 20.00
#4,5	Same, flour or sugar	25.00 – 28.00
#6	Glasbake, red cup	55.00 – 65.00
#7,8	Shakers, ea.	10.00 – 12.00
#9	Reamer, tab handle, red	35.00 – 45.00

Row 5:
#1	Oval 7" jar, black	35.00 – 40.00
#2,3	Shaker (go-with #1-3 in Row 4)	8.00 – 10.00
#4	Rolling pin, white	90.00 – 110.00

Row 6:
#1	Mustard (Gemco set)	8.00 – 10.00
#2	Salt bowl, same	22.00 – 25.00
#3	Sugar shaker, same	28.00 – 35.00
#4	Hazel-Atlas sugar canister	75.00 – 85.00
#5	Same, coffee	65.00 – 75.00
#6	Same, tea	60.00 – 70.00
#7	Hocking tea canister	50.00 – 75.00

Page 68

Row 1:
#1-4	Shakers, ea.	8.00 – 9.00
#5	Cup w/red handle	4.00 – 5.00
#6	Black shaker	12.50 – 15.00
#7	Small sugar shaker	25.00 – 35.00
#8	Small striped canister	18.00 – 22.00

Row 2:
#1	Dutch bowl, 7"	20.00 – 25.00
#2	Dutch cereal, 5"	15.00 – 20.00
#3	Oil or vinegar bottle	12.00 – 15.00
#4	Apothecary jar	18.00 22.00
#5	Drippings jar (turned backwards)	40.00 – 45.00
#6	Glasbake measure pitcher	30.00 – 35.00

Row 3:
#1	Hazel-Atlas flour canister	80.00 – 90.00
#2,5	Syrup, ea.	22.00 – 28.00
#3	Batter bowl, Colonial Rim	55.00 – 60.00
#4	Knobs, ea.	18.00 – 22.00
#6	Carafe	6.00 – 8.00

Row 4:
#1-4	Pyrex bowl set	30.00 – 38.00
#1	Yellow	10.00 – 12.00

Row 4 (Continued):
#2	Red	8.00 – 10.00
#3	Green	8.00 – 10.00
#4	Blue	4.00 – 6.00

Row 5:
#1,2	Multi-colored Glasbake "Lipton" soup cups, ea.	5.00 – 6.00
#3	Pyrex 3½" x 4¾", yellow, refrigerator dish	10.00 – 12.00
#4	Pyrex 4¼" x 6¾", blue, refrigerator dish	12.00 – 15.00
#5	Cobalt tumbler w/red, white Dutch scene	15.00 – 18.00
#6	Crystal pitcher w/Dutch scene	30.00 – 35.00
#7	Same as #4, red	12.00 – 15.00
#8	Same as #3, orange	10.00 – 12.00
#9	Pyrex 7" x 9", yellow refrigerator dish	18.00 – 22.00

Page 69

Row 1:
#1	Canister, yellow	90.00 – 100.00
#2	Canister, ribbed green	45.00 – 55.00
	Canister, small (tea) not shown	35.00 – 45.00
#3	Shaker	18.00 – 22.00
#4	Hazel-Atlas coffee	65.00 – 75.00
#5	Same, tea	60.00 – 70.00
#6	Hocking tea canister	85.00 – 100.00

Row 2:
#1	Milk pitcher, 16 oz.	18.00 – 25.00
#2,3	Same, cream, 8 oz.	8.00 – 10.00
#4	Syrup	22.00 – 28.00
#5	Gemco shaker	28.00 – 35.00
#6	Shaker, Hocking	15.00 – 18.00

Row 3:
#1-3	Hocking refrigerator dish, 5½" x 4¾"	25.00 – 30.00
	Same, 9" x 5¼"	30.00 – 35.00
#4	Water bottle w/clear lid	45.00 – 50.00

Row 4:
#1-3	Round refrigerator bowl, 5½", ea.	18.00 – 22.00
#4	Pitcher, 20 oz.	60.00 – 65.00

Row 5:
#1-3	Dutch shakers, ea. (set/4: also green boy)	20.00 – 25.00
#4,5	Tappan shakers, pr.	12.50 – 15.00
#6,7	Shakers, ea.	12.00 – 15.00
#8	"Crisscross" design bowl, 5¼"	12.50 – 15.00

Green

The items pictured on page 71 have been found labeled "Cavalier Emerald-Glo Hand-Made." You will find additional pieces to this set; let me hear what you find! Most pieces are cut with a star. Those with a star cut were made by Paden City. Pieces without a star cut were made by both Paden City and Fenton. Fenton's pieces are a darker green shade when set side by side with those of Paden City. All Emerald-Glo was made for Rubel.

Page 71 Emerald-Glo

Row 1:	#1	Fenton double relish with holder	60.00 – 70.00
	#2	Two tier tidbit	45.00 – 50.00
	#3	Fenton oil & vinegar set in holder	70.00 – 75.00
Row 2:	#1	Handled relish	30.00 – 35.00
	#2	Salad bowl	40.00 – 45.00

Row 2 (Continued):			
	#3	Condiment set	60.00 – 65.00
Row 3:	#1	Ice tub with tongs	65.00 – 70.00
	#2	Shaker	10.00 – 12.50
	#3,4	Metal candle holders	15.00 – 20.00
	#5	Relish server	50.00 – 55.00

Forest Green
Page 72

Row 1:	#1	Owens-Illinois vinegar or water bottle w/tray	40.00 – 45.00
		Same wo/tray	20.00 – 25.00
	#2	Hocking water bottle w/top	75.00 – 95.00
	#3	Duraglas water bottle	30.00 – 35.00
	#4	Emerald-Glo syrup	45.00 – 55.00
	#5	Emerald-Glo oil & vinegar set	65.00 – 75.00
Row 2:	#1,2	Owens-Illinois canisters (ovoid shape), ea.	55.00 – 65.00
		Same, medium size TEA, RICE (not shown)	50.00 – 60.00
	#3	Same, shaker size	22.50 – 25.00
		Prices for #1, 2, 3 (30% to 40% less w/missing lettering)	
	#4	Owens-Illinois embossed COFFEE w/flip top	100.00 – 125.00

Row 2 (Continued):			
	#5	Owens-Illinois water bottle	25.00 – 30.00
Row 3:	#1-3	Owens-Illinois 40 oz. diagonal ridged canister, ea.	40.00 – 45.00
	#4,5	Same, 20 oz. (TEA, RICE)	40.00 – 45.00
	#6	Same, 10 oz.	17.50 – 22.50
	#7,8	Shakers, ea.	8.00 – 9.00
Row 4:	#1	New Martinsville batter jug	125.00 – 135.00
	#2	Same, syrup jug	75.00 – 85.00
	#3	Cruet	40.00 – 45.00
	#4	Sugar shaker (1950s)	125.00 – 135.00
Row 5:	#1,2	Curtain rings, ea.	17.50 – 22.50
	#3	Rolling pin	150.00 – 175.00
	#4, 5	Shakers, pr.	20.00 – 25.00

Green "Clambroth," etc.
Page 73

Row 1:	#1-4	Hocking canisters w/glass lid, 47 oz., ea.	90.00 – 100.00
	#5-8	Hocking shakers, 8 oz., ea.	30.00 – 35.00
Row 2:	#1	Hocking oval refrig. dish, 8"	55.00 – 65.00
	#2	Same, 7"	45.00 – 55.00
	#3	Same, 6"	35.00 – 40.00
	#4	Refrigerator jar, 4¼" x 4¾"	40.00 – 45.00
	#5	Hocking drippings jar (possibly powder jar)	45.00 – 50.00
	#6	Hocking 2-cup measure	150.00 – 175.00
Row 3:	#1	Hocking 1-cup measure	225.00 – 275.00
	#2	Hocking reamer	175.00 – 195.00
	#3	Fenton reamer top for pitcher	125.00 – 150.00
	#4	Jadite Sunkist (there is one that is much more translucent than this)	50.00 – 95.00

Row 3 (Continued):			
	#5	Cold cream jar	30.00 – 35.00
	#6	Mug	50.00 – 55.00
Row 4:	#1	Owl "tumble-up" nite set (pitcher & glass as top)	135.00 – 150.00
	#2	Butter dish	165.00 – 195.00
	#3	McKee Hall's refrigerator dish, 4" x 6"	35.00 – 40.00
	#4	Water dispenser w/crystal top	145.00 – 165.00
Row 5:	#1	Ice bucket, Fenton	65.00 – 75.00
	#2	Whipped cream pail	45.00 – 55.00
	#3	Fenton pitcher missing lid (as pictured) 3 pt., #1639	95.00 – 110.00
	#4	Towel bar holders, pr.	25.00 – 30.00
	#5	Sugar shaker	50.00 – 60.00
	#6	"Serv-All" napkin holder	200.00 – 220.00

As with "Clambroth" white, the term "Clambroth" refers to a collector name for the translucent green pictured on pages 73 and 75. It is not a company name. Shown on pages 76 and 77 are a combination of different companies' Jadite. Hocking spelled their color Jade-ite. The only spouted Jadite measuring cup that I have heard about is shown at the top of page 76. On page 77 in Row 3 is a Jade-ite skillet with a label reading, "Yours with Gold Medal Flour; 1 w 25 lb. sack; 2 w 50 lb. sack; New Fire-King Oven Ware."

Page 75 "Clambroth"

Row 1:	#1	Fenton #100 pitcher	110.00 – 125.00
	#2	Fenton #100 matching tumbler	17.50 – 20.00
	#3	Fenton #1681 macaroon jar & lid	150.00 – 160.00
	#4	Tumbler, ftd.	15.00 – 17.50
	#5	Sherbet	12.00 – 15.00
	#6	Door knob set	135.00 – 150.00
Row 2:	#1	Mixing bowl, 8¾"	85.00 – 90.00
	#2	Same, 7¾"	75.00 – 85.00
	#3	Same, 6¾"	65.00 – 75.00
	#4	Powder shaker?	55.00 – 65.00
Row 3:	#1	Ashtray	8.00 – 10.00
	#2	Wall tumbler holder w/bracket	25.00 – 30.00
	#3	Coaster	8.00 – 10.00
	#4	Furniture "foot rest" (per 1920s Montgomery Ward catalog)	8.00 – 10.00
	#5	Jadite towel bar in rear	55.00 – 65.00

Row 3 (Continued):			
	#6	Soap dish	20.00 – 25.00
	#7	Jade ashtray	12.00 – 15.00
	#8	Jade makeup holder	20.00 – 22.50
Row 4:	#1, 2	Canisters, fired-on ea.	100.00 – 125.00
	#3	Decanter, pinched	145.00 – 160.00
	#4	Water bottle	250.00 – 275.00
	#5	Bowl, 4¾" twist design	30.00 – 35.00
	#6	*McKee bottoms up w/coaster (coaster 100.00 – 120.00)	165.00 – 185.00
Row 5:	#1	Jadite vinegar cruet	295.00 – 325.00
	#2	Refrigerator dish, wedge shaped	60.00 – 70.00
	#3	Refrigerator w/jade lid	45.00 – 55.00
	#4	Cigarette ashtray	40.00 – 45.00
	#5	Bowl, 4½"	25.00 – 30.00

* Reproductions do not have patent number

Page 76 Jadite

Row 1:	#1	Jeannette souvenir shakers, pr.	250.00 – 300.00
	#2	Spouted ½ cup measure	150.00 – 175.00
Row 2:	#1	Jadite miniature skillet	40.00 – 45.00

	#2-5	Child's size 3" canister, ea. (don't confuse w/reg. 3" spice shakers, p. 79)	300.00 – 350.00
Row 3:	#1-4	Jeannette toiletry shakers, ea.	150.00 – 160.00

Page 77 Jadite and Jade-ite

Row 1:	#1	Hocking Jade-ite 7½" bowl, 2 qt. (decorated)	300.00 – 350.00
	#2	McKee embossed salt	200.00 – 250.00
	#3	McKee 4" x 5" drippings	125.00 – 145.00
	#4	Jeannette Epsom Salt	150.00 – 160.00
	#5	Hocking Jade-ite 6½" bowl 1 qt. (decorated)	400.00 – 450.00
Row 2:	#1	Hocking embossed Fire-King mug	100.00 – 125.00
	#2	Hocking 7 oz. mug	12.00 – 14.00
	#3	Hocking 16 oz. pitcher	195.00 – 225.00
	#4	Hocking St. Denis cup	12.00 – 15.00
	#5	Hocking 6 oz. straight cup	12.00 – 14.00
Row 3:	#1	"Swedish Modern," "Jade-ite," 8⅜" mixing bowl, 3 qt.	100.00 – 125.00
		Same, 7¼", 2 qt. (not shown)	90.00 – 100.00

Row 3 (Continued):			
		Same, 6", 1 qt. (not shown)	100.00 – 125.00
	#2	Same, 5", 1 pt.	50.00 – 55.00
	#3	Jade-ite ¼ pound butter	110.00 – 125.00
	#4	Jade-ite one spout skillet	75.00 – 80.00
		Same w/label	110.00 – 125.00
Row 4:	#1	Leftover refrigerator jar	45.00 – 55.00
	#2,3	Plate, 9⅝", 5 compartment	25.00 – 28.00
		Cup, 6 oz.	9.00 – 12.00
	#4	Handiwhip w/beater	85.00 – 95.00
Row 5:	#1	Jade-ite Mixing bowl, 9"	28.00 – 30.00
	#2	Same, 8"	25.00 – 28.00
	#3	Same, 7"	22.50 – 25.00
	#4	Same, 6"	25.00 – 28.00

Colorations

Page 79 (Jeannette Glass Co.)

Row 1:	#1-4	Canister, square, 5½" high, 48 oz., ea.	175.00 – 200.00
		Same, Floral pattern inside lid	175.00 – 200.00
	#5	Beater bowl, w/beater	80.00 – 95.00
Row 2:	#1,2	Jadite, light, salt or pepper	35.00 – 45.00
	#3,4	Same, flour or sugar, #580	55.00 – 65.00
	#5,6	Jadite, dark, salt or pepper	35.00 – 45.00
	#7,8	Same, flour or sugar	55.00 – 65.00
	#9	Butter, light, #5175	125.00 – 145.00
Row 3:	#1	Orange reamer, lg., light, #379	50.00 – 55.00
	#2	Same, dark	50.00 – 55.00
	#3	Refrigerator dish, 5" x 5" (floral lid)	65.00 – 75.00
	#4	Butter, dark	125.00 – 145.00

Row 4:	#1-4	Canister, #543 sq., 29 oz., ea.	175.00 – 200.00
	#5	Refrigerator dish, 10" x 5", (Floral lid)	75.00 – 95.00
Row 5:	#1-4	Spice canister, #5162, 3", ea.	135.00 – 150.00
	#5	Child's size canister "sugar" (others include coffee, cereal, tea)	300.00 – 350.00
	#6	Refrigerator dish, 4" x 4", #352	30.00 – 35.00
	#7	Same, 4" x 8", #353	55.00 – 65.00
Row 6:	#1	Ice box jug #370 (bottom only, $60.00)	325.00 – 375.00
	#2	Salt box, #5114	350.00 – 375.00
	#3	Reamer pitcher, 2 cup, light	85.00 – 95.00
	#4	Same, dark (price varies as top & bottom match correctly)	85.00 – 95.00

Page 80 (Jeannette Glass Co.)

Row 1:	#1,2	Canister, round, screw-on lid, 40 oz. coffee, light/dark	175.00 – 200.00
	#3	Same, sugar	200.00 – 225.00
	#4,5	Same, 16 oz., tea	135.00 – 150.00
	#6	Vase #519, bud	20.00 – 25.00
Row 2:	#1,3	Salt or pepper, #590	30.00 – 35.00
	#2	#544 drippings (no lettering, $40.00)	95.00 – 110.00
	#4,5	Flour or sugar	55.00 – 65.00
	#6,7	Decorated salt or pepper	35.00 – 40.00
	#8-10	Bicarbonate soda or mouth wash	150.00 – 160.00
Row 3:	#1	Round crock, #5031, 40 oz.	85.00 – 95.00
	#2	Tumbler, 10 oz., #528	30.00 – 35.00
	#3	Sugar shaker, dark, #2051	165.00 – 175.00

Row 3	(Continued):		
	#4	Sugar shaker, light, #2051	165.00 – 175.00
	#5	Round refrigerator dish, 32 oz.	75.00 – 85.00
Row 4:	#1	Bowl, 5½", horizontal rib	50.00 – 60.00
	#2	Bowl, 8", vertical rib	60.00 – 65.00
	#3	Same, 7"	45.00 – 50.00
	#4	Same, 6"	50.00 – 55.00
		Same, 9" (not shown)	60.00 – 65.00
Row 5:	#1	Match holder, #5170 w/lettering (egg cup wo/lettering)	75.00 – 95.00 / 18.00 – 20.00
	#2	Ashtray #530	12.00 – 15.00
	#3	Reamer, small, light	50.00 – 55.00
	#4	Same, dark	50.00 – 55.00
Row 6:	#1	Bowl, 9¾", horizontal rib	90.00 – 110.00
	#2	Same, 7½"	75.00 – 95.00
	#3	Bowl, 9¾", vertical rib	60.00 – 65.00

Page 81

Row 1:	#1-4	Canisters, 28 oz., square, ea.	225.00 – 275.00
	#5	Measure pitcher, 4 cup	125.00 – 135.00
	#6	Columned canister, 48 oz. (rare)	400.00 – 450.00
	#7	Same, 20 oz.	350.00 – 400.00
	#8	Measure pitcher (sans handle), 4 cup	700.00 – 800.00
Row 2:	#1	Refrigerator dish, 4" x 4"	35.00 – 40.00
		Same 8" x 4"	55.00 – 65.00
	#2,3	Shakers, salt or pepper, ea.	35.00 – 40.00
	#4,5	Shakers, flour or sugar, ea.	50.00 – 60.00
	#6	"Soap Powder," unusual label	150.00 – 175.00
	#7	Refrigerator water dispenser	225.00 – 250.00
Row 3:	#1	Butter dish	150.00 – 165.00
	#2	2 spout measure cup	225.00 – 275.00
	#3	Shaker, Roman arch side panel, pepper	55.00 – 65.00
	#4	Same, flour	85.00 – 100.00
	#5	Same, spice	125.00 – 150.00
	#6	Covered coaster holder for 6 coasters	65.00 – 80.00
		Coasters for above, ea.	8.00 – 10.00
	#7	Water tumbler	25.00 – 30.00
	#8	Bowl w/spout (egg beater)	65.00 – 95.00

Row 4:	#1	Drippings dish (unusual)	125.00 – 145.00
		Refrigerator dish 4" x 8"	55.00 – 65.00
	#2	Flanged lid refrigerator dish, 6"	65.00 – 75.00
	#3	Square refrigerator dish	95.00 – 120.00
	#4	Sunkist reamer wo/embossing	150.00 – 165.00
	#5	Nude "Bottoms Up" mug	185.00 – 195.00
Row 5:	#1,2	Canisters, 48 oz. round	150.00 – 160.00
	#3	Same, 40 oz.	75.00 – 85.00
	#4	Same, 24 oz.	60.00 – 65.00
		Same, 10 oz.	40.00 – 50.00
	#5	Water bottle	250.00 – 275.00
Row 6:	#1-3	Mixing bowl set (4)	120.00 – 140.00
		9" (not shown)	60.00 – 65.00
		8"	60.00 – 65.00
		7"	50.00 – 55.00
		6"	50.00 – 55.00
	#4	Bowl, 8", flanged rim w/spout	50.00 – 55.00
	#5	Cracker bowl, swirl design, hard to find	30.00 – 35.00

The once plentiful supply of Hocking green is a thing of the past. New collectors are finding that many pieces are not to be found. The "Vegetable Freshener" (embossed on top) that is shown in Row 3 on page 85 is missing from many collections.

Hocking canisters are the most popular of all those shown in this book, ostensibly because they can be found and prices are well within the range of most collectors. Finding canisters with perfect glass lids is a difficult task; the screw-type metal lid style is harder to find, but less in demand. In Florida, I prefer the screw-type because they are somewhat more moisture proof.

Page 83 Hocking

Row 1: #1-5 Canisters, 47 oz. w/glass
lid — 75.00 – 85.00
#6-8 Shakers, ea. — 25.00 – 28.00
Row 2: #1 Canister, screw-on lid,
64 oz. — 75.00 – 85.00
#2, 3 Same, 40 oz. — 75.00 – 85.00
#4 Same, 20 oz. — 75.00 – 85.00
#5 Shaker, 8 oz., labeled
"Domino Sugar" — 28.00
#6, 7 Shakers, ea. — 25.00 – 28.00
Row 3: #1-4 Provision jars, 64 oz. — 35.00 – 40.00
Same, 32 oz. — 30.00 – 35.00
Same, 16 oz. — 25.00 – 28.00

Row 3 (Continued):
Same, 8 oz. — 20.00 – 25.00
Same, 4 oz. (not shown) — 50.00 – 55.00
#5, 7 Round shakers, pr. — 70.00 – 80.00
#6 Drip jar — 50.00 – 55.00
Row 4: #1 Canister — 45.00 – 50.00
#2-5 Smooth sided canister,
40 oz., screw-on lid — 40.00 – 45.00
Same, 20 oz. — 35.00 – 40.00
Same, 8 oz., ea. — 20.00 – 22.00
#6, 7 Shakers (sold individually
as sugar shakers), ea. — 30.00 – 35.00
#8, 9 Milk bottle caps, ea. — 6.00 – 8.00

Page 84 Hocking

Row 1: #1-3 Paneled mixing bowl, $11^{1}/_{2}$" — 65.00 – 75.00
$10^{1}/_{4}$" — 50.00 – 55.00
$9^{1}/_{2}$" — 40.00 – 45.00
Row 2: #1, 3, 4
$8^{1}/_{2}$" — 30.00 – 35.00
$7^{1}/_{2}$" — 25.00 – 30.00
$6^{3}/_{4}$" — 20.00 – 25.00
#2 $8^{1}/_{2}$" bowl, embossed Diamond
Crystal Salt — 35.00 – 45.00

Row 3: #1-4 Mixing bowl, $9^{1}/_{2}$" — 35.00 – 40.00
$8^{3}/_{4}$" — 30.00 – 35.00
$7^{3}/_{4}$" — 25.00 – 30.00
$6^{3}/_{4}$" — 20.00 – 25.00
Row 4: #1 Mixing bowl, $10^{1}/_{2}$" — 40.00 – 45.00
#2 Batter bowl, handled — 55.00 – 65.00
#3 Batter bowl — 35.00 – 40.00

Page 85 Hocking

Row 1: #1 Butter dish — 55.00 – 75.00
#2 Block Optic butter dish — 55.00 – 65.00
#3 Refrigerator dish, Block design,
$4^{1}/_{4}$" x $4^{3}/_{4}$" — 30.00 – 35.00
Row 2: #1-3 Panelled refrigerator dish,
8" x 8" — 50.00 – 55.00
Same, 4" x 8" — 40.00 – 45.00
Same, 4" x 4" — 22.00 – 28.00
Row 3: #1 "Vegetable Freshener"
embossed on top — 150.00 – 165.00
#2, 3 Indent handle, 4" x 4",
refrigerator dish — 30.00 – 35.00
Same, 4" x 8" — 50.00 – 55.00

Row 4: #1-4 Oval refrigerator jars
(2 style knobs), 8" — 50.00 – 55.00
Same, 7" — 40.00 – 45.00
Same, 6" — 30.00 – 35.00
Row 5: #1 Crock, 8" — 50.00 – 55.00
Crock, $6^{1}/_{2}$" (not shown) — 40.00 – 45.00
#2 Crock, 5" — 35.00 – 40.00
#3, 4 Round refrigerator jar and
cover, 9" — 50.00 – 55.00
Same, 7" (not shown) — 40.00 – 45.00
Same, 5" — 30.00 – 35.00

Colorations

To save my answering letters, note that newly made labels for Hocking or Owens-Illinois canisters can be ordered from Lorrie Kitchen, 2258 Sylvania Ave., Toledo, OH 43613, or Geri and Dan Tucker, 3905 Torrance Dr., Toledo, OH 43612. Write for price and styles if your labels are missing.

Colorations

Page 87 Hocking

Row 1:	#1	Cocktail shaker	45.00 – 50.00
	#2	Cocktail shaker (pinched-in sides), #151	50.00 – 60.00
	#3	Onion chopper	40.00 – 45.00
	#4	Cigarette jar, ashtray on top	35.00 – 40.00
	#5	Toothpick	25.00 – 30.00
	#6	Electric beater	65.00 – 75.00
Row 2:	#1	Measure cup	75.00 – 85.00
	#2-4	Measure cups, ea.	30.00 – 35.00
	#5	Syrup	50.00 – 55.00
	#6	Cruet	40.00 – 45.00
	#7	Ash tray	15.00 – 18.00
Row 3:	#1	2-piece reamer	55.00 – 65.00
	#2	Reamer pitcher	35.00 – 40.00
	#3	2-piece reamer-ribbed pitcher	75.00 – 85.00
	#4	2-piece reamer	55.00 – 65.00
Row 4:	#1	Reamer, odd shade	30.00 – 35.00
	#2	"Coke" bottle green	30.00 – 35.00
	#3	Reamer, shade most collected	30.00 – 35.00
	#4	Tab-handled reamer	25.00 – 28.00
	#5	Tab-handled reamer	25.00 – 28.00

Page 88 Hocking

Row 1:	#1	Decanter, #102, pinched in	65.00 – 75.00
	#2	Water bottle	50.00 – 60.00
	#3	Water bottle	30.00 – 35.00
	#4	Water bottle	45.00 – 50.00
	#5	Decanter #2 (same stopper as Cameo)	50.00 – 55.00
Row 2:	#1-6	Pretzel Set (pitcher, jar, 4 #636 mugs)	335.00 – 370.00
		Pitcher, 60 oz.	40.00 – 45.00
Row 2 (Continued):			
		Mug, ea.	40.00 – 45.00
		Pretzel jar, #695	135.00 – 145.00
Row 3:	#1, 2	Water bottles, 32 oz., 2 styles	35.00 – 45.00
	#3	Same, 62 oz.	40.00 – 50.00
	#4, 5	Water bottles, raised panels, 32 oz	40.00 – 45.00
		Same, 62 oz.	45.00 – 50.00

Page 89 All Jeannette Glass Co.

Row 1:	#1	"Hex Optic" reamer bucket	45.00 – 50.00
	#2	Beater bowl	45.00 – 55.00
	#3	Cruet, w/correct stopper	75.00 – 85.00
	#4	Jenkins batter jug	175.00 – 195.00
Row 2:	#1	"Hex Optic" sugar shaker, #300	200.00 – 220.00
	#2	Sugar shaker	125.00 – 135.00
	#3	Sugar shaker, #2051	125.00 – 135.00
	#4	Mug, #516	40.00 – 45.00
	#5	Measure cup, tab handle	30.00 – 35.00
	#6	2-cup measure (Sunflower bottom)	110.00 – 125.00
Row 3:	#1	"Hex Optic" 4¹/₂" x 5" 'frige' jar	30.00 – 35.00
Row 3 (Continued):			
	#2	Same, dark	30.00 – 35.00
	#3	Same, butter	85.00 – 90.00
	#4	"Floral," 5" x 5"	65.00 – 75.00
Row 4:	#1	Reamer, large	30.00 – 35.00
	#2	Tab reamer	25.00 – 28.00
	#3	Reamer top (fits pitcher or bucket)	20.00 – 25.00
	#4	Butter	65.00 – 75.00
Row 5:	#1	Covered 9" bowl	50.00 – 55.00
	#2	Salt box, 6", "SALT" on lid, #10	250.00 – 275.00
	#3	Butter, 2-lb. box	180.00 – 200.00

Colorations

Possibly the most coveted green canister set collectors are searching for is the Sneath set shown in Row 2, page 93. Very few sets have been completed over the years. The "Zipper" set shown in Row 3 is also very desirable and can be found with less difficulty.

Page 91

Row 1:	#1	Canister, Hazel-Atlas	60.00 – 65.00
	#2	Canister, McKee (RARE)	75.00 – 80.00
	#3	Oil bottle	50.00 – 55.00
	#4	Syrup, Hazel-Atlas	50.00 – 55.00
	#5	Syrup, Paden City	50.00 – 55.00
	#6	"Orasorb" container	50.00 – 60.00
Row 2:	#1, 2	Shaker, embossed salt or pepper	55.00 – 60.00
	#3, 4	Same, embossed flour or sugar	80.00 – 90.00
	#5	FAN FOLD napkin holder	150.00 – 175.00
	#6	Measure cup, 3 spout, Federal	40.00 – 45.00
	#7	Hazel-Atlas tumbler	15.00 – 17.50
	#8	Measure cup, Paden City	135.00 – 150.00
Row 3:	#1	Mixing bowl, 9"	35.00 – 40.00

Row 3 (Continued):		Same, 8" (not shown)	30.00 – 35.00
	#2	Same, 7"	25.00 – 30.00
	#3	Same, 6"	20.00 – 25.00
	#4	Same, 5"	18.00 – 22.00
Row 4:	#1	Butter, Hazel-Atlas	75.00 – 85.00
	#2	Cheese plate ?	25.00 – 35.00
	#3	Measure cup (slightly oval)	55.00 – 65.00
	#4	Reamer top (scalloped edges)	45.00 – 50.00
Row 5:	#1	Fry tray, 'Not heat resisting glass'	125.00 – 135.00
	#2	Lattice design refrigerator jar	30.00 – 35.00
	#3	Warming dish, two inserts	75.00 – 90.00

Page 92 Tufglas

Row 1:	#1	J.E. Marsden Glassworks mixing bowl, 5 pt., 10"	45.00 – 50.00
	#2	Same, 3 pt., 9", made in Ambler, Pa.	40.00 – 45.00
	#3	Same, 2 pt., 8", also not for oven use	35.00 – 40.00
	#4	Same, 1½ pt., 7", for mixing, cooling & storing food	35.00 – 40.00
Row 2:	#1	Butter dish	65.00 – 75.00
	#2	Refrigerator dish, 3" x 6"	30.00 – 35.00
	#3	Refrigerator dish, 6½" sq.	40.00 – 45.00
	#4	"Tufglas Refrigerator Hydrator" No. 1	65.00 – 75.00
Row 3:	#1	Tufglas tab-handled spouted bowl	60.00 – 65.00
	#2	1-handled "No Splash Mixer"	60.00 – 65.00
	#3	Measure pitcher, 36 oz.	150.00 – 160.00
	#4	Funnel	65.00 – 75.00
	#5	Custard, "Trade Mark Tufglas Registered"	8.00 – 10.00

Row 4:	#1	Reamer	100.00 – 125.00
	#2	Bowl, round, 4"	15.00 – 18.00
	#3	"Kold or Hot" small covered casserole	30.00 – 35.00
	#4	Gelatin mold	30.00 – 35.00
	#5	"Kold or Hot" Sanitary Food Mold	25.00 – 30.00
Row 5:	#1	4-cup "Kold or Hot" measure pitcher	80.00 – 90.00
	#2	Round refrigerator dish, "To seal, turn cover"	30.00 – 35.00
	#3	"Sanitary Butter Box," top only	30.00 – 35.00
	#4	Round bowl, wrinkled ridge, "Kold or Hot"	12.00 – 15.00
	#5	Custard w/ridges, "Kold or Hot"	8.00 – 10.00

Page 93

Row 1:	#1	Straw holder, tall	425.00 – 450.00
	#2	Straw holder, fancy base	450.00 – 500.00
	#3	Straw holder, short	400.00 – 425.00
	#4	Paden City, 'Rena' line tumbler, Line 154, 9 oz.	12.00 – 14.00
	#5	Same, pitcher, 72 oz.	40.00 – 45.00
Row 2:	#1	Paden City syrup w/liner	60.00 – 65.00
	#2	Bullet-shaped sugar shaker w/dots on top, made by McKee	220.00 – 240.00
	#3-9	Sneath spice shakers, ea	55.00 – 65.00
	#10	Sneath embossed TEA	225.00 – 250.00
	#11	Same, embossed COFFEE	295.00 – 325.00

Row 3:	#1	"Zipper" large canister	225.00 – 250.00
	#2	Same, embossed COFFEE	225.00 – 250.00
	#3	Same, embossed TEA	200.00 – 225.00
	#4-6	Same, spice shakers	40.00 – 45.00
	#7	Holt soapsaver dish	20.00 – 25.00
Row 4:	#1	Syrup or milk jug, Paden City, w/lid	100.00 – 110.00
	#2	Paden City "Party Line" napkin holder	135.00 – 150.00
	#3	Grape juice pitcher, Baronial #6859, Tiffin	35.00 – 45.00
	#4	Jenkins pitcher	50.00 – 55.00

Colorations

Page 95

Row 1:	#1	Churn	375.00 – 425.00
	#2	L.E. Smith cookie	110.00 – 125.00
	#3	Imperial cocktail shaker	65.00 – 75.00
	#4	Cocktail shaker (Sweet Ad-aline painted on side)	45.00 – 50.00
Row 2:	#1	Reamer, called "Speakeasy" by collectors	40.00 – 45.00
	#2	Hocking pinched-in decanter	75.00 – 85.00
	#3	Cookie jar	65.00 – 75.00
	#4	Jar	30.00 – 35.00
	#5	Paden City ftd. tumbler	18.00 – 20.00
	#6	Glass straw	10.00 – 12.00

Row 3:	#1	Paden City Tulip sundae, Line 210	18.00 – 22.00
	#2	Covered round dish, 7¼"	35.00 – 40.00
	#3	Same, 8¼"	40.00 – 45.00
	#4	Crock, 6¼"	40.00 – 45.00
Row 4:	#1	Tufglas refrigerator dish, 5⅞" sq.	35.00 – 40.00
	#2	Cold cream jar	20.00 – 25.00
	#3	Twisted towel bar	25.00 – 35.00
	#4	Coffee pot lid	20.00 – 25.00
	#5	Drawer pull	20.00 – 25.00

Page 96

Row 1:	#1	Sanitary jar	150.00 – 165.00
	#2	U.S. Glass reamer pitcher (snowflake in bottom)	85.00 – 90.00
	#3	Slick-handled 9" covered bowl	65.00 – 75.00
		wo/lid	45.00 – 50.00
Row 2:	#1	Fluted sundae	18.00 – 22.00
	#2	Soda	18.00 – 20.00
	#3	Canning funnel	45.00 – 50.00
	#4	Cruet	40.00 – 45.00
	#5	Batter syrup (see page 123 Row 3, #2)	125.00 – 135.00
	#6	U.S. Glass, 5" x 5"	30.00 – 35.00

Row 3:	#1	Flask (hard day in kitchen!)	45.00 – 50.00
	#2	"Tea Room" banana split	90.00 – 95.00
	#3	Fluted sundae	18.00 – 22.00
	#4	Cup, slick handle	10.00 – 12.00
	#5	Banana split	25.00 – 35.00
Row 4:	#1,3	Flat banana split, ea.	25.00 – 35.00
	#2	9-oz. tumbler	10.00 – 12.00
	#4	U.S. Glass covered dish	30.00 – 35.00
Row 5:	#1,2	Salad set	130.00 – 150.00
	#3	Spoon holder	175.00 – 200.00
	#4	Mug, Fenton	30.00 – 35.00

Page 97

Row 1:	#1	Canister, sugar	150.00 – 175.00
	#2	Cocktail shaker	40.00 – 45.00
	#3	Ring cocktail shaker	40.00 – 45.00
	#4	Apothecary jar	40.00 – 45.00
	#5	Cookie, frosted	50.00 – 60.00
Row 2:	#1	Spouted mixing bowl	35.00 – 40.00
	#2	Butter tub	35.00 – 40.00
	#3-5	Three jar set	105.00 – 120.00
		w/black tray (not shown)	140.00 – 155.00
	#6	Mustard	25.00 – 30.00
	#7	Spouted bowl, 4½"	55.00 – 65.00

Row 3:	#1	Canister, similar to first item in Row 1	35.00 – 40.00
	#2	Punch ladle	65.00 – 75.00
	#3	Cambridge fork	70.00 – 80.00
	#4	Knife rest	22.00 – 25.00
Row 4:	#1	Jenkins reamer pitcher w/lid shown beside it	400.00 – 450.00
	#3	Canister embossed TEA	125.00 – 130.00
	#4	Salt	85.00 – 95.00
	#5	Large salt	90.00 – 110.00

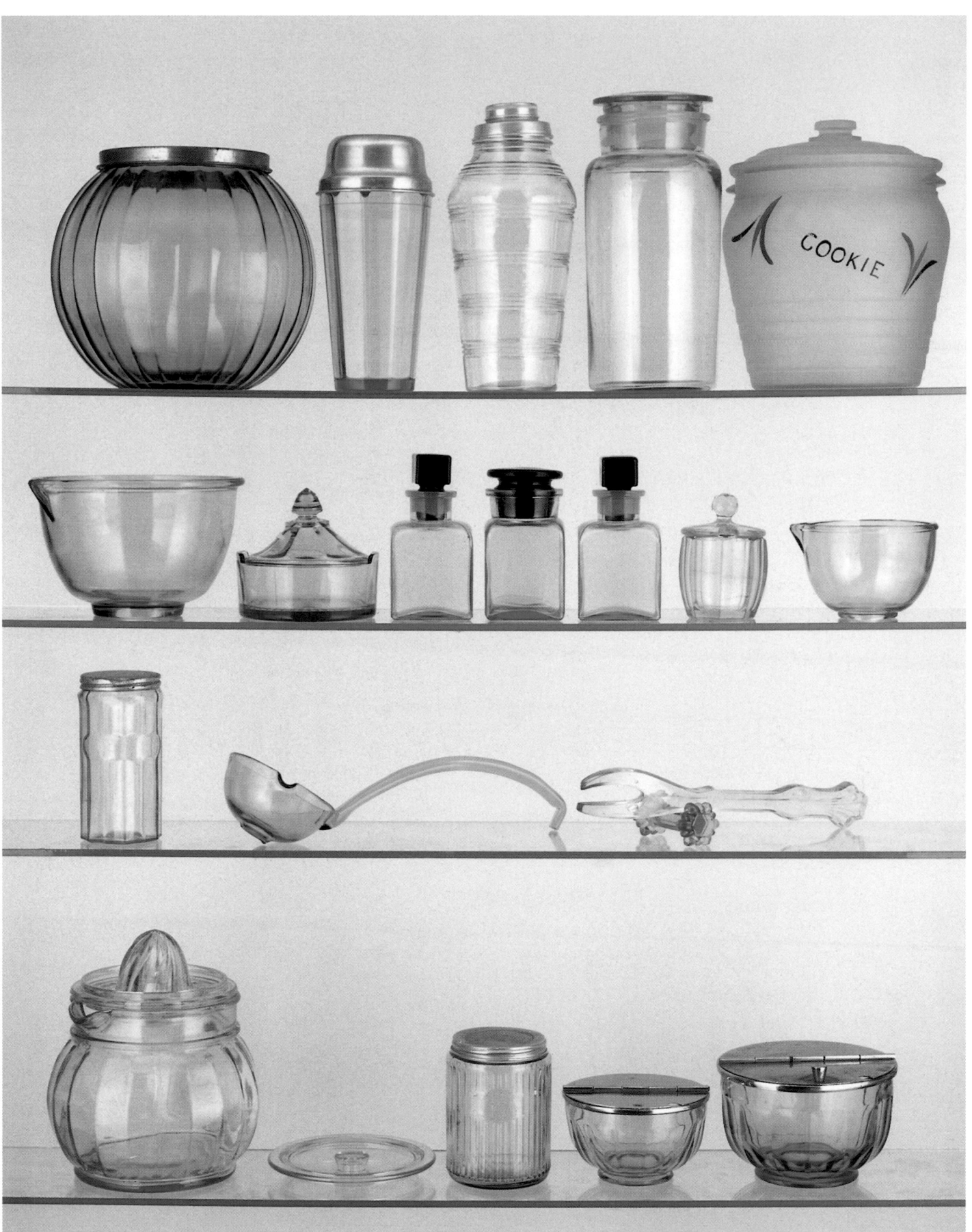

Colorations

Page 98 (below)

Small scoop, 40.00 – 45.00; Large scoop, 55.00 – 60.00; set as pictured, in box, 1,000.00 – 1,100.00

Page 99

Row 1:	#1	"Busy Betty" washing machine	250.00 – 300.00
	#2	Barrel cookie jar	70.00 – 80.00
	#3	4-cup measure pitcher	800.00 – 850.00
	#4	Single doorknob	60.00 – 65.00
	#5	Canister, embossed COFFEE	150.00 – 175.00
Row 2:	#1	Rolling pin	450.00 – 500.00
	#2	"Zipper" canister, embossed TEA	200.00 – 225.00

Row 3:	#1	Child's washboard, embossed CRYSTAL	150.00 – 200.00
	#2	Double towel bar	85.00 – 95.00
	#3	Double doorknob	125.00 – 135.00
Row 4:	#1, 5	Paden City 290 Vase, ea.	25.00 – 35.00
	#2	Pickle jar	110.00 – 125.00
	#3	Door hook (screw-in type)	25.00 – 30.00
	#4	Wall coffee dispenser	400.00 – 450.00

Page 100

Row 1:	#1	Cambridge oil and vinegar	100.00 – 125.00
	#2	Paden City parfait	18.00 – 20.00
	#3	Ice bucket w/metal drainer	45.00 – 50.00
	#4	Georgian ice bucket	40.00 – 45.00
Row 2:	#1	Tissue holder	250.00 – 300.00
	#2	Moisture proof salt shaker	55.00 – 60.00
	#3	Small scoop	40.00 – 45.00
	#4	Large scoop	55.00 – 60.00
Row 3:	#1	Owens-Illinois shaker	8.00 – 10.00
	#2	Tie back w/screw	20.00 – 22.50
	#3-5	Assorted knobs, ea.	18.00 – 25.00
	#6,7	Spoon and fork, set	85.00 – 95.00
	#8	"Holt Soap Saver;" Duro Hock Co.; Chicago	20.00 – 25.00
	#9	Shaker	8.00 – 10.00

Row 4:	#1	Mixing bowl, 6½"	20.00 – 25.00
	#2	Same, 5¾"	18.00 – 22.00
	#3	"Tea Room" banana split	90.00 – 95.00
	#4	Refrigerator dish ("To seal, turn cover to drop to slots")	30.00 – 35.00
Row 5:	#1	Mixing bowl, 9½"	40.00 – 45.00
	#2,3	Heisey frosted spoon and fork	125.00 – 145.00
	#4	Pyrex casserole	35.00 – 45.00
	#5,6	Cambridge spoon and fork set	140.00 – 175.00
	#7	U.S. Glass slick handle bowl w/cover	65.00 – 75.00

Page 101

Row 1:	#1	Paden City "Party Line" crushed fruit/cookie jar	75.00 – 80.00
	#2-4	Cambridge set, etched, #732	315.00 – 345.00
		Pitcher	50.00 – 60.00
		Covered plate	90.00 – 100.00
		Shaker	175.00 – 185.00
Row 2:	#1	Stack sugar/creamer/plate	85.00 – 95.00
	#2, 3	Marmalade, ea.	35.00 – 40.00
	#4	Breakfast stack set: Westmoreland sugar/creamer/plate/shakers	110.00 – 125.00
	#5, 6	Curtain tie back, ea.	17.50 – 22.50
	#7	Ashtray	12.00 – 15.00
Row 3:	#1	Cambridge gravy & underliner	125.00 – 135.00
	#2	Bowl, 7¾"	28.00 – 32.00
	#3	Toothbrush holder, frosted	25.00 – 30.00
	#4	Fenton "Ming" reamer	350.00 – 395.00
	#5	Measure cup, 20 oz.	150.00 – 175.00
Row 4:	#1	Bottom to jar or canister	20.00 – 25.00
	#2	Kompakt dish units, 8" x 4" (Pat. June 16, 1925)	65.00 – 75.00

Row 4 (Continued):	#3	Towel bar	55.00 – 65.00
	#4, 5	Curtain tie backs, pr.	35.00 – 45.00
	#6-8	Drawer pulls, ea. (large backs 6.00 – 8.00); small backs, ea.	18.00 – 25.00
	#9	Double drawer pull	20.00 – 25.00

That pair of embossed salt and pepper shakers on page 106 Row 5 have been reproduced in pink, green, and cobalt blue; the latter was never made originally. See Reproduction Section on pages 266 – 270 for items with asterisk.

Some of the pink items you need to watch for include "Tricia" reamer (page 103 Row 4, # 4); Paramount napkin holder (page 105 Row 2, #2); "Ming" reamer (page 105 Row 3, #3) and the dispenser mentioned in the next paragraph. I imagine that you could look at the prices and surmise that on your own.

It turns out that the "so-called" sugar dispenser shown on page 103 Row 4, #5 (shown complete on page 105 Row 2, #1) is a liquid dispenser for syrup or soap.

Page 103

Row 1:	#1	Hex Optic stack set, Jeannette	75.00 – 85.00
		base (18.00 – 20.00); lid (20.00 – 25.00)	
	#2	Hex Optic flat-rim mixing bowl, 9"	30.00 – 35.00
		Same, 10" (not shown)	35.00 – 40.00
		Same, 8¼" (not shown)	25.00 – 30.00
		Same, 7¼" (not shown)	20.00 – 25.00
	#3	Hex Optic ruffled-edge mixing bowl, 8¼"	25.00 – 30.00
		Same, 9" (not shown)	30.00 – 35.00
		Same, 7¼" (not shown)	20.00 – 25.00
	#4	Ice bucket w/lid, Fry	225.00 – 245.00
Row 2:	#1	Butter box, 2 lb., embossed "B," Jeannette	200.00 – 225.00
	#2	Round salt	275.00 – 295.00
	#3, 4	Flat Jennyware shakers, ea.	35.00 – 45.00
	#5	Tumbler, #500 Jeannette	18.00 – 22.00
	#6	Cruet	50.00 – 55.00
	#7	Barber bottle	45.00 – 50.00
Row 3:	#1, 2	Moisture proof shakers, pr.	200.00 – 225.00
	#3	Reamer, probably foreign	45.00 – 55.00
		Same, sun-colored amethyst (not shown)	35.00 – 45.00
		Same, crystal (not shown)	20.00 – 25.00
	#4	Tumbler, imprinted Mission Juice	25.00 – 30.00
	#5, 6	Quilted refrigerator jars, w/lid 8 oz.	40.00 – 45.00
		4 oz.	30.00 – 35.00
	#7	Stack sugar, creamer, and lid	85.00 – 95.00
	#8	Same only with place for salt and pepper	40.00 – 45.00
		Set w/salt and pepper on above	110.00 – 125.00
Row 4:	#1	MacBeth Evans stack set	75.00 – 85.00
	#2	Ice bucket	40.00 – 45.00
	#3	Ice bucket w/Sterling bear	55.00 – 60.00
	#4	Reamer, called "Tricia" by collectors	950.00 – 1,000.00
	#5	Dispenser w/insert (insert not shown)	200.00 – 225.00
Row 5:	#1	Reamer, unembossed "Orange Juice Extractor"	200.00 – 225.00
	#2	Paden City #11, syrup jug	75.00 – 85.00
	#3	New Martinsville syrup jug	125.00 – 135.00
	#4, 5	Heisey Twist cruet, 2½ oz.	140.00
		and 4 oz.	110.00
	#6	Heisey Twist mustard w/spoon	90.00
		wo/spoon	60.00 – 75.00
	#7	Cambridge syrup	85.00 – 95.00
Row 6:	#1	Bowl, 9¾", marked Cambridge	35.00 – 45.00
	#2	Bowl, 7¾", plain bottom	22.00 – 25.00
	#3	Bowl, 8", concentric rings in bottom	22.00 – 25.00
	#4	Butter dish, bow-handled top	65.00 – 75.00

Colorations

Page 105

Row 1: #1 Paden City "Party Line" #191
crushed fruit/cookie jar 75.00 – 85.00

#2 Jenkins batter pitcher 225.00 – 250.00

#3 Cambridge batter jug for
waffle set 110.00 – 125.00

#4 Cocktail shaker 85.00 – 95.00

Row 2: #1 Dispenser (possibly liquid
soap or syrup) 200.00 – 225.00

#2 Paramount napkin holder
(U.S. Glass) 400.00 – 450.00

#3 U.S. Glass "SHARI" cosmetic
holder (2 pc.) 125.00 – 150.00

#4 Breakfast set: sugar/creamer/plate
shakers; Westmoreland 110.00 – 125.00

Row 3: #1 Cambridge double gravy boat 70.00 – 80.00

#2 Imperial gravy boat 55.00 – 65.00

#3 Fenton "Ming" 2-pc. reamer 350.00 – 395.00

#4 Tufglas gelatin mold 55.00 – 65.00

Row 4: #1 Paden City Party Line ice tub 40.00 – 45.00

#2 U.S. Glass 2-cup measure 200.00 – 225.00

#3 Cambridge 1-cup measure 275.00 – 295.00

#4 Stack sugar/creamer/lid 85.00 – 95.00

#5, 6 Curtain tie backs, ea. 18.00 – 22.50

Row 5: #1, 2 Curtain tie backs, ea. 18.00 – 22.50

#3 Drawer pull, single 18.00 – 25.00

#4, 5 Single towel rods, 18", ea.
w/bracket 60.00 – 65.00

#6 Double towel rod w/bracket 85.00 – 95.00

Page 106

Row 1: #1 Pretzel jar, Hocking 125.00 – 150.00

#2-4 Canisters, plain, 40 oz. 60.00 – 65.00

16 oz. (not shown) 40.00 – 50.00

8 oz. 45.00 – 55.00

#5 Refrigerator dish, 4" x 4",
indented handles 30.00 – 35.00

#6 Measure pitcher, 2 cup,
ribbed 60.00 – 70.00

Row 2: #1-4 Mixing bowl set (4) 110.00 – 130.00

$9^{1}/_2$" 35.00 – 40.00

$8^{1}/_2$" 30.00 – 35.00

$7^{1}/_2$" 25.00 – 30.00

$6^{1}/_2$" 20.00 – 25.00

Row 3: #1,2 & 4 Refrigerator dish set (3) 120.00 – 135.00

8" x 8" 50.00 – 55.00

4" x 8" 40.00 – 45.00

4" x 4" 30.00 – 35.00

#3 Refrigerator dish,
$3^{3}/_4$" x $5^{3}/_4$", w/legs 35.00 – 45.00

#5 Butter dish, ¼ lb. 55.00 – 65.00

Row 4: #1 Butter dish, 1 lb. 65.00 – 75.00

#2 4" x 4" vegetable embossed
lid (asparagus) 35.00 – 40.00

Row 4 (Continued):

4" x 8" vegetable embossed
lid (not shown) 45.00 – 50.00

#3,4 Round refrigerator dish, $4^{1}/_2$" 30.00 – 35.00

Same, $5^{1}/_2$" 25.00 – 30.00

#5 Reamer, Federal 110.00 – 125.00

Row 5: #1,2 Mixing bowls, $11^{5}/_8$"
(not shown) 65.00 – 75.00

$10^{5}/_8$" (not shown) 45.00 – 55.00

$9^{5}/_8$" 35.00 – 40.00

$8^{5}/_8$" (not shown) 30.00 – 35.00

$7^{5}/_8$" 25.00 – 30.00

$6^{5}/_8$" (not shown) 20.00 – 25.00

#3,4 Salt or pepper, embossed *60.00 – 65.00

#5 Cruet 55.00 – 60.00

#6 Milk pitcher, #3027 Hazel-Atlas 45.00 – 50.00

Row 6: #1-4 REST-WELL mixing
bowl set (5) 150.00 – 175.00

$9^{1}/_2$" 40.00 – 45.00

$8^{1}/_2$" 35.00 – 40.00

$7^{1}/_2$" 30.00 – 35.00

$6^{1}/_2$" (not shown) 25.00 – 30.00

$5^{1}/_2$" 20.00 – 25.00

Page 107

Row 1: #1 Utility pitcher 65.00 – 75.00

#2 Slick-handle measure pitcher 50.00 – 55.00

#3 Measure cup 60.00 – 65.00

#4 Cruet 55.00 – 60.00

#5 Cruet 55.00 – 60.00

#6 Apothecary jar 30.00 – 35.00

Row 2: #1 Heisey cigarette and ashtray 75.00 – 85.00

#2 Cruet set 100.00 – 120.00

#3 Mixing bowl, 7" 30.00 – 35.00

Same, 5" 25.00 – 28.00

Same, 9" 35.00 – 40.00

#4 Mug, "Adams Rib," #900
Diamond Glass Co. 35.00 – 40.00

#5 Ice pail 35.00 – 40.00

Row 3: #1 Round crock, 8", lid fits outside 65.00 – 75.00

#2 Same, $6^{1}/_2$" 45.00 – 55.00

Row 3 (Continued):

#3 Round refrigerator dish, tab
handle 45.00 – 55.00

#4 "Kompakt" dish unit 75.00 – 80.00

Row 4: #1 Slick-handle mixing bowl,
$8^{3}/_4$" w/lid, spouted 65.00 – 75.00

Same wo/lid 40.00 – 45.00

#2 Slick-handle mixing bowl,
9", (2 handles, spouted) 40.00 – 45.00

Same w/lid 65.00 – 75.00

#3 Slick handle bowl, $7^{1}/_2$",
spouted, "D&B" embossed 40.00 – 45.00

Row 5: #1 Slick handle 9" concentric
ring bowl 40.00 – 45.00

Same, w/lid 65.00 – 75.00

#2 Snowflake cake plate 30.00 – 35.00

#3 2-handle bowl, no spout, 9" 40.00 – 45.00

Red & Fired-on Red

By putting all these reds together, we made this section unappealing, I know; but when taken in small measures, the fired-on red colors can add a little "spice" to kitchen labor. Those red water bottles (with the unfortunate shape) are readily available which amazes me since they're awkward as anything to handle when filled with liquid!

We turned the Hocking Vitrock bowl over in the last row to show you the design and "foot" these bowls have. I've seen few red kitchens around, but red is a dramatic accent color, so there is a lot of demand for the red pieces shown here and on the next page. Fired-on colors really photograph nicely as you can see on page 111.

Page 109

Row 1:	#1	Hocking tumbler w/Old Reliable tea bags	10.00 – 12.00
	#2, 3	Hocking water bottles, plain or ribbed	225.00 – 250.00
	#4	Food chopper	35.00 – 45.00
	#5	Straw holder (possibly 60s)	135.00 – 150.00
	#6	Hocking 24 oz. beater jar	50.00 – 60.00
Row 2:	#1	Cambridge "Mt. Vernon" ice bucket	95.00 – 110.00
	#2	Hocking ice bucket	35.00 – 45.00
	#3	Cruet	100.00 – 125.00
	#4	Sugar shaker	175.00 – 200.00
	#5, 6	Wheaton Nuline shakers, pr.	50.00 – 60.00
	#7, 8	Hocking shakers, pr.	35.00 – 45.00
Row 3:	#1	Imperial gravy & platter	175.00 – 200.00
	#2	Butter w/crystal top	120.00 – 130.00
	#3	Mixing bowl set (3)	220.00 – 255.00

Row 3 (Continued):			
		9¼"	100.00 – 120.00
		7¾"	70.00 – 80.00
		6½"	50.00 – 55.00
Row 4:	#1	Percolator top	22.50 – 25.00
	#2	Knob escutcheon plate for door	18.00 – 20.00
	#3	Double drawer pull	35.00 – 45.00
	#4	Single drawer pull	20.00 – 25.00
	#5, 6	Curtain rings, ea.	18.00 – 20.00
	#7, 8	Feathered curtain tie backs, pr.	35.00 – 45.00
Row 5:	#1	Trivet	40.00 – 50.00
	#2	Tray (possibly for a New Martinsville set)	45.00 – 50.00
	#3, 4	Fork & spoon set	225.00 – 250.00

Page 110

Row 1:	#1	Boot cocktail shaker	300.00 – 350.00
	#2	Silex coffee pot	200.00 – 250.00
	#3	Decanter w/shot glass stopper	110.00 – 120.00
Row 2:	#1	Cocktail shaker	60.00 – 75.00
	#2	3 oz. tumbler that goes w/#1	8.00 – 10.00
	#3	Barbell cocktail shaker (possibly New Martinsville)	125.00 – 135.00

Row 2 (Continued):			
	#4	Duncan Miller cocktail shaker	65.00 – 75.00
	#5	Cocktail shaker	65.00 – 75.00
Row 3:	#1	McKee batter pitcher	150.00 – 160.00
	#2	Batter pitcher w/tray	250.00 – 275.00
	#3, 4	Tumble-up set	200.00 – 225.00

Page 111

Row 1:	#1	Sugar canister, press-on lid	75.00 – 85.00
	#2,3	Shakers, ea.	20.00 – 25.00
	#4-6	Hocking canisters, 40 oz.	90.00 – 100.00
		Same, 20 oz.	45.00 – 60.00
		Shakers, 8 oz., ea.	25.00 – 30.00
Row 2:	#1, 2	Hocking ribbed canisters, 47 oz., glass lid	50.00 – 60.00
	#3,4	Shakers, ea.	25.00 – 30.00
	#5	Drip jar	40.00 – 45.00
	#6	Water bottle	45.00 – 50.00
	#7	Tappan shaker	10.00 – 12.00
Row 3:	#1-4	Owens-Illinois canisters (ovoid shape), Coffee	65.00 – 75.00

Row 3 (Continued):			
		Tea	65.00 – 75.00
		Shakers, ea.	35.00
	#5	MacBeth Evans canister, "Gold Medal Flour"	55.00 – 65.00
	#6	Sugar shaker (Gemco)	28.00 – 35.00
Row 4:	#1	McKee water bottle (tumbler makes top)	50.00 – 60.00
	#2	McKee water bottle, stopper	30.00 – 35.00
	#3-5	Hocking canister set	58.00 – 72.00
		(20.00 – 25.00; 20.00 – 25.00; 18.00 – 22.00)	
Row 5:	#1	Hocking 10½" mixing bowl	40.00 – 45.00
	#2	Vitrock, 6¾" bowl	30.00 – 35.00
	#3	Federal 5" bowl	15.00 – 18.00

White

White kitchenware is very versatile in a decorating scheme and more abundant than many colors! Prices reflect that abundance; so, today's collectors are using this color in their kitchens.

Page 113 McKee Glass Company

Row 1:	#1-4	Canister, 48 oz., ea	180.00 – 200.00
	#5,6	Large shakers, salt, pepper, ea.	60.00 – 70.00
	#7,8	Flour, sugar, ea.	70.00 – 80.00
Row 2:	#1,2	Shakers, salt, pepper, ea.	22.50 – 25.00
	#3,4	Flour, sugar, ea.	30.00 – 35.00
	#5,6	Salt, pepper, ea.	20.00 – 25.00
	#7,8	Flour, sugar, ea.	30.00 – 35.00
	#9	Canister, same design	250.00 – 275.00
	#10	Dots 48 oz. canister	225.00 – 275.00
Row 3:	#1	Grapefruit reamer	200.00 – 250.00
	#2	Tea w/lid	85.00 – 95.00

Row 3 (Continued):			
	#3	Bowl, 9" w/decal	45.00 – 50.00
	#4	2 cup measure w/decal	50.00 – 55.00
Row 4:	#1	Bowl, 9"	30.00 – 35.00
	#2, 3	Shakers (good lettering!)	20.00 – 25.00
	#4	Reamer, small	25.00 – 30.00
	#5	Sunkist reamer	10.00 – 20.00
Row 5:	#1	Water dispenser	150.00 – 165.00
	#2	Glasbake measure cup	65.00 – 75.00
	#3	Shaker, salt	18.00 – 20.00
	#4,5	Shaker, flour or sugar	25.00 – 28.00
	#6	Diamond Check shaker	35.00 – 40.00

Page 114 Hocking Glass Company Vitrock

Row 1:	#1	Canister w/glass lid (rare)	85.00 – 100.00
	#2	Canister, 20 oz. screw-on lid	60.00 – 65.00
	#3	Shaker	18.00 – 22.00
	#4-5	Mixing bowl, 6¾"	15.00 – 22.00
		Same, 7½" (not shown)	22.00 – 28.00
		Same, 8½" (not shown)	25.00 – 30.00
		Same, 9½" (not shown)	30.00 – 35.00
		Same, 10½" (not shown)	35.00 – 38.00
		Same, 11¼"	40.00 – 45.00
Row 2:	#1	"Blue Circle" flour	85.00 – 95.00
	#2,3	Same, shakers, salt or pepper	20.00 – 30.00
	#4,5	Same, flour or sugar	25.00 – 35.00
	#6, 7	"Black Circle" shakers, ea.	22.00 – 30.00

Row 3:	#1	Grease wo/label	40.00 – 45.00
	#2	2 cup measure w/lid	65.00 – 75.00
	#3	Reamer	28.00 – 35.00
	#4	Bowl, 10", red trim	35.00 – 40.00
Row 4:	#1-3	"Red Circle" w/screw-on lids	85.00 – 95.00
	#4-6	Same, shakers, salt/pepper ea.	20.00 – 25.00
		sugar	25.00 – 30.00
Row 5:	#1	"Red Circle w/flowers," canister w/screw-on lid	65.00 – 75.00
	#2	Tab handle reamer	100.00 – 110.00
	#3	4" x 4" refrigerator dish	25.00 – 30.00
	#4	8" x 8" refrigerator dish	55.00 – 65.00

Page 115

Row 1:	#1,2	Oval refrigerator set (3)	90.00 – 105.00
		Same, 8"	35.00 – 40.00
		Same, 7"	30.00 – 35.00
		Same, 6" (not shown)	25.00 – 30.00
	#3	Canister, 20 oz. screw lid w/label	60.00 – 65.00
		wo/label	45.00 – 55.00
	#4-6	Shakers w/label	18.00 – 22.00
	#7	Reamer, embossed Vitrock	28.00 – 35.00
		Same, not embossed	25.00 – 30.00
Row 2:	#1,2	Decorated bowl	35.00 – 40.00
		Same, 5¼"	12.00 – 15.00
	#3	Refrigerator dish, 4" x 4"	25.00 – 30.00
		Same, 4" x 8" (not shown)	45.00 – 55.00
		Same, 8" x 8"	55.00 – 65.00
	#4	Reamer, 2 piece	40.00 – 45.00

Row 3:	#1,2	Mixing bowls, 7½"	22.00 – 28.00
		6¾", Hocking Vitrock	15.00 – 22.00
	#3,5	Shakers, ea.	18.00 – 22.00
	#4	Dripping jar	40.00 – 45.00
	#6	Ashtray wo/ad	8.00 – 10.00
		w/ad (*Lancaster Eagle-Gazette* 1809 – 1937)	12.00 – 15.00
Row 4:	#1-3	Mixing bowls as in Row 3, 11½"	40.00 – 45.00
		Same w/ad (Bertman Pickle Co.)	55.00 – 65.00
		10¼"	35.00 – 38.00
		9½"	30.00 – 35.00
		8½" (not shown)	25.00 – 30.00

Yellow ===================

Opaque

Colorations

McKee's opaque yellow is called "Seville." This color is sometimes confused with Custard by beginning collectors. Custard leans to the white with a beige tint while "Seville" **is** yellow. The item that nearly everyone who collects this needs is the little two spout measuring cup at the end of Row 2, page 117. Memorize it. The canisters come with both screw-on and press-on lids.

Pages 117 and 118 give a representative example of this color that can be compared to Hocking's opaque yellow shown on page 119. Even though Hocking's yellow is more rare, there are fewer collectors, and that limits its price potential. Most yellow opaque pieces are found with black lettering, but there are exceptions to that rule. Some Hocking pieces have been seen with green lettering!

Page 117 McKee

Row 1:	#1	Canister, 48 oz., screw-on lid	200.00 – 225.00
	#2-4	Canister, 48 oz., press-on lid	140.00 – 150.00
	#5,6,8	Sugar or flour shaker, 8 oz.	30.00 – 35.00
	#7	Shaker, pepper 8 oz.	18.00 – 20.00
Row 2:	#1,2	Round canister, 48 oz., w/lid	95.00 – 110.00
	#3	Same, 40 oz.	65.00 – 75.00
	#4	Same, 24 oz.	45.00 – 55.00
		Same, 10 oz. (not shown)	40.00 – 45.00
	#5	Measuring cup, 2 spout	180.00 – 200.00
Row 3:	#1-3	Mixing bowl set (3)	90.00 – 103.00
		9"	35.00 – 40.00
		7½"	30.00 – 35.00
		6"	25.00 – 28.00
	#4	Pitcher, 2 cup measure	135.00 – 140.00

Row 4:	#1	Bowl, ribbed "Manning Bowman," 9½"	40.00 – 45.00
	#2	Bowl, ribbed, 6½"	22.00 – 28.00
	#3	Bowl, "Hamilton Beach," 9¼"	20.00 – 25.00
	#4	"Bottoms Up" mug	185.00 – 195.00
Row 5:	#1	Mixing bowl, 7", part of set	25.00 – 30.00
		Same, 9" (not shown)	35.00 – 40.00
		Same, 8" (not shown)	30.00 – 35.00
		Same, 6" (not shown)	20.00 – 25.00
	#2	Bowl, 7" w/spout	30.00 – 35.00
	#3	Bowl, 4½"	10.00 – 12.00
	#4	Pitcher, 2 cup measure	40.00 – 45.00

Page 118 McKee Glass Company

Row 1:	#1	Pinch decanter	125.00 – 140.00
	#2	Measure, 4 cup, no handle	500.00 – 600.00
	#3	Measure, 4 cup, ftd. w/handle	135.00 – 140.00
	#4	4 cup dry measure (mug)	200.00 – 225.00
Row 2:	#1	Bottoms down mug	185.00 – 195.00
	#2	Measure, 2 cup	40.00 – 45.00
	#3-9	Salt or pepper, ea.	18.00 – 20.00
		Flour or sugar, ea.	30.00 – 35.00

Row 3:	#1	Grapefruit reamer	225.00 – 250.00
	#2	Sunkist reamer	55.00 – 60.00
	#3	Refrigerator dish, 7¼" square	45.00 – 50.00
Row 4:	#1	Butter dish	125.00 – 135.00
	#2	4" x 5" refrigerator dish	30.00 – 35.00
	#3	Measure cup, 2 spout	180.00 – 200.00
	#4	Bowl, 4¼"	10.00 – 12.00
Row 5:	#1	Mixing bowl, 9¼"	35.00 – 40.00
	#2	Same, 7½"	30.00 – 35.00
	#3,4	Canister, 48 oz., ea.	225.00 – 250.00

Page 119 Hocking Glass Company

Row 1:	#1-3	Canister, 40 oz., ea.	175.00 – 225.00
	#4,5	Canister, 20 oz., ea.	165.00 – 200.00
Row 2:	#1	Refrigerator jar, 4" x 4"	12.00 – 15.00
		Same, w/lid	30.00 – 35.00
	#2,3	Shaker, flour or sugar	40.00 – 50.00
	#4	Refrigerator dish, 6" x 6"	35.00 – 40.00

Row 3:	#1	Measure pitcher	175.00 – 200.00
	#2	Batter bowl	125.00 – 135.00
Row 4:	#1	Refrigerator dish, 8" x 8"	65.00 – 75.00
	#2, 4	Salt or pepper	25.00 – 30.00
	#3	Grease jar	70.00 – 75.00

Colorations

Transparent

Colorations

Page 120

Chesterfield, Imperial Glass #600 Line, pitcher and lid		175.00 – 200.00
Chesterfield mug		30.00 – 35.00

Page 121

Row 1:
#1	Paden City ice bucket	145.00 – 155.00
#2	U.S. Glass reamer pitcher	650.00 – 750.00
#3	Glass matching pitcher above	15.00 – 17.50
#4	Fostoria ice bucket	55.00 – 65.00
#5	Fostoria oil and vinegar	100.00 – 110.00
#6	Fostoria "Mayfair" cruet	100.00 – 125.00

Row 2:
#1	Fostoria oil and vinegar	55.00 – 65.00
#2	Fostoria "Mayfair" syrup & liner	65.00 – 75.00
#3	Sugar shaker	375.00 – 395.00
#4	Hazel-Atlas 2 cup reamer set	350.00 – 375.00
#5	Hazel-Atlas mug	50.00 – 55.00
#6	Duncan "Festive" sauce dish & ladle	45.00 – 55.00

Row 3:
#1	Heisey syrup	75.00 – 85.00
#2	Heisey "Old Sandwich"	170.00
#3	Hazel-Atlas 1 cup measure, 3 spout	295.00 – 325.00
#4	Hazel-Atlas egg cup	8.00 – 10.00
#5	Canning funnel "C.W. Hart," Troy, N.Y.	40.00 – 45.00
#6	Hazel-Atlas refrigerator dish, 4½" x 5"	40.00 – 45.00

Row 4:
#1	Hazel-Atlas REST-WELL, mixing bowl, 8¾"	35.00 – 40.00
#2	Same, 7¾"	30.00 – 35.00
#3	Same, 6¾"	22.00 – 25.00
#4	Same, 5¾"	18.00 – 20.00

Row 5:
#1	U.S. Glass slick handled batter bowl	35.00 – 40.00
#2	Soap dish	20.00 – 25.00
#3	Cambridge sugar cube tray	75.00 – 85.00
#4	Spoon, salad size	60.00 – 70.00
#5	Spoon, regular size	45.00 – 50.00

PART 3 – KITCHEN ITEMS
Batter Jugs & Bowls

Batter jugs were usually parts of sets consisting of a batter jug with lid, syrup with lid, and drip tray. Although these sets were made by several different companies in a myriad of colors, cobalt blue and red are the most popular colors with collectors.

Page 125 shows a collection of batter bowls. They came in many shapes and sizes, although all those shown were made by Hocking. The "Mayfair" blue in Row 2 and the "Turquoise Blue" in Row 4 are most coveted by collectors. It took us four years to find the "Turquoise Blue" when we were collecting that color.

The Hocking canister in Row 3 was a late arrival, and since this was an all Hocking page, I included it there. The top shows that "ARCO" Coffee was originally in the jar; but when empty, the jar could become your cookies' home.

Page 123

Row 1:	#1	Paden City #11, crystal w/black lids set, 9 oz. syrup/30 oz. batter	175.00 – 190.00
	#2	Paden City black set	275.00 – 300.00
	#3	Paden City pink w/black tray set	225.00 – 250.00
Row 2:	#1	Paden City syrup	65.00 – 75.00
	#2	Paden City batter jug	90.00 – 95.00
	#3	Paden City milk jug	90.00 – 95.00
	#4	Paden City green batter jug	100.00 – 110.00
	#5	Cambridge pink batter jug for waffle set	110.00 – 125.00

Row 2 (Continued):			
	#6	Cambridge amber syrup jug	55.00 – 60.00
Row 3:	#1	Jenkins #570 green batter jug	175.00 – 195.00
	#2	Green batter jug	125.00 – 135.00
	#3	Square green batter jug	195.00 – 220.00
	#4	Jenkins green batter jug	225.00 – 250.00
Row 4:	#1	Jenkins pink batter jug	225.00 – 250.00
	#2	Jeannette Jadite (bottom only, 50.00)	325.00 – 375.00
	#3	Liberty "American Pioneer" batter jug	225.00 – 250.00
	#4	Same, syrup jug	200.00 – 225.00

Page 124

Row 1:	#1	New Martinsville cobalt blue batter set	350.00 – 400.00
	#2	Same, amber	200.00 – 220.00
	#3	Red batter jug & liner	250.00 – 275.00
Row 2:	#1	New Martinsville green batter jug	100.00 – 125.00
	#2	Same, syrup jug	70.00 – 75.00
	#3	New Martinsville crystal batter w/green top	60.00 – 65.00

Row 2 (Continued):			
	#4	New Martinsville pink syrup jug	75.00 – 85.00
Row 3:	#1	McKee black batter	150.00 – 160.00
	#2	Same, white	95.00 – 120.00
	#3	Same, blue	150.00 – 160.00
	#4	Same, red	150.00 – 160.00
Row 4:	#1	Federal Batter Bowl	40.00 – 50.00
	#2	New Martinsville pink batter jug	125.00 – 135.00

Page 125 All Anchor Hocking Glass Company

Row 1:	#1	Ribbed green	55.00 – 60.00
	#2	Opaque yellow	125.00 – 135.00
Row 2:	#1	Ribbed crystal	28.00 – 35.00
	#2	Spiraled green	45.00 – 55.00
	#3	"Mayfair" blue	350.00 – 400.00
		"Mayfair" green (not shown)	100.00 – 125.00
Row 3:	#1	Cookie jar w/coffee lid	80.00 – 90.00

Row 3 (Continued):			
	#2	Fire-King (peach/grape)	200.00 – 225.00
Row 4:	#1	Same, Jade-ite	
		¾" band at top	40.00 – 45.00
		1" band at top (not shown)	35.00 – 40.00
	#2	Same, "Turquoise Blue"	300.00 – 350.00

Butter & Cheese Dishes & Canisters

Butter dishes can be found in several sizes and shapes from quarter pound to two pounds. Many were premium items as indicated by the advertising found imprinted or embossed on them. In Row 2, #4 on page 127, the top says "Ask for Iowa creamery butter, always good!" So many older canisters are finding their way into today's kitchens that I have included a page of some odd ones. After all, it was canisters with screw-on lids that Cathy began buying 23 years ago that eventually evolved into this book.

Page 127

Row 1:	#1	Custard, McKee	75.00 – 95.00
	#2	Skokie green, McKee	150.00 – 175.00
	#3	Seville yellow, McKee	125.00 – 135.00
Row 2:	#1	Ships, McKee	60.00 – 70.00
	#2	Red Dots	155.00 – 175.00
	#3	Delphite, McKee	425.00 – 475.00
	#4	Jadite bottom, metal top ad	75.00 – 95.00
Row 3:	#1,2	Amber ¼ lb., Federal, ea.	40.00 – 45.00
	#3	Crystal frosted, ¼ lb., Federal	25.00 – 28.00
	#4	Amber 1 lb., Federal	40.00 – 45.00
	#5	Amber tub, Federal	40.00 – 45.00
Row 4:	**Jeannette** tops embossed "BUTTER"		
	#1	Delphite,	425.00 – 475.00

Row 4 (Continued):			
	#2	Jadite, dark,	125.00 – 145.00
	#3	Jadite, light,	125.00 – 145.00
	#4	Green	65.00 – 75.00
	#5	Pink (all pink)	85.00 – 95.00
Row 5:	#1	Ultra-marine, "Jennyware"	175.00 – 195.00
	#2	Same, crystal	65.00 – 75.00
	#3	Same, pink	175.00 – 195.00
	#4	Pink, embossed Scotty	45.00 – 55.00
Row 6:	#1	Green, embossed "B," 2 lb.	180.00 – 200.00
	#2	Green (or pink), "Hex Optic"	85.00 – 90.00
	#3	Pink, embossed "B," 2 lb.	200.00 – 225.00

Page 128

Row 1:	#1	Green, unknown	50.00 – 55.00
	#2	Green, Hocking	55.00 – 75.00
	#3	Green, "Block Optic," Hocking	50.00 – 65.00
Row 2:	#1	Green, unknown	55.00 – 75.00
	#2	Green "Clambroth," Hocking	165.00 – 195.00
	#3	Green, unknown	45.00 – 55.00
	#4	Refrigerator dish (sold as butter)	35.00 – 45.00
Row 3:	**Hazel-Atlas** tops embossed "BUTTER COVER"		
	#1	Green	65.00 – 75.00
	#2	Crystal	35.00 – 45.00
	#3	White	45.00 – 55.00

Row 3 (Continued):			
	#4	Cobalt blue	300.00 – 325.00
Row 4:	#1, 3	"Crisscross," 1 lb., green or pink	60.00 – 65.00
	#2	Same, crystal	25.00 – 28.00
	#4	Same, cobalt blue	135.00 – 145.00
Row 5:	#1, 3	Same, ¼ lb., green or pink	60.00 – 65.00
	#2	Same, crystal	25.00 – 28.00
	#4	Same, cobalt blue	135.00 – 145.00
Row 6:	#1	"Sanitary Refrigerator Jar"	150.00 – 165.00
	#2	Cheese, blue (foreign?)	125.00 – 140.00
	#3	"Hot & Cold" embossed	45.00 – 50.00
	#4	Cheese "Sanitary Preserver"	40.00 – 45.00

Page 129

Row 1:	#1	Fleur-de-lis pepper	8.00 – 12.00
	#2	Fleur-de-lis salt	12.00 – 15.00
	#3-5	Fleur-de-lis coffee, sugar, flour, ea.	25.00 – 35.00
	#6	Large canister wo/label	15.00 – 20.00
	#7	Small canister wo/label	4.00 – 6.00
Row 2:	#1	Teal stacking jar set	45.00 – 55.00
	#2	Sugar shaker	20.00 – 22.00
	#3-7	Spice canisters (match canisters in Row 1), ea.	15.00 – 18.00
	#8	Refrigerator container	18.00 – 22.00
	#9	Teal canister	25.00 – 30.00
Row 3:	#1	Canister, 64 oz.	20.00 – 25.00

Row 3 (Continued):			
	#2	Canister, 32 oz.	20.00 – 25.00
	#3-5	Canister, 8 oz., ea.	18.00 – 22.00
	#6	Canister, 16 oz., "Three Bears"	12.50 – 15.00
Row 4:	#1,2	Canister white w/Mexican decal, ea.	18.00 – 22.00
	#3	Canister, 128 oz.	45.00 – 55.00
	#4	Hazel-Atlas flour canister	80.00 – 90.00
Row 5:	#1	"Clambroth" large canister	65.00 – 85.00
	#2	Same, medium	55.00 – 75.00
	#3	Same, small	20.00 – 25.00
	#4	L.E.Smith jar	55.00 – 65.00
	#5	L.E.Smith jar, larger version	50.00 – 65.00

Kitchen Items

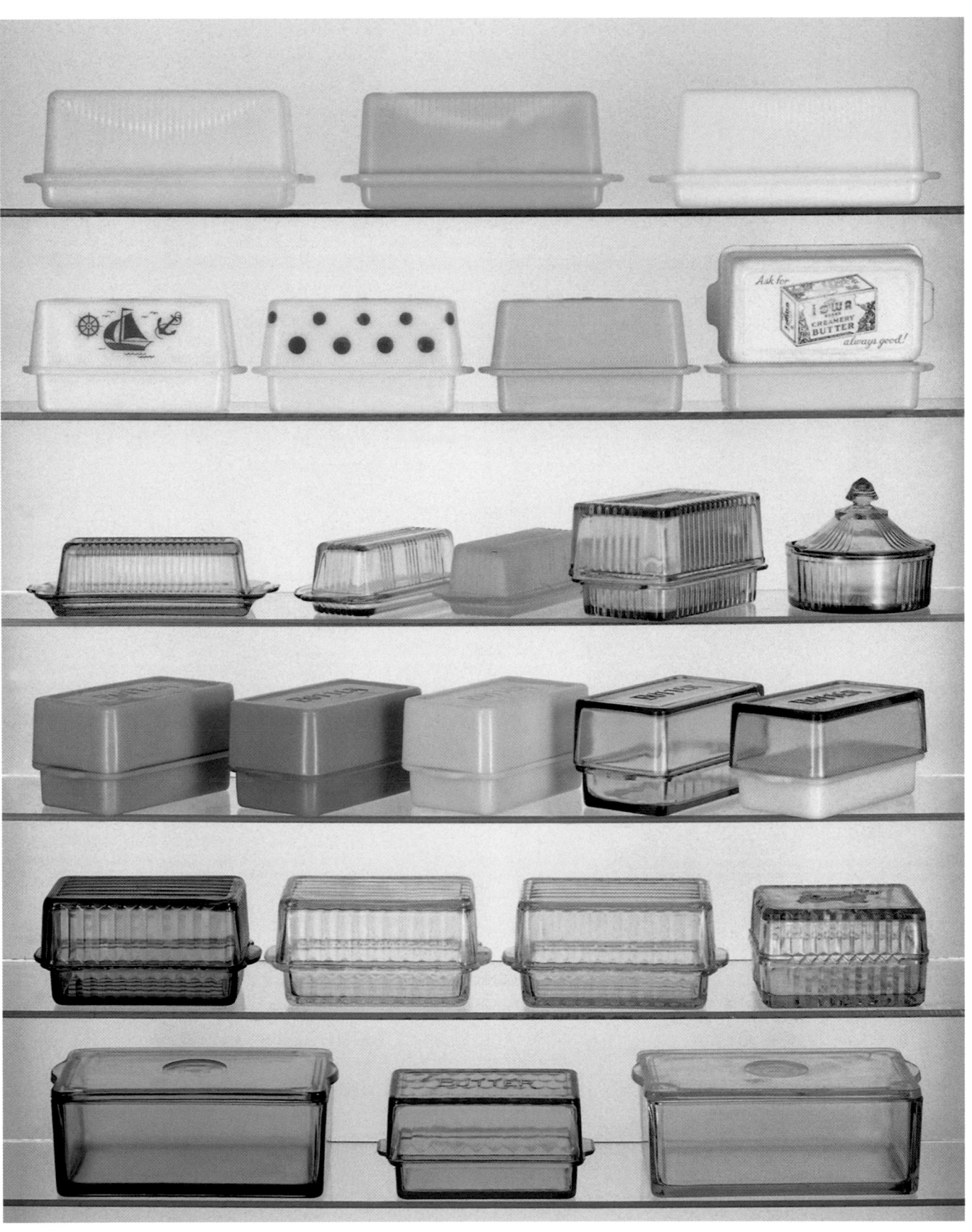

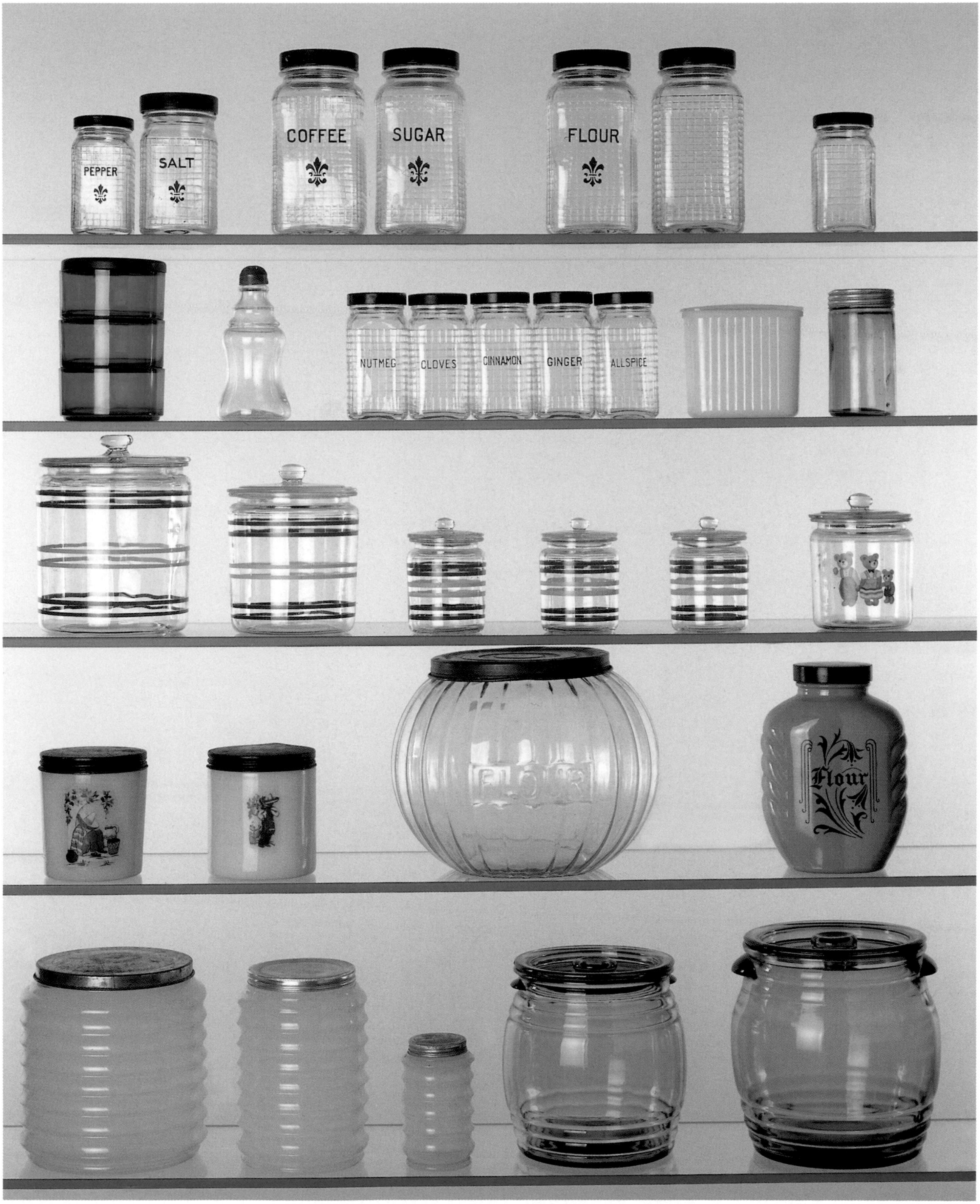
PEPPER
SALT
COFFEE
SUGAR
FLOUR
NUTMEG
CLOVES
CINNAMON
GINGER
ALLSPICE
FLOUR
Flour

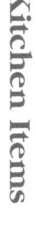

Kitchen Items

Page 131

Row 1:	Moon and Star canisters		
	#1,5 Pint	18.00 – 20.00	
	#2 Half gallon	25.00 – 28.00	
	#3 Gallon	28.00 – 30.00	
	#4 Quart	20.00 – 25.00	
Row 2:	#1 Two quart with decal	20.00 – 22.00	

Row 2 (Continued):

#2	Gallon, crystal	20.00 – 25.00
	Same, green	65.00 – 75.00
#3	Quart, red coffee	90.00 – 100.00
Row 3:	All 2 qt. Dutch decals, ea.	18.00 – 22.00
Row 4:	All 2 qt. assorted decals, ea.	18.00 – 22.00

Page 132

Row 1:	#1 Gallon w/floral decal, Hall Red Poppy	65.00 – 75.00
	#2 8 oz. striped provision jar	18.00 – 22.00
	#3 Same, 64 oz.	20.00 – 25.00
	#4 Same, 32 oz.	20.00 – 25.00
Row 2:	#1 Crystal SUGAR embossed canister	45.00 – 65.00
	#2 Same, TEA	45.00 – 65.00
	#3 Same, FLOUR	45.00 – 65.00
	#4 Same, RICE	45.00 – 65.00
	#5 Geo. A. Bayle store jar for Pretzels and Crackers, Saratoga Chip Potatoes, Salted Corn (see page 133 for close-ups)	75.00 – 100.00
Row 3:	#1 White "Mixed Vegetables,"	

	quart	15.00 – 18.00

Row 3 (Continued):

#2	White "Cherries," 2 qt.	18.00 – 20.00
#3	White "Mixed Vegetables," 2 qt.	18.00 – 20.00
#4	Provision jar, 8 oz.	18.00 – 22.00
#5	Crystal spice jar	45.00 – 55.00
#6	Teal stacking set	45.00 – 55.00
Row 4: #1	Green gallon jar	75.00 – 95.00
#2	Same, half gallon	75.00 – 95.00
#3	Same, pint	45.00 – 55.00
#4	Flour canister	65.00 – 75.00
#5	Green, rectangular, half gallon	75.00 – 100.00
#6	Green, rectangular, gallon	100.00 – 125.00

Page 133

Row 1:	#1 Green paneled provision jar, 32 oz.	75.00 – 95.00
	#2 Green, rectangular half gallon	75.00 – 100.00
	#3 Green, rectangular gallon	100.00 – 125.00
Row 2:	Hocking blue quart canister	300.00 – 350.00

Row 3:	Three views of Geo. A. Bayle store jars for Salted Corn, Saratoga Chip Potatoes, Pretzels and Crackers	75.00 – 100.00

Coffee & Tea Pots

Shown in Row 1, page 137, Cory coffee makers with glass insert rods were selling in 1946 for about $5.00 according to catalog information. However, by 1954, Silex electric coffee percolators were $13.95. On that same page, in Row 2, notice the wire "star" that some companies included to put between the burner and the glass pot to prevent breakage.

Kitchen Items

Page 135

Row 1:	#1	Silex, w/lid, large	200.00 – 250.00
	#2	Silex, "2 cupper, drip model"	35.00 – 40.00
	#3	Red Silex, marked on bottom & band at center	200.00 – 250.00
	#4	Silex dripolator	50.00 – 60.00
Row 2:	#1	Blue band dripolator w/creamer, sugar	45.00 – 50.00

Row 2 (Continued):			
	#2	Flashed red set: dripolator/creamer/ sugar/carafe	65.00 – 75.00
		Dripolator	45.00 – 50.00
		Creamer/sugar, pr.	20.00 – 25.00
Row 3:	#1	Cory coffee maker	25.00 – 30.00
	#2	McKee Glasbake dripolator	85.00 – 100.00
	#3,4	Glasbake ring decorated pots, ea.	35.00 – 40.00

Page 136

Row 1:	#1	Glasbake, tea kettle, white	45.00 – 50.00
	#2	Same, coffee pot	40.00 – 45.00
	#3	Same, unusual style	40.00 – 45.00
	#4	Rectangular casserole, probably made for Westinghouse	15.00 – 18.00
Row 2:	#1	Glasbake, gelatin mold	12.00 – 15.00
	#2	Same, rectangular casserole	15.00 – 18.00
	#3	Same, tube cake pan	12.50 – 15.00
Row 3:	#1	"Safe Bake," Saben Glass Co., heart shape 9½" or 10½" ea.	18.00 – 20.00

Row 3 (Continued):			
	#2	"Flamex" teapot	12.00 – 15.00
	#3	Same, double boiler	20.00 – 25.00
Row 4:	#1	Same as #1 in Row 3, 8½" casserole	25.00 – 30.00
	#2	Same, 6½"	12.00 – 15.00
	#3	Glasbake, 4¼" square	12.00 – 15.00
	#4	Same, 4¼" x 8"	15.00 – 18.00

Page 137

Row 1:	#1	Silex coffee pot w/lid	200.00 – 250.00
	#2	Cory coffee maker	25.00 – 30.00
	#3	Silex dripolator w/burner,	75.00 – 85.00
		wo/burner	50.00 – 60.00
Row 2:	#1	Glasbake teapot	45.00 – 50.00
	#2	Crystal teapot w/wire rack; detachable handle	12.00 – 15.00
	#3	Crystal Silex teapot	25.00 – 30.00
	#4	Silex individual coffee	35.00 – 40.00

Row 3:	#1-3	Pyrex 4 piece set w/handles	30.00 – 35.00
		Individual skillet wo/handle	6.00 – 7.00
		Same w/handle	8.00 – 10.00
Row 4:	#1	Box for set in Row 3	4.00 – 5.00
	#2	Cory double boiler	22.00 – 25.00
	#3	Glasbake teapot	35.00 – 40.00

Cruets & Dispensers

Page 139

Row 1: #1 Imperial "Canary Yellow" (vaseline) — 55.00 – 60.00
#2 Imperial green — 55.00 – 65.00
#3 Imperial "Cape Cod" — 30.00 – 35.00
#4 Imperial ribbed & beaded, pink — 55.00 – 60.00
#5 Same, no beads — 55.00 – 60.00
#6 Heisey, crystal — 35.00 – 40.00

Row 2: #1 Lancaster Glass Company, yellow — 50.00 – 60.00
#2 Same, green — 55.00 – 65.00
#3 Pink blown (probably foreign) — 40.00 – 45.00
#4 Pink — 55.00 – 60.00
#5 Fostoria "Garland" — 50.00 – 60.00
#6 Amber — 30.00 – 35.00

Row 3: #1 Heisey "Old Sandwich" w/stopper — 150.00 – 170.00
#2 Heisey "Yeoman" — 60.00 – 70.00
#3 Heisey "Twist," 4 oz., "Moongleam" green — 100.00 – 120.00

Row 3 (Continued):
#4 Same, "Flamingo" pink — 100.00 – 110.00
#5 Same, 2½ oz. — 120.00 – 140.00
#6 Imperial "Cape Cod" — 25.00 – 35.00
#7 Duncan "Caribbean" blue — 85.00 – 95.00

Row 4: #1 Duncan "Canterbury" — 25.00 – 30.00
#2 Red — 100.00 – 120.00
#3 Green — 50.00 – 55.00
#4 Imperial's "Verde" green from Heisey "Crystolite" mold — 20.00 – 25.00
#5 Hazel-Atlas green — 40.00 – 45.00
#6 Same, pink — 55.00 – 60.00

Row 5: #1, 2 U.S. Glass (?) dark green, ea. — 40.00 – 45.00
#3 Pink — 55.00 – 60.00
#4 Green — 40.00 – 45.00
#5 Crystal — 20.00 – 25.00
#6 Hocking green — 40.00 – 45.00

Page 140

Row 1: #1 Fostoria yellow "Trojan" — 300.00 – 325.00
#2 Fostoria blue "Fairfax," w/stopper — 175.00 – 200.00
#3 Fostoria amber "Fairfax," w/stopper — 85.00 – 100.00
#4 Fostoria green "Mayfair" — 100.00 – 125.00
#5 Same, yellow, w/stopper — 100.00 – 125.00

Row 2: #1 Fostoria "Colony" — 40.00 – 45.00
#2 Fostoria yellow "Baroque," w/stopper — 250.00 – 275.00
#3 Paden City pink #210 line — 75.00 – 85.00
#4 Same, green — 65.00 – 75.00
#5 Jadite "Vinegar" — 295.00 – 325.00

Row 3: #1 U.S. Glass (?) set on tray — 90.00 – 100.00
#2 Imperial blue (not Heisey experimental blue) — 85.00 – 95.00
#3 Same as #1, pink — 100.00 – 120.00

Row 3 (Continued):
#4 Pink — 55.00 – 60.00

Row 4: #1 U.S. Glass green — 45.00 – 50.00
#2 Same, crystal — 22.00 – 25.00
#3 Same, pink — 55.00 – 60.00
#4 Imperial, pink — 50.00 – 55.00
#5 New Martinsville "Janice" blue — 85.00 – 100.00
#6 New Martinsville "Radiance" crystal — 30.00 – 35.00

Row 5: #1 Cambridge green — 65.00 – 75.00
#2 Same, amber — 40.00 – 45.00
#3 Cambridge, "Caprice" blue — 80.00 – 100.00
#4 Cambridge, "Apple Blossom" pink — 150.00 – 195.00
#5 Cambridge, amber in Faberware — 28.00 – 32.00

Page 141 Dispensers

Row 1: #1 Mission Orange — 350.00 – 400.00
#2 South Seas Brand Pineapple Juice — 350.00 – 400.00
#3 Fowler's Cherry Smash — 275.00 – 300.00

Row 2: #1 Blue 2 pc. with lid — 400.00 – 450.00
#2 Orange Crush — 275.00 – 325.00
#3 Pink Nesbitts' — 200.00 – 250.00

Antique shows that feature old advertising items are among the best places to find kitchenware collectibles. In days past, that was where I bought many of my colored straw holders as well as other kitchen related collectibles. Today, all that has changed is advertising dealers now attend Depression Glass shows to buy our kitchenware to take to their shows. I miss the $150.00 – 200.00 prices for green straw jars at those shows!

The popularity of these remnants from restaurant and soda fountain days is awesome, as my son used to say! Advertising shows draw collectors with megabucks. There are usually four or five of these dispensers at one of the larger shows. Rarely are there any unsold, if priced fairly, when it is over. One impediment, when it comes to exhibiting them, is size. However, because of lingering nostalgic memories, most are finding homes on antique bars in the den or game room.

Page 143

Row 1:	#1	"Middleby Quality"	125.00 – 150.00
	#2	"Orange Crush" type	200.00 – 250.00
	#3	Manufactured by E.B. Evans Co., Philadelphia 33, Pa.	225.00 – 250.00
Row 2:	#1	Crystal and green (no name)	200.00 – 250.00
	#2	Samovar, green w/copper holder	300.00 – 325.00

Page 144

Row 1:	#1	Samovar, yellow (possibly Paden City)	300.00 – 350.00
	#2	Mission Orange	350.00 – 400.00
	#3	Mission Grapefruit	350.00 – 400.00
Row 2:	#1	Paden City percolator, 3 piece, green	400.00 – 450.00
		Amber (not shown)	275.00 – 295.00
		Blue w/lid (p. 141, Row 2, #1)	400.00 – 450.00
	#2	Mission Real Fruit Juice (pink)	225.00 – 250.00
	#3	Mission Real Fruit Juice (green)	225.00 – 250.00

Page 145

Row 1:	#1	Bireley's Orange Juice	400.00 – 450.00
	#2	Amber barrel and green base	350.00 – 375.00
	#3	Samovar, green (possibly Paden City)	300.00 – 350.00
Row 2:	#1	Orange Crush	250.00 – 300.00

Kitchen Items

Ice Buckets, Funnels* & Gravy Boats ▄▄▄

Collectors of ice buckets tell me the first fifty buckets are found rather easily; the next fifty come with some difficulty; and once you have approximately one hundred, you can no longer find those you don't already own or the room to display them! I've seen photos of some super collections, and most of them have been very artfully displayed.

Page 147

Row 1:	#1	Jeannette "Hex Optic" w/reamer top, green	45.00 – 50.00
	#2	Van Deman "Black Forest," pink	110.00 – 125.00
	#3	Fostoria "Polar Bear"	55.00 – 65.00
	#4	McKee, green	40.00 – 45.00
Row 2:	#1	Fostoria "Swirl," blue	75.00 – 85.00
	#2	Fostoria "Colony"	125.00 – 135.00
	#3	Cambridge etched grapes	50.00 – 55.00
	#4	Fostoria, yellow	55.00 – 65.00
Row 3:	#1	Fostoria, pink	75.00 – 85.00
	#2	Fenton, jade	65.00 – 75.00
	#3	Same, black	65.00 – 75.00
	#4	Pink w/etched flower & square bottom	40.00 – 45.00
Row 4:	#1	Cambridge, "Decagon," amethyst	65.00 – 85.00
	#2	Same, amber	50.00 – 55.00
	#3	Cambridge, green	55.00 – 65.00
	#4	Cambridge, #731 or "Rosalie," blue	100.00 – 120.00
Row 5:	#1	Hocking "Frigidaire Ice Server"	30.00 – 35.00
	#2	Hocking, "Ring"	35.00 – 38.00
	#3	Central Glass Co., pink	75.00 – 85.00
	#4	Crystal, Made in U.S.A. (English, other languages on side)	30.00 – 35.00

Page 148

Row 1:	#1	Fry w/lid, pink	225.00 – 250.00
	#2	Same, green	225.00 – 250.00
	#3	Paden City, w/lid, yellow	145.00 – 155.00
	#4	Fenton, w/lid, jade	150.00 – 160.00
Row 2:	#1	Cambridge "Mt. Vernon," red	95.00 – 110.00
	#2	Fenton, w/lid, green	85.00 – 95.00
	#3	Fenton "Plymouth," red	85.00 – 95.00
	#4	Green w/metal lid	50.00 – 60.00
Row 3:	#1	Pink "Diamond"	45.00 – 50.00
	#2	Green "Zig-Zag"	45.00 – 50.00
	#3	Green Westmoreland #101	85.00 – 110.00
Row 3 (Continued):			
	#4	Paden City "Party Line" w/etched flowers, pink	45.00 – 55.00
Row 4:	#1	Paden City "Party Line," pink	45.00 – 55.00
	#2	Same, amber	40.00 – 45.00
	#3, 4	Paden City "Cupid," green or pink	300.00 – 350.00
Row 5:	#1	Paden City "Cupid" ice tub, pink	300.00 – 325.00
	#2, 3	Paden City "Party Line" ice tub, ea.	40.00 – 45.00
	#4	Green ice tub	40.00 – 45.00

Page 149

Row 1:	#1	Funnel*, 11", crystal	25.00 – 30.00
	#2	Funnel, 9", crystal	20.00 – 25.00
	#3	Funnel, 5", crystal	12.00 – 15.00
	#4,5	Funnel, 4" or 4½", crystal, ea.	10.00 – 15.00
Row 2:	#1,2	Funnel, 4½", ribbed or plain green	40.00 – 45.00
	#3	Funnel, 4½", plain pink	40.00 – 45.00
	#4	Funnel, yellow canning	40.00 – 45.00
	#5	Funnel, Tufglas	65.00 – 75.00
Row 3:	#1	Funnel, Radnt	45.00 – 50.00
	#2	Cambridge green gravy & platter	125.00 – 135.00
	#3	Duncan "Festive" sauce & ladle	45.00 – 55.00
Row 4:	#1	Imperial, red gravy & platter	175.00 – 200.00
	#2	Same, pink wo/platter	55.00 – 65.00
	#3	Same, blue wo/platter	65.00 – 85.00
Row 5:	#1	Cambridge, double gravy wo/platter, amber	45.00 – 55.00
	#2	Same, pink	70.00 – 80.00
	#3	Same, blue	85.00 – 95.00
	#4	Cambridge cream sauce boat for asparagus platter	40.00 – 45.00

* No original jadite funnels were made; new ones are being produced in two sizes.

Kitchen Items

Knives

Knife prices have now stabilized. "Comparable" colors are selling in the same price range. All rarer knives are commanding higher prices!

Boxes add $1.00 – 5.00 to the price if in excellent condition. Boxes are placed near the knife found in that box. The box on the right in Row 1 on page 151 says "New York World's Fair," and, so labeled, will fetch a higher price.

Kitchen Items

Some knives are priced but not shown.

Page 151

Row 1:			Pink (lt/dk)	Blue	Crystal	Green
Row 1:	#1-3	3 Star, 8½"	32.00 – 35.00	32.00 – 35.00	10.00 – 15.00	——
	#4-6	3 Star, 9¼"	32.00 – 35.00	32.00 – 35.00	10.00 – 15.00	——
Row 2:	#1,2	3 Leaf Dur-X, 8½"	32.00 – 35.00	35.00 – 40.00	10.00 – 15.00	35.00 – 38.00
	#3,4	3 Leaf, Dur-X, 9¼"	32.00 – 35.00	——	10.00 – 15.00	——
	#5	Same (light amber)	225.00 – 275.00	——	——	——
	#6-8	5 Leaf, Dur-X, 8½"	——	35.00 – 40.00	10.00 – 15.00	35.00 – 38.00

			Pink (lt/dk)	Amber	Crystal	Green
Row 3:	#1,2	Rose spray, 8½"	*200.00 – 250.00	275.00 – 295.00	80.00 – 90.00	*200.00 – 250.00
	#3	Plain handle, 8½"	——	——	12.00 – 15.00	35.00 – 40.00
	#4-6	Plain handle, 9¼"	50.00 – 60.00	——	——	35.00 – 40.00
	#7	Same (pinkish/amber)	100.00 – 125.00	——	——	——

Page 152

			Pink (lt/dk)	Amber	Crystal	Green
Row 1:	#1-3	Block, 8¼"	45.00 – 50.00	——	15.00 – 22.00	40.00 – 45.00
	#4-8	AER FLO, 7½"	70.00 – 80.00	300.00 – 350.00	30.00 – 40.00	70.00 – 75.00
	#9	Same (Forest Green)	350.00 – 395.00			
Row 2:	#1-3	Steel-ite	90.00 – 100.00	——	35.00 – 45.00	90.00 – 100.00
	#4	Stonex, 8¼", (white)	300.00 – 350.00	——	——	——
	#5-8	Same, light or dark	——	275.00 – 295.00	——	65.00 – 75.00
Row 3:	#1	Candlewick, 8½"	——	——	450.00 – 500.00	——
	#2	Dagger, 9¼"	——	——	150.00 – 165.00	——
	#3	Westmoreland, #1800 Thumbguard, 9¼"	——	——	135.00 – 150.00	
	#4	Westmoreland #1801 Thumbguard	——	——	25.00 – 28.00	*350.00 – 395.00
	#5	Same, miniature (sample?)	——	——	150.00 – 175.00	——
	#6-8	Buffalo Knife (B.K.Co.), 9¼"	*350.00 – 395.00	——	15.00 – 18.00	40.00 – 45.00

Page 153

Row 1:	#1-5	Colored handles/blades, ea.	15.00 – 28.00
	#6,7	Plain	15.00 – 18.00
	#8	Pinwheel	6.00 – 12.00
Rows 2 & 3:		Boxes illustrated.	
		Add $1.00 – 5.00 depending on condition of box and rarity of knife.	

* not shown

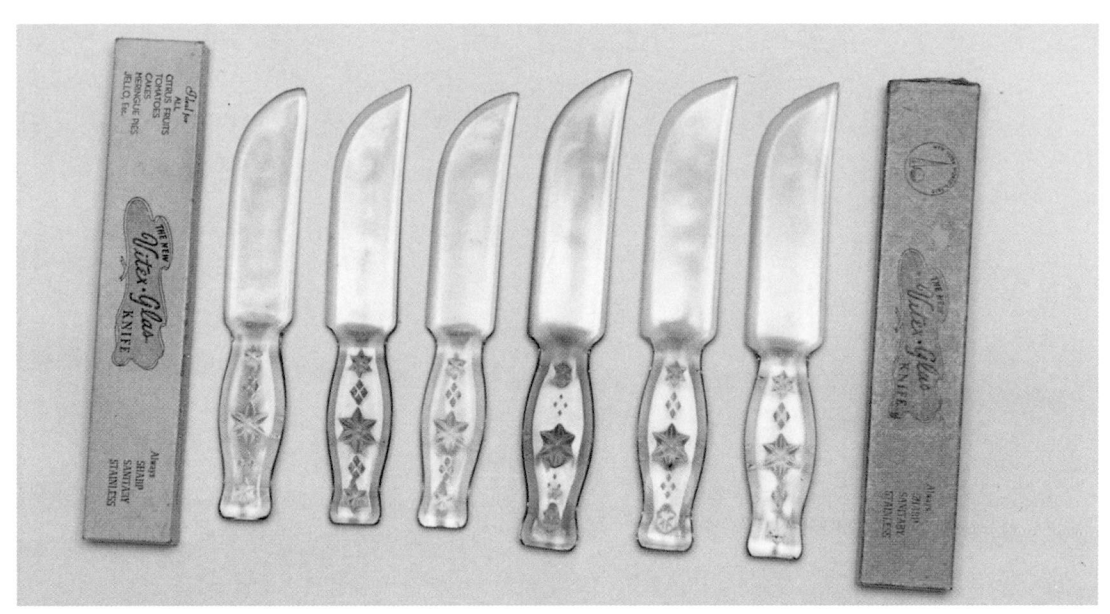

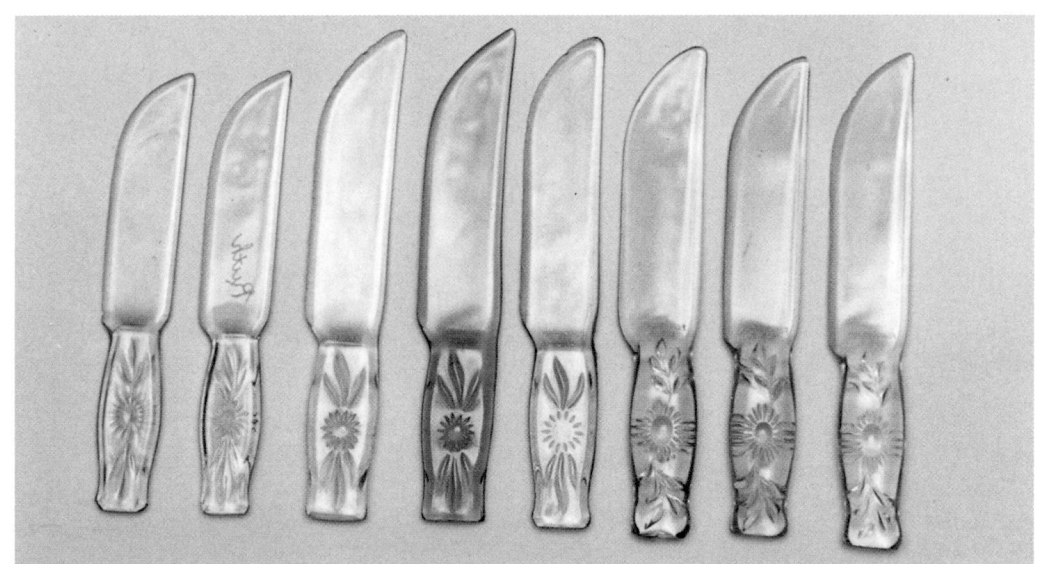

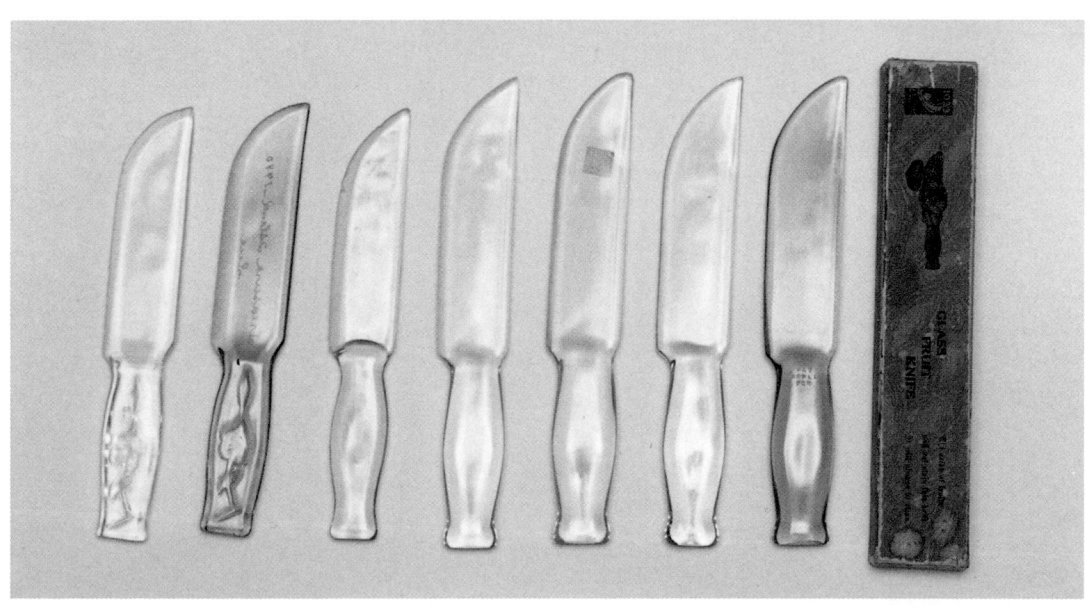

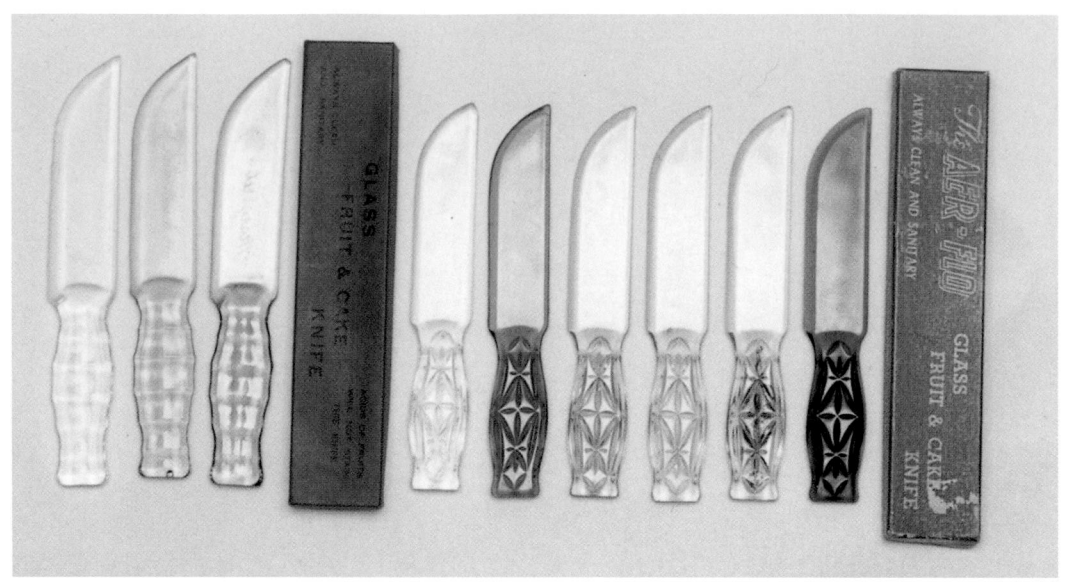

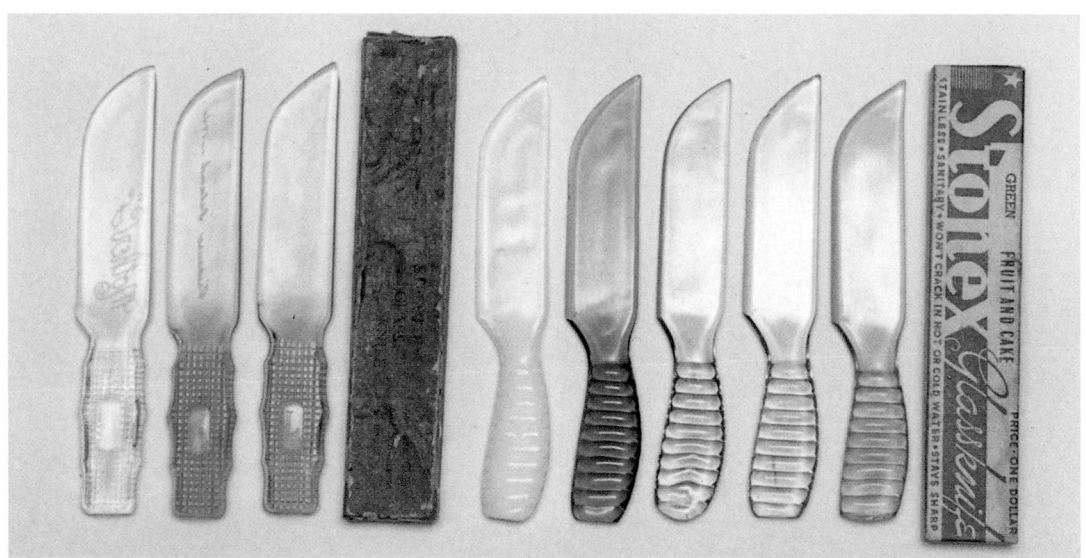

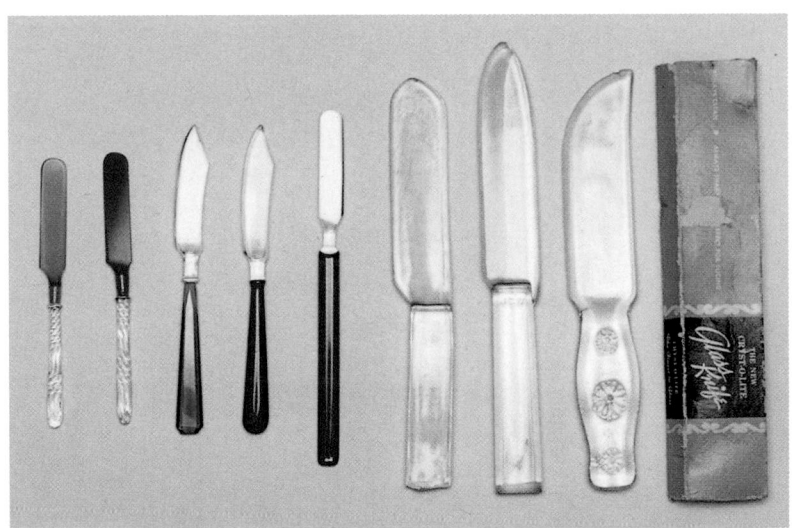

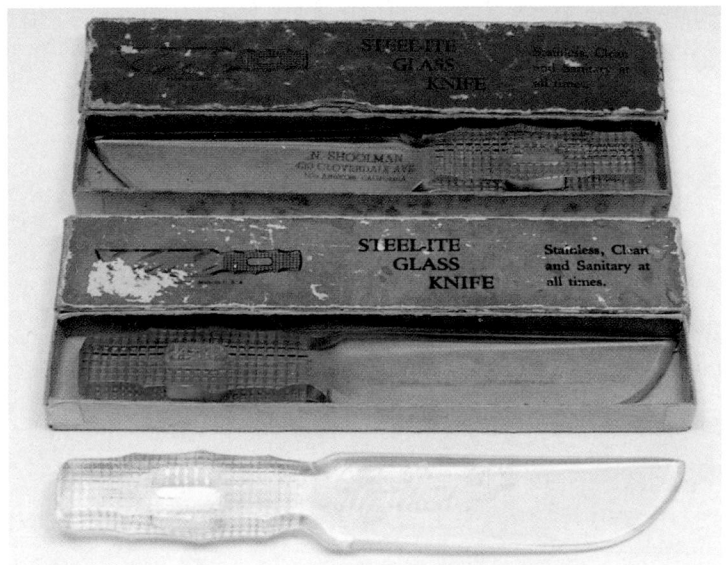

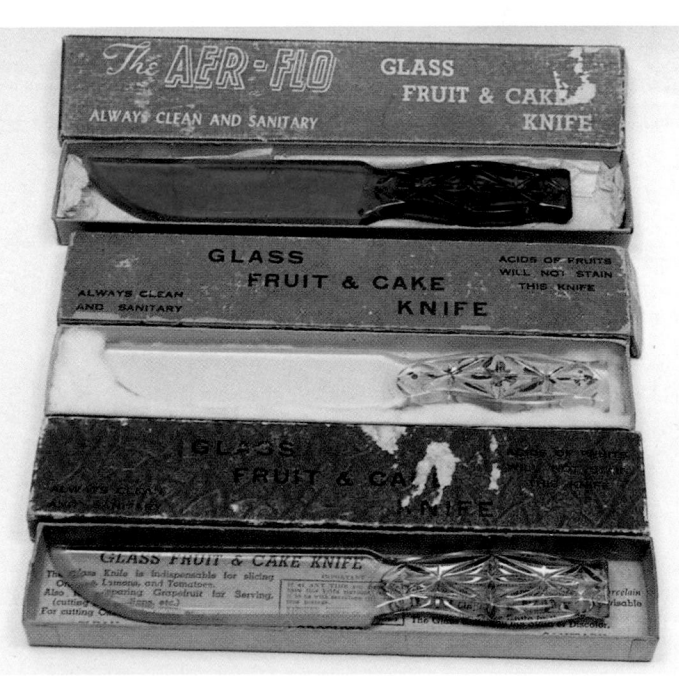

Ladles

Heisey, Fostoria, and Cambridge ladles are the most in demand, although other companies' ladles are collected. An abundance of black ladles with a dwindling demand for them has caused the price of those to plunge.

Page 155

Row 1: #1	Duncan, "Festive"	22.00 – 25.00	
#2	Pink	18.00 – 22.00	
#3,4	Blue, pink	22.00 – 25.00	
#5	Blue	30.00 – 35.00	
Row 2: #1	Cambridge, pink	22.00 – 25.00	
#2,3	Same, green	22.00 – 25.00	
#4	Same, Forest Green	25.00 – 28.00	
#5	Same, Moonlight blue	35.00 – 40.00	
#6	Same, amber	20.00 – 22.00	
Row 3:	Ladle w/pointed bottom	25.00 – 30.00	

Column 1:

#1,2	Green or amber crisscross	20.00 – 22.00
#3	Blue, crisscross design	25.00 – 28.00
#4,5	Green or yellow	20.00 – 22.00

Column 2:

#1	Fostoria, crystal	15.00 – 18.00
#2	Pink, same	30.00 – 35.00

Column 2 (Continued):

#3	Same, yellow	30.00 – 35.00
#4	Same, amber	25.00 – 27.50
	(green, not shown)	30.00 – 35.00
#5	Same, light blue	45.00 – 50.00
#6	Same, cobalt blue	50.00 – 55.00

Column 3:

#1	Cambridge, blue	35.00 – 40.00
#2-4	Same, green	22.00 – 25.00
#5	Same, crystal	10.00 – 12.00

Column 4:

#1	Cambridge, amberina	50.00 – 55.00
#2	Same, Ivory	35.00 – 45.00
#3	Same, Primrose	35.00 – 45.00
#4	Same, Azurite	45.00 – 50.00
#5	Ebony	35.00 – 40.00

Page 156

Row 1: #1	Crystal, side spout	12.00 – 15.00	
#2-4	Candlewick, ea.	15.00 – 22.00	
#5	Higbee, signed bee in bottom	20.00 – 25.00	
Row 2: #1-4	Crystal, unusual shapes, ea.	12.00 – 15.00	

Columns 1 & 2: **All ladles have rounded bottoms.**

#1,4-6	Crystal, plain & etched	10.00 – 15.00
#2	Green	22.00 – 25.00
#3	Black	30.00 – 35.00
#7	Amethyst	30.00 – 35.00

Column 2:

#1,2	Blue	30.00 – 35.00
#4	Clambroth	35.00 – 40.00
#3	Cobalt blue	40.00 – 45.00
#5	Pink	22.00 – 25.00

Column 2 (Continued):

#6	Amber	18.00 – 22.00
#7	Black	30.00 – 35.00

Column 3: **All ladles have wedge shaped handles.**

#1,10	White	15.00 – 18.00
#2	Black	25.00 – 30.00
#3,4,8	Blue, ea.	25.00 – 28.00
#5	Crystal	12.00 – 15.00
#6,7,9	Yellow, pink or green	22.00 – 25.00

Column 4: **All ladles have rounded handles.**

#1	Forest green	18.00 – 22.00
#8	Light blue	25.00 – 28.00
#2,5,10	Crystal, ea.	12.00 – 15.00
#3,4,6	Pink or green	22.00 – 25.00
#7	Amber	18.00 – 22.00
#9	Black	25.00 – 30.00

Page 157

Row 1: #1-3	All iridized carnival colors	45.00 – 50.00	
Row 2: #1,2	Heisey, Flamingo, ea.	30.00 – 40.00	
#3,4	Same, Hawthorne	45.00 – 55.00	
#5	Same, Moongleam	35.00 – 45.00	

Columns 1 & 2: **All ladles have flat bottoms.**

Column 1:

#1,5	Flashed or amber	12.00 – 15.00
#2,4, 6,7	Yellow, green or pink	22.00 – 25.00
#3	Blue	30.00 – 35.00
#8	Cobalt blue, etched	40.00 – 45.00

Column 2:

#1	Cobalt blue	40.00 – 45.00
#2	Amethyst	30.00 – 35.00

Column 2 (Continued):

#3	Amber	18.00 – 22.00
#4,6	Frosted blue or vaseline	30.00 – 35.00
#5	Crystal	12.00 – 18.00

Column 3: **All ladle knobs end in triangle shape.**

#1	Amber	18.00 – 22.00
#2	Green	22.00 – 25.00
#3,5	Amethyst or vaseline	30.00 – 35.00
#4	Red	40.00 – 50.00

Column 4: **All ladle knobs end in straight line.**

#1	Red	40.00 – 50.00
#2,4	Frosted & vaseline	30.00 – 35.00
#3,6	Flashed or amber	18.00 – 22.00
#5	Green	22.00 – 25.00

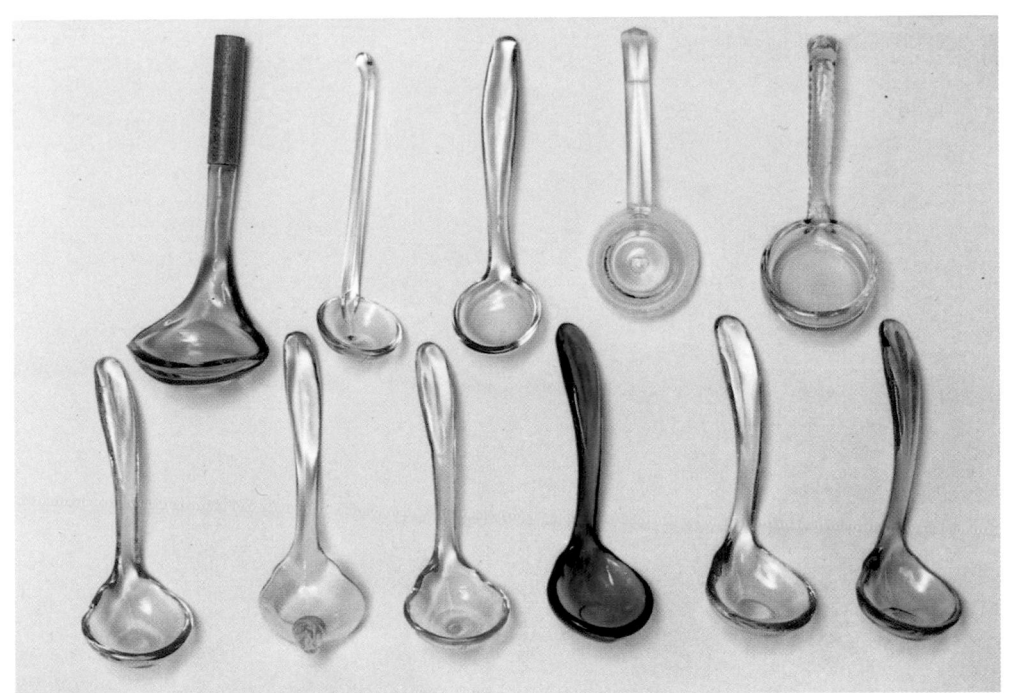

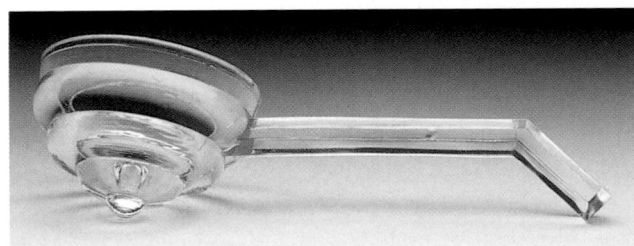

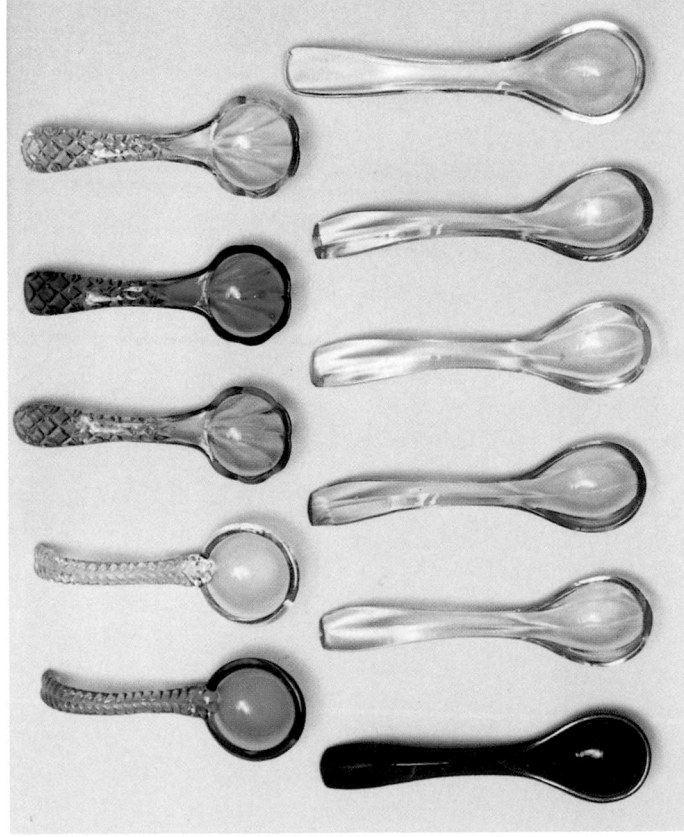

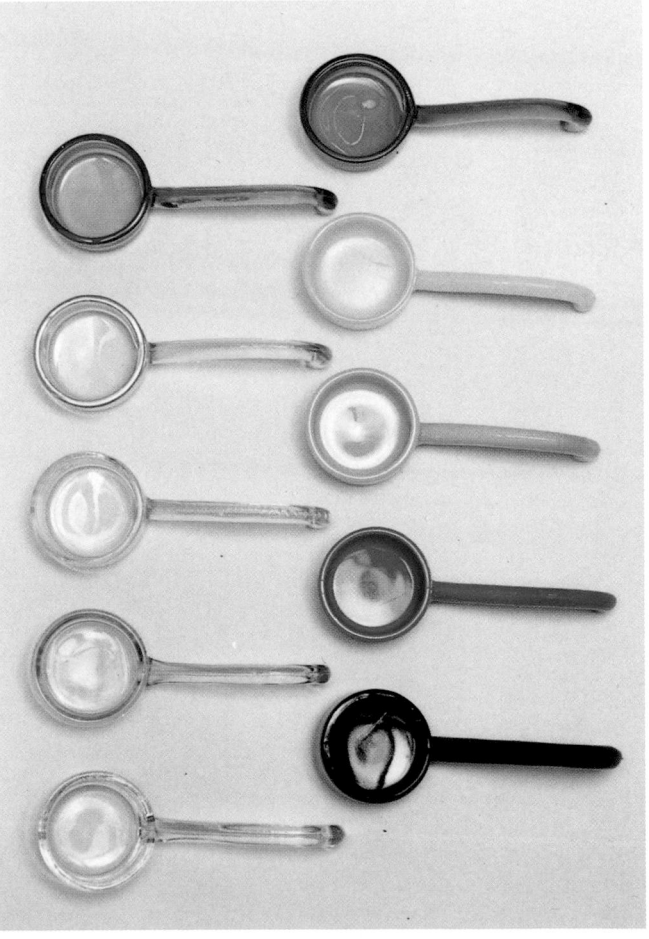

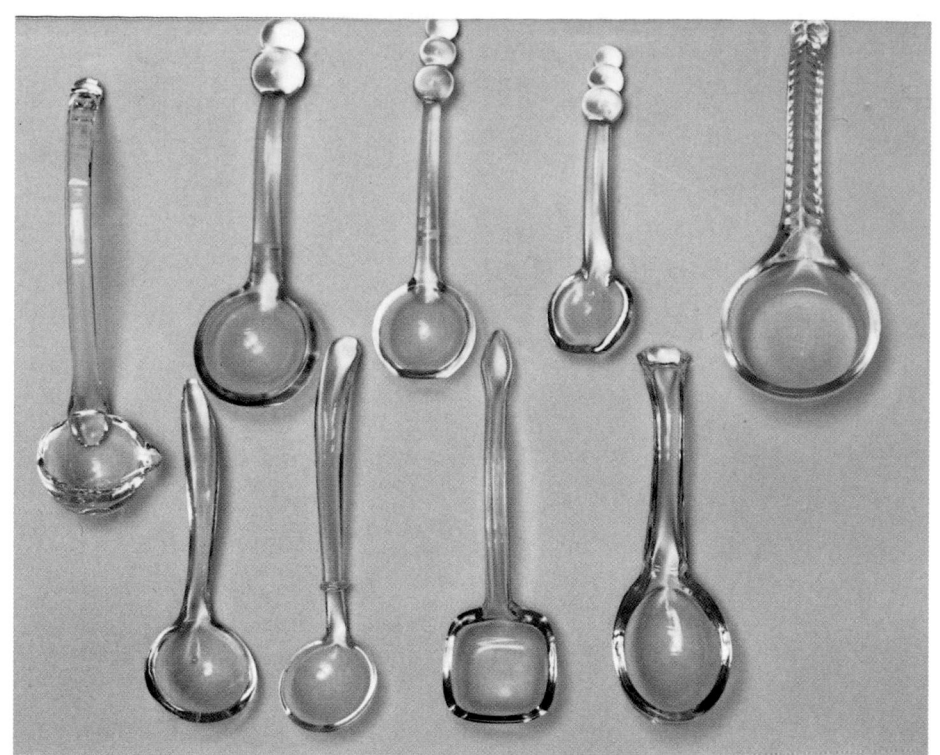

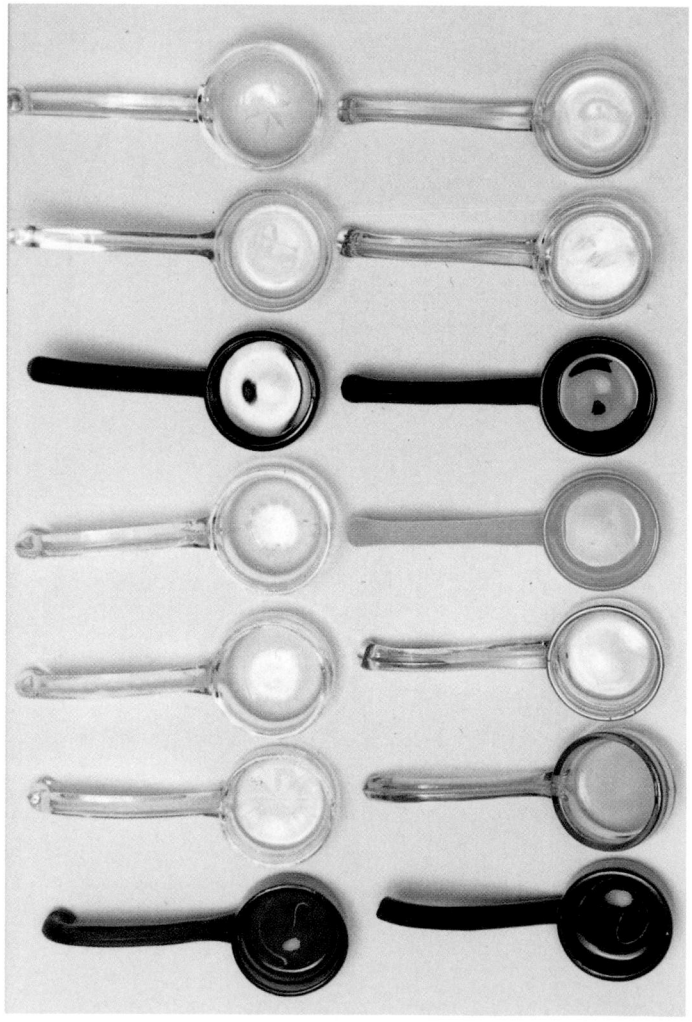

Measuring Cups

You will notice a large price range on these measuring cups. One of the major problems that I had in pricing this book, with dealers from the East and the West, was a big discrepancy in prices obtained from them. In the case of advertising cups, collectors of advertising will pay more than collectors of measuring cups. A large price range is evidence such disparity of values exists between the two collectible categories. That is just one of the things that makes pricing a book such FUN! Actually, only two people determine price — the buyer and the seller.

Page 159

Row 1:	#1	"CREAM DOVE" Brand Peanut Butter Salad Dressing Cream Dove Mfg. in Binghamton, NY	30.00 – 38.00
	#2	"FLUFFO," "Be sure of success, use Fluffo shortening & Salad oil"	30.00 – 38.00
	#3	"EASY," Combination washer/dryer with confidence built in	25.00 – 30.00
	#4	"ARMOUR," Use Armour's extract of beef	30.00 – 38.00
	#5	"PET MILK," Use Pet Milk, my pet cup	20.00 – 25.00
Row 2:	#1	"TIPPE CANOE," Kitchen Cabinets, none better	30.00 – 38.00
	#2	"Owen & Co."	30.00 – 38.00
	#3	"NAPANEE" Dutch Kitchen Cabinet, world's finest kitchen	30.00 – 38.00
	#4	"HEALTH CLUB" Baking Powder for Success in every baking	30.00 – 38.00
	#5	"CLOVERDALE" quality (4-leaf clover in red)	30.00 – 38.00
	#6	"ALONZOO BLISS CO.," our native herbs, Washington, D.C., 2 Tbsps.	12.00 – 15.00
Row 3:	#1	"SILVER'S," Brooklyn, Trademark (picture Brooklyn Bridge)	30.00 – 38.00
	#2	"PICKERINGS," Your credit is good, complete home furnishings, 10th & Penn, Pittsburgh	30.00 – 38.00
	#3	"SELLER'S," Pat. Dec. 8, 1925	30.00 – 38.00
	#4	"BROWN EKBERG" Golden Rule Store	30.00 – 38.00
	#5	"SAGINAW MILLING CO."	30.00 – 38.00
	#6	"ROOT-TEA-NA," For health use ROOT-TEA-NA, Akron, Oh., 4 Tbsps.	20.00 – 25.00
Row 4:	#1	"STICKNEY & POOR" Spice Co.	30.00 – 38.00
	#2	Same, BOSTON	30.00 – 38.00
	#3	"SILVER & CO.," 8 oz. tumbler	25.00 – 30.00
	#4	"Higbee" (bee in bottom)	25.00 – 30.00
	#5	Same, only dry measure	25.00 – 30.00
	#6	Dry measure (cup shape)	25.00 – 30.00
Row 5:	#1	Odd shade	15.00 – 20.00
	#2	Log handle	20.00 – 25.00
	#3	Kellogg's	30.00 – 38.00
	#4	Square	24.00 – 30.00
	#5	Crystal	20.00 – 25.00
Row 6:	#1-3	Westmoreland wo/measure lid, pat. 1897 (reproduced)	50.00 – 60.00
		Same w/measure lid (Most have advertising in base such as "Finley Acker & Co.," highest grade at lowest cost.)	95.00 – 110.00
	#4,5	Measurements below spout; wo/measure lid	95.00 – 110.00
		w/lid	95.00 – 110.00

Page 161

Rows 1-3: Jeannette sets except *Row 2:* Green $30.00 – 35.00; Pink $35.00 – 40.00

		Ultra-marine	Pink	Crystal	Delphite	Jadite*
	1 cup	70.00 – 75.00	70.00 – 75.00	40.00 – 45.00	75.00 – 85.00	75.00 – 85.00
	½ cup	60.00 – 65.00	60.00 – 65.00	40.00 – 45.00	55.00 – 65.00	55.00 – 65.00
	⅓ cup	60.00 – 65.00	60.00 – 65.00	35.00 – 40.00	55.00 – 65.00	55.00 – 65.00
	¼ cup	50.00 – 55.00	50.00 – 55.00	35.00 – 40.00	45.00 – 50.00	45.00 – 50.00
	Set	240.00 – 260.00	240.00 –260.00	150.00 – 170.00	230.00 – 265.00	230.00 – 265.00

Row 4:	#1	Glasbake (A.J. Novite & Sons; Charleston, 3 S.C.)	20.00 – 25.00
	#2	Box for Jeannette set	10.00 – 15.00
	#3	Fry, 1 spout	85.00 – 95.00
	#4	Fry, 3 spout	85.00 – 95.00
	#5	"Ideal" teas. & Tbsp. measure (Pat. 5/26/95)	40.00 – 45.00
Row 5:	#1	McKee, crystal, 2 spout	75.00 – 90.00
	#2	Radnt, crystal, 2 spout or Glasbake, 1 spout	90.00 – 100.00
	#3	Glasbake, white, 1 spout	65.00 – 75.00
	#4,5	Glasbake, crystal, 1 spout, ea.	45.00 – 65.00
Row 6:	#1-5	McKee 2 spout (turned to show from all angles): (prices below by color)	

Seville Yellow	Caramel	Black	Jadite	Chalaine Blue
180.00 – 200.00	550.00 – 650.00	800.00 – 900.00	225.00 – 275.00	800.00 – 900.00

* reproduced in 2002

Page 162

Row 1 & 2: Hocking Glass Co.

	#1	"Fire-King" 1 spout	25.00 – 28.00
	#2	Box w/measure cup/thermometers for room/bath/food	75.00 – 80.00
	#3	"Fire-King" 3 spout	28.00 – 32.00
	#4,5	Green 1 spout, ea.	30.00 – 35.00
Row 2:	#1,4	Green Clambroth, ea.	225.00 – 275.00
	#2,3	Crystal, ea.	18.00 – 22.00
	#5	Green	30.00 – 35.00
	#6	Crystal "Fire-King"	12.00 – 15.00
Row 3:	#1	Hocking, crystal, 3 spout	18.00 – 22.00
	#2	Hazel-Atlas, 3 spout, cobalt blue	300.00 – 350.00
	#3	Same, yellow	295.00 – 325.00
	#4	Same, unembossed pink	35.00 – 40.00
	#5	Same, unembossed green	30.00 – 35.00
	#6	Same, embossed "Urban's Liberty Flour"	75.00 – 85.00
Row 4:	#1	Hazel-Atlas, 3 spout, red flashed	55.00 – 65.00
	#2	Same, green flashed	55.00 – 65.00
	#3	Same, opalescent white	45.00 – 55.00

Row 4 (Continued):

	#4,5	Same, flat white, w/red trim	55.00 – 65.00
	#6	Same, embossed Kellogg's, pink	40.00 – 45.00
Row 5:	#1	Same, embossed Kellogg's, green	35.00 – 40.00
	#2	Hazel-Atlas, 1 spout, pink	35.00 – 40.00
	#3	Same, green	30.00 – 35.00
	#4	Federal, green, no hdl., 3 spout	35.00 – 40.00
	#5	Same, crystal	20.00 – 25.00
	#6	Same, amber	35.00 – 40.00
	#7	Federal, green, 1 spout, solid handle	40.00 – 45.00
Row 6:	#1	Federal, 3 spout, open handle, amber	35.00 – 40.00
	#2	Same, pink	40.00 – 45.00
	#3	Same, crystal	18.00 – 22.00
	#4,5	Federal, 3 spout, solid handle, green	40.00 – 45.00
	#6	Same, crystal	22.00 – 25.00

Page 163

Row 1:

	#1	U.S. Glass 1 spout, pink	60.00 – 65.00
	#2	Same, green	35.00 – 40.00
	#3	U.S. Glass 3 spout, green	35.00 – 40.00
	#4	U.S. Glass 1 spout, crystal	22.00 – 25.00
	#5	U.S. Glass dry measure, white	175.00 – 200.00
Row 2:	#1	U.S. Glass 2 spout, slick hdl./green	40.00 – 45.00
	#2	Same, pink	50.00 – 55.00
	#3	Dry measure, embossed E.E. Hamm, Hanover, Pa.	50.00 – 60.00
	#4	Same, embossed Sellers	55.00 – 65.00
	#5	U.S. Glass, 1 spout, slick hdl./grn.	40.00 – 45.00
Row 3:	#1	Tufglas	65.00 – 75.00
	#2,5	Green, 1 spout	75.00 – 85.00
	#3	Amber, 1 spout	300.00 – 325.00
	#4	Crystal, 1 spout	22.00 – 25.00

Row 3 (Continued):

Row 4:	#1	Glasbake, red flashed	55.00 – 65.00
	#2	Glasbake, white w/red trim	65.00 – 75.00
	#3	Pyrex, 1 spout	18.00 – 22.00
	#4	Pyrex	10.00 – 12.00
	#5	Pyrex, 2 spout	22.00 – 25.00
Row 5:	#1	Cambridge, crystal	20.00 – 25.00
	#2	Paden City, crystal	20.00 – 25.00
	#3,4	Cup or dry measure embossed "Kanton Kitchen Kup," ea.	20.00 – 25.00
	#5	Heisey cup	275.00 – 300.00
Row 6:	#1	Crystal, oval	22.00 – 25.00
	#2	Green, oval	55.00 – 65.00
	#3	Blue foreign EJKRONT (measures tea, coffee, wine)	75.00 – 85.00
	#4	Foreign (liters) etched 1895	18.00 – 22.00
	#5	Foreign "Sepdelen"	75.00 – 85.00

It is difficult to obtain an accurate price on items that have not been sold in years. For example, a Chalaine blue four cup measure without handles was bought for $100.00 in 1980. One of these just sold for $1,600.00. Are the others known worth the same — or more? How many collectors are willing to pay that much for the privilege of owning a Chalaine blue four cup measure?

Kitchen Items

Page 165

Row 1:	#1	McKee Chalaine blue, 4 cup, no handle	1,500.00 – 1,600.00
	#2	Same, Seville yellow	500.00 – 600.00
	#3	Same, Jadite green	700.00 – 800.00
	#4	Same, crystal	150.00 – 165.00
	#5	Tufglas, 4 cup	80.00 – 90.00
Row 2:	#1	McKee Seville yellow, 4 cup, ftd. w/hdl	135.00 – 140.00
	#2	Same, Chalaine blue	500.00 – 550.00
	#3	Same, Jadite	125.00 – 135.00
	#4	Same, Custard	50.00 – 55.00
Row 3:	#1	Cambridge dry measure, green	300.00 – 325.00
	#2	Cambridge, 1 spout, 1 cup, pink	275.00 – 295.00
	#3	Same, green	275.00 – 295.00
	#4	U.S. Glass, 2 cup, pink	200.00 – 225.00
		(Not shown: green, 175.00 – 200.00; crystal, 75.00 – 95.00)	
Row 4:	#1	McKee, 4 cup, Caramel	700.00 – 750.00
	#2	Same, Delphite	600.00 – 650.00
	#3	Unknown, green, 2 cups = 1 pt. & 20 oz. = 1 pt. on side	150.00 – 175.00
Below:		Peacock blue, 1 cup, dry measure	225.00 – 250.00

Measuring Pitchers

There are more measuring cup collectors than there are measuring pitcher collectors. Owning decorated McKee two cup pitchers alone could fill several shelves in your china cabinet! Just take a look at the top four rows on Page 168. Considering that each of those designs could come on white or Custard as well as all the different colors gives an idea how many reamer tops you would need to complete these sets. See Reproduction Section, pages 266 – 270, for items marked with an asterisk (*).

See Reproduction Section, pages 266 – 270

Kitchen Items

Page 167

Rows 1-4 Hazel-Atlas 2 cups

Row 1:	#1-3	White w/dots	45.00 – 55.00
	#4	Green w/white dots	50.00 – 60.00
	#5	Black flower decal	45.00 – 55.00
Row 2:	#1,2	White w/decorated bands	40.00 – 45.00
	#3	White	25.00 – 30.00
	#4	Opalescent white	25.00 – 30.00
	#5	Fired-on red	50.00 – 55.00
Row 3:	#1	Yellow	275.00 – 295.00
	#2	Iridized	100.00 – 125.00
	#3	Green	45.00 – 50.00
	#4	Cobalt blue	*250.00 – 275.00

Row 4:	#1,2	Pink or light pink	110.00 – 125.00
	#3	Crystal	25.00 – 28.00
	#4	Embossed A & J	22.00 – 25.00
Row 5:	#1	Hocking, 2 cup, ribbed, green	60.00 – 70.00
	#2	Same, pink	60.00 – 70.00
	#3	Same, crystal	25.00 – 28.00
	#4	Vitrock w/lid	65.00 – 75.00
Row 6:	#1	Hocking, 2 cup, green	40.00 – 45.00
	#2	Same, green Clambroth	150.00 – 175.00
	#3	Fire-King, 16 oz., 2 spout	28.00 – 32.00
	#4	Made in Italy 1971, "Grandma's Old Time Measure"	18.00 – 25.00

Page 168

Rows 1 – 4 All McKee 2 cups

Row 1:	#1,2	Ships	45.00 – 50.00
	#3-5	Black, red bows or wild rose flower	50.00 – 55.00
Row 2:	#1,2	Red or black "Diamond Check"	50.00 55.00
	#3,4	Red or green dots on white	50.00 – 55.00
Row 3:	#1	Fired-on green	45.00 – 55.00
	#2	Jadite	65.00 – 75.00
	#3	Delphite	110.00 – 125.00
	#4	Seville yellow	40.00 – 45.00
	#5	Custard	30.00 – 35.00

Row 4:	#1,2	Black or orange dots on custard	50.00 – 60.00
	#3	Custard w/red trim	40.00 – 45.00
	#4	Glasbake crystal	30.00 – 35.00
Row 5:	#1	Iridized carnival	35.00 – 45.00
	#2	Crystal	20.00 – 25.00
	#3	U.S. Glass slick hdl., grn.	45.00 – 50.00
	#4	Same, crystal	25.00 – 30.00
	#5	Same, pink	50.00 – 55.00
Row 6:		All Jeannette	
	#1,2	Light or dark Jadite	65.00 – 75.00
	#3	Delphite	110.00 – 125.00
	#4	Transparent green	110.00 – 125.00

Page 169

Row 1:	#1	"Ocean Mills," Montreal, Canada (Man holding box of Chinese starch), 2½ pt.	60.00 – 75.00
	#2	"Davis Baking Powder," ½ gal.	60.00 – 75.00
	#3	½ gal.	40.00 – 50.00
Row 2:	#1	1 qt.	45.00 – 55.00
	#2	1 qt., green	800.00 – 850.00
	#3	Cambridge, 1 qt., measure top	100.00 – 125.00
	#4	Baby formula, 20 oz. (foreign) Estans Materna	30.00 – 35.00
Row 3:	#1	Umpire Glass Co., Pittsburgh, 1 qt.	25.00 – 30.00

Row 3 (Continued):			
	#2	Silvers Brooklyn Trademark, 1 qt.	25.00 – 30.00
	#3	Sanitary Bess Mixer (embossed "4" inside a large "1")	175.00 – 200.00
	#4	Lighting Dasher Egg Beater Co., 1 pt.	25.00 – 30.00
	#5	Hazel-Atlas 4 cup crystal	22.00 – 28.00
Row 4:	#1	Hazel-Atlas frosted green	*25.00 – 30.00
	#2	White w/red trim, ea.	30.00 – 35.00
	#3	Hazel-Atlas A&J green	30.00 – 35.00
	#4	White w/black trim	30.00 – 35.00

Mechanical Attachments

Shown on the right below and in the middle of Row 3 on page 171 are two different "Cold Water Coffee Extractors." Neither of these was ever used, so they may have been a great idea that wasn't popular.

Page 170

Row 1:	#1	Economy dispenser	40.00 – 50.00
	#2	Filtron cold water coffee extractor	100.00 – 125.00

Page 171

Row 1:	#1	Mayonnaise maker	20.00 – 22.00
	#2	Sugar shaker (one tsp. measure top)	40.00 – 45.00
	#3	Honey or other liquid dispenser	20.00 – 25.00
	#4	Syrup dispenser	15.00 – 20.00
	#5	"Vidrio" electric mixer w/green base	75.00 – 95.00
Row 2:	#1	Mixer	15.00 – 18.00
	#2	Food chopper	22.00 – 28.00
	#3	Mixer	18.00 – 22.00
	#4	Mixer, bands at 4-8-12 oz. marks	22.00 – 25.00
	#5	Electric beater	30.00 – 40.00
Row 3:	#1	Mixer	35.00 – 40.00
	#2	Measure for CoffeeX coffee extractor	12.50 – 15.00
	#3	CoffeeX cold water coffee extractor	100.00 – 125.00
	#4	Green butter churn	375.00 – 425.00

Kitchen Items

Kitchen gadgets abound and this is only a tip of the iceberg as to what it is possible to collect from that era. You will notice that some of these have motors, but the majority were hand-cranked.

Kitchen Items

Page 173

Row 1:	#1	Food or drink mixer, crackle pattern	22.00 – 28.00
	#2	Ultra-marine beater	65.00 – 75.00
	#3	Ice cream mixer, Consolidated Mfg. Co.	75.00 – 100.00
	#4	Evenfull beater	55.00 – 65.00
	#5	Crystal beater	20.00 – 28.00
	#6	Electric beater w/custard bottom (Chicago Elec.)	60.00 – 70.00
		w/milk green bottom	75.00 – 95.00
Row 2:	#1	Naxon Electric Co. electric beater	45.00 – 55.00
	#2	Food or drink mixer, pat. Jan. 6, 1920	15.00 – 20.00
	#3	Waldorf Sealtop shaker and mixer	15.00 – 20.00
	#4	Hot toddy mixer, "a meal in a glass"	15.00 – 20.00
	#5	Vidrio electric mixer	75.00 – 95.00
Row 3:	#1	Keystone beater, Pat. Dec. 1885, North Bros.	75.00 – 100.00
	#2, 3	Ladd beater, green or pink, complete	65.00 – 75.00
	#4	Chopper, qt. capacity	20.00 – 28.00
	#5, 6	Mixers, bands indicate 4, 8, 12 oz. marks, ea.	25.00 – 30.00
	#7	Air-O-Mixer, Bentley-Beatle, Inc., "Egg beater, drink mixer, cream whipper, mayonnaise mixer"	25.00 – 30.00

ELECTRIC MIXERS

"Polar Cub Junior"—7½x 9½, steel frame, drawn steel motor housing, standard "Universal" motor, base of motor holder and motor gray enameled, other metal parts nickel plated, delft blue finish hardwood handle, toggle switch in head of motor, cord and 2 pc. attachment plug, crystal mixing bowl.
1H3153—1 in box.
Each $3.75
3 or more, **Each 3.50**

"Eskimo"—10½ in., high speed heavy duty motor, **toggle switch**, 5 in. driving rod, 2 types of agitators, heavy cast frame, battleship gray enameled, white enameled handle, rubber feet, cord and plug, 16 oz. glass bowl.
1H3556—1 in box.
Each $4.95
3 or more, **Each 4.50**

"POLAR CUB" ELECTRIC FRUIT JUICE EXTRACTOR

1H3190—9½ in. high, 6¾x3½ juice shell, spun aluminum, highly polished, aluminum spout, gray enameled steel body, juice extractor heavily ribbed, designed to extract all juice from fruit, aluminum bottom, rubber tipped to prevent creeping, on and off **toggle switch** cord and attachment plug. 1 in box. Retails $14.50.
Each $11.50
6 or more, **Each 11.05**

"A & J" EGG BEATER SET

1H5320—Nickel plated steel egg beater, blue tipped white enameled handle, 4½x4½ glass bowl, graduated from ½ to 2 cups, and ¼ to 1 pt., nickel plated cover. 1 doz. in spaced shipping carton.
Doz $4.00

I recently received a letter from a reader requesting instructions on how to work the two ice cream makers. These sanitary freezers, as they were called, are shown in the middle of Row 1 on page 175 and at the end of Row 1 on page 176. The instructions for operating the one on page 175 were in it, but I did not take them out to see how it was done. I suspect they were the "Ronco" of the radio age. You probably stir, put in ice box, stir later, and put back in ice box, hoping not to blow up the glass container. It eventually will work.

These accessory items make up some of the more unusual items in kitchenware collecting. For those who collect colors, there are mechanical or hand beaters in almost every color. If you collect Fire-King, there is even a popcorn maker.

A one quart ice cream maker is shown at the bottom of page 176. An ice crusher is attached to it. I thought this was a great idea, but it was the first I had seen; so it may not have been too popular! I *do* know how to make this one work! I have done that chore! This piece is quite heavy; we had to triple the glass shelves to hold the mixer and the ice cream maker.

Page 175

Row 1:	#1	"Keystone" beater, Pat. Dec. 1885, North Bros.	75.00 – 100.00
	#2	Jewel "Beater Mixer" (mfg. by Juergens Bros., Minn., Mn.)	65.00 – 75.00
	#3	Sanitary glass ice cream freezer (Consolidated Mfg. Co.)	75.00 – 100.00
	#4	Mixer, 1 qt. capacity	25.00 – 28.00
	#5	"Ladd" beater, green or pink (not shown)	75.00 – 95.00
Row 2:	#1	Hydraulic "Niagara" food mixer (attaches to faucet)	50.00 – 55.00
	#2	Thermos (mercury lined), "Higbee Hot/Cold Sanitary Bottle"	75.00 – 100.00

Row 2 (Continued):			
	#3	Criss Cross food mixer (baby face on side)	85.00 – 95.00
	#4	Mixer, bands at 4-8-12 oz. marks, Kamkap, Inc., U.S.A.	25.00 – 30.00
	#5	Fire-King popcorn popper	35.00 – 40.00
Row 3:	#1	"Vidrio" electric mixer w/ cobalt blue base	125.00 – 135.00
	#2	Same, w/custard slag base	60.00 – 70.00
	#3	"Chicago Electric" beater w/ Jadite bottom	85.00 – 95.00
	#4	"Challenge" w/Custard bottom	60.00 – 70.00
	#5	"Kenmore" electric beater	30.00 – 40.00

Page 176

Row 1:	#1	Delphite beater bowl	80.00 – 95.00
	#2	Jadite beater bowl	80.00 – 95.00
	#3	White beater bowl	30.00 – 35.00
	#4	Iridized beater bowl	40.00 – 45.00
	#5	Sanitary freezer	75.00 – 100.00
Row 2:	#1	Handy Andy Juice Extractor	40.00 – 50.00
	#2	Juice extractor	175.00 – 195.00
	#3	Ser-Mor Juice Extractor Pat.	70.00 – 75.00

Row 2 (Continued):			
	#4	Vidrio Products Corp. "Gem Squeezer" Cicero, Il.	55.00 – 65.00
Row 3:	#1	Mixer, w/Chalaine bowl	125.00 – 150.00
	#2	"Deluxe Lightning One Quart Ice Cream Maker" w/Lightning ice cube breaker by North Brothers	80.00 – 100.00

Page 177

Row 1:	#1	"J. Hutchanson" trademark S&S Long Island (Mayonnaise)	125.00 – 150.00
	#2	Cobalt beater	100.00 – 125.00
	#3	Ultra-marine beater	65.00 – 75.00
	#4	Pink beater	60.00 – 70.00

Row 2:	#1	"Bromo-Seltzer" dispenser	135.00 – 150.00
	#2	"Ladd" mixer churn #2	100.00 – 125.00
	#3	Mixer (similar to Keystone)	55.00 – 65.00
	#4	"Silver & Co." food mixer	35.00 – 40.00
	#5	"Bordens" Pat. Mar. 30, 1915	25.00 – 30.00

Miscellaneous

Page 179

Row 1: #1 5" fired-on mixing bowl — 12.00 – 15.00
#2 6" fired-on mixing bowl — 15.00 – 18.00
#3 7" fired-on mixing bowl — 18.00 – 22.00
#4 Witch ice tub — 20.00 – 25.00
#5 McKee 6" fired-on mixing bowl — 22.00 – 28.00
#6 Same, 7" — 25.00 – 30.00
#7 Same, 8" — 30.00 – 35.00
#8 Same, 9" — 30.00 – 35.00
Row 2: #1 Drippings — 30.00 – 35.00
#2,3 Fry custard, ea. — 10.00 – 12.00
#4 Fire-King oval baking dish — 4.00 – 5.00
#5 Drippings lid — 18.00 – 20.00
Row 3: #1, Mixing bowl, 6" w/green lettering — 35.00 – 40.00

Row 3 (Continued):
#2 Anchor Hocking batter bowl (rare design) — 60.00 – 65.00
#3 Tufglass bowl — 12.00 – 15.00
#4 Pink 2 qt. measure pitcher — 250.00 – 300.00
Same, crystal (not shown) — 20.00 – 25.00
Row 4: #1 Anchor Hocking Swirl mixing bowl, 9" — 25.00 – 27.50
#2 Signed Georges Briard, silver decorated casserole — 30.00 – 35.00
#3 Black Ships 9½" mixing bowl — 40.00 – 45.00
Row 5: #1 Anchor Hocking red stripe batter bowl — 55.00 – 60.00
#2 Drippings jar w/stripes — 35.00 – 40.00
#3 White storage jar — 10.00 – 12.00
#4 Federal batter jug w/stars — 45.00 – 50.00

Page 180

Row 1: #1-5 Shakers, ea. — 10.00 – 12.00
#6 Shaker or spice set in rotating tray — 40.00 – 50.00
#7 Tall yellow shaker — 10.00 – 12.00
#8 Amber shaker — 12.00 – 15.00
#9,10 Hocking opaque yellow, ea. — 25.00 – 30.00
Row 2: #1-16 Cattail, shakers, ea. — 10.00 – 12.00
Row 3: #1,2 Delphite "basket wave," pr. — 30.00 – 35.00
#3 Delphite blue Roman arch pepper — 125.00 – 150.00
#4 Sellers spice shaker — 12.00 – 15.00
#5 Hocking, crystal — 3.00 – 4.00
#6 Owens-Illinois green — 8.00 – 10.00
#7 Green, plain — 8.00 – 10.00
#8 Green, "Moisture Proof" — 55.00 – 60.00
#9,10 Jennyware, flat, pink, w/labels, ea. — 35.00 – 45.00

Row 3 (Continued):
#11 Amber — 15.00 – 20.00
Row 4: #1,2 Hazel-Atlas "Skating Dutch" flour or sugar, ea. — 35.00 – 40.00
#3,4 Hocking "Modern Tulips" salt or pepper, ea. — 20.00 – 22.50
#5-7 Roastmeat seasoning — 65.00 – 70.00
Same, salt or pepper, ea. — 30.00 – 35.00
#8,9 "Clambroth" white embossed salt or pepper, ea. — 20.00 – 22.50
Row 5: #1 Black pepper — 30.00 – 35.00
#2 Black sugar — 45.00 – 50.00
#3-6 Scotty dog salt or pepper — 45.00 – 50.00
Flour or sugar — 45.00 – 50.00
#7 Sitting bird, pr. — 75.00 – 80.00
#8,9 Black flour or sugar, ea. — 45.00 – 55.00

Page 181

Row 1: #1 Blue canister — 12.50 – 15.00
#2 Cactus decorated container — 25.00 – 30.00
#3 Green paneled provision jar, 32 oz. — 75.00 – 100.00
#4 Owens-Illinois water bottle — 15.00 – 20.00
#5 McKee Diamond Check 24 oz. canister — 60.00 – 70.00
#6 McKee white 24 oz. canister — 20.00 – 25.00
Row 2: #1 Criss Cross ¼ lb. butter, satinized green — 60.00 – 65.00
#2 Hocking left-over jar — 6.00 – 8.00
#3 McKee red rim, 5" x 8", refrigerator w/lid — 35.00 – 38.00
#4 Crystal decorated, satinized 4" x 4" — 12.50 – 15.00
Row 3: #1 Wedge shaped left-over container w/lid — 20.00 – 25.00
#2 Same, w/Jadite top — 45.00 – 55.00
#3 Mixing bowl, 1 qt. — 10.00 – 12.00

Row 3 (Continued):
#4 Revolving 10 piece left-over set — 85.00 – 95.00
Row 4: #1 Engraved "Mother" mug — 40.00 – 45.00
#2 Carafe — 6.00 – 8.00
#3, Dots on white tumbler — 12.00 – 15.00
#4,6,8 Dots on frosted glass tumblers, ea. — 8.00 – 10.00
#5,7 Soup mugs — 3.00 – 4.00
#9,11 Advertising measure glasses, ea. — 12.50 – 15.00
#10 Engraved advertising mug — 35.00 – 40.00
Row 5: #1,2 Cory dripolator with original packing and labels — 35.00 – 40.00
#3,4 Tumblers to match cocktail shaker, ea. — 6.00 – 9.00
#5 Cocktail shaker — 25.00 – 30.00
#6 Advertising measure — 8.00 – 10.00
#7 Cory flashed red dripolator — 45.00 – 50.00

Kitchen Items

SUGGESTED COFFEE MEASURE FOR
9
8
7
6
5
4
3
2
1
AVERAGE CUPS
FRIGIDAIRE
GENERAL MOTORS
RANGES
WATER HEATERS
and other products giving
A FULL MEASURE OF VALUE
MANHATTAN
STRAINEX

Every time you have a large photography session for a book, there are items that do not fit in the categories you are presently working on. Also, there are times that a quantity of harder to find items are available to be photographed when you are not even working on a book. That is how pages 183, 184, and 185 came to be.

Page 183

Row 1:	#1	Fry covered jug	275.00 – 295.00
	#2	Unusual Fry pitcher	225.00 – 250.00
	#3	Paden City cobalt blue sugar shaker	900.00 – 1,000.00
Row 2:	#1	Green sugar shaker	275.00 – 325.00
	#2	Pink sugar shaker	275.00 – 325.00
	#3	Cobalt blue 3 ftd. sugar shaker (New Martinsville?)	850.00 – 950.00
	#3,4	Green door knobs, pr.	125.00 – 145.00
	#5,6	Cobalt blue door knobs, pr.	200.00 – 225.00
Row 3:	#1	"Paramount" napkin holder, black	400.00 – 450.00
	#2	Same, pink	400.00 – 450.00
	#3	Candlewick knife	450.00 – 500.00
Row 4:	#1	Hocking "Mayfair blue" reamer	1,000.00 – 1,200.00
	#2	Teal measure cup	225.00 – 250.00
	#3	Salad set, cobalt blue	275.00 – 300.00

Page 184

Row 1:	#1,5	Hocking batter dispenser	30.00 – 35.00
	#2,4	Syrup dispensers to match above	22.00 – 25.00
	#3	Pitcher to match #1,2	30.00 – 35.00
Row 2:	#1	Red mug	35.00 – 40.00
	#2	Crown Tuscan mug	55.00 – 65.00
	#3	Crystal McKee "Bottoms Down" mug	185.00 – 195.00
	#4	"Elsie" sundae	12.50 – 15.00
	#5	Striped cocktail shaker	25.00 – 28.00
	#6	Cambridge pinch decanter	85.00 – 95.00
Row 3:	#1-7	Comic cocktail shaker set, "Sweet Ad-aline" (shaker, 45.00 – 50.00; glasses, ea., 8.50 – 10.00)	85.00 – 100.00
	#8	Tumbler, 8 oz., matches #9	6.00 – 9.00
	#9	Cocktail shaker "Gay '90s" scene	25.00 – 30.00
	#10	Tumbler, 4 oz., matches #9	6.00 – 9.00
	#11	New Martinsville "Prelude" cocktail shaker, 32 oz.	185.00 – 195.00

Page 185

Row 1:	#1	"Pyrex" red bottle	90.00 – 100.00
	#2	Cobalt, large jar, L.E. Smith	75.00 – 80.00
	#3	Jadite decorated coffee, Jeannette	225.00 – 275.00
	#4	Red sugar shaker, signed "Hawkes"	350.00 – 400.00
	#5	Pink sugar shaker	55.00 – 75.00
	#6	Ultra-marine electric beater	80.00 – 95.00
Row 2:	#1	Mixing bowl, 7½", kitchen utensils decor	20.00 – 28.00
	#2	"Red Willow" decorated, 5" bowl, Hazel-Atlas	20.00 – 22.00
	#3	Pink spoonholder, marked "Clamborne"	40.00 – 55.00
	#4,5	Cambridge sugar cube tray, pink or green	55.00 – 65.00
Row 3:	#1	Chalaine blue mixing bowl, 9"	125.00 – 135.00
	#2	Iridized, 9½", mixing bowl, Federal	30.00 – 35.00
	#3	Amethyst, 9⅝" mixing bowl, Hazel-Atlas	45.00 – 50.00
Row 4:	#1	"White King" dispenser	125.00 – 135.00
	#2	"Sanitol" jar	12.50 – 15.00
	#3	Colonial Block creamer	125.00 – 150.00
	#4	Peacock blue measure cup	200.00 – 225.00
	#5	Cobalt blue creamer, "Chevron" like stripes	15.00 – 22.00
	#6	Same, milk pitcher	18.00 – 25.00

Kitchen Items

111111111 11111111111111111111 111111

Mixing Bowls

Splash Proof bowls are the most abundant of all Anchor Hocking mixing bowls. If you only own one Anchor Hocking mixing bowl, chances are it's a Splash Proof, and more often than not, a two-quart one. Showing every possible Splash Proof mixing bowl would have been redundant and used valuable book space needed for other things. A sampling of all styles of decorated bowls is illustrated and prices are given for those that have been corroborated in collections.

Page 187	6¾" **1 qt.**	7⅝" **2 qt.**	8½" **3 qt.**	9½" **4 qt.**
Crystal	20.00 – 22.00	22.00 – 24.00	25.00 – 28.00	28.00 – 30.00
Ivory	18.00 – 20.00	10.00 – 12.00	18.00 – 20.00	20.00 – 22.00
Jade-ite	250.00 – 300.00	60.00 – 65.00	90.00 – 100.00	90.00 – 100.00
Turquoise blue	25.00 – 30.00	30.00 – 35.00	30.00 – 35.00	——
White	18.00 – 20.00	10.00 – 12.00	18.00 – 20.00	20.00 – 22.00

Page 188	6¾" **1 qt.**	7⅝" **2 qt.**	8½" **3 qt.**	9½" **4 qt.**
Apples, Tulips on white	30.00 – 35.00	25.00 – 30.00	30.00 – 35.00	35.00 – 40.00
Black Dots	30.00 – 35.00	30.00 – 35.00	30.00 – 35.00	30.00 – 35.00
Kitchen Aids*	100.00 – 125.00	*65.00 – 75.00	90.00 – 100.00	90.00 – 100.00
Modern Tulip, black	20.00 – 22.50	18.00 – 20.00	18.00 – 20.00	20.00 – 22.50
Modern Tulip, navy blue	75.00 – 90.00	65.00 – 75.00	65.00 – 75.00	65.00 – 75.00
Red Dots, Tulips on ivory	20.00 – 22.50	20.00 – 22.50	25.00 – 27.50	27.50 – 30.00

* Skags Anniversary, 75.00 – 90.00

Page 189 top, 400 Line

	5"	6"	7¼"	8⅜"
"Granite Ware"	35.00 – 40.00	25.00 – 30.00	30.00 – 35.00	35.00 – 40.00
Dutch Clover	3.00 – 4.00	5.00 – 6.00	6.00 – 8.00	8.00 – 10.00
Bold colors, black rim	5.00 – 6.00	6.00 – 8.00	8.00 – 10.00	10.00 – 12.00

Page 189 bottom, Swedish Modern

	5"	6"	7¼"	8⅜"
Anchorwhite	12.50 – 15.00			
*Jade-ite	50.00 – 55.00	100.00 – 125.00	90.00 – 100.00	100.00 – 125.00
Turquoise blue	25.00 – 30.00	30.00 – 35.00	30.00 – 35.00	55.00 – 60.00

* add $35.00 – 40.00 for box set

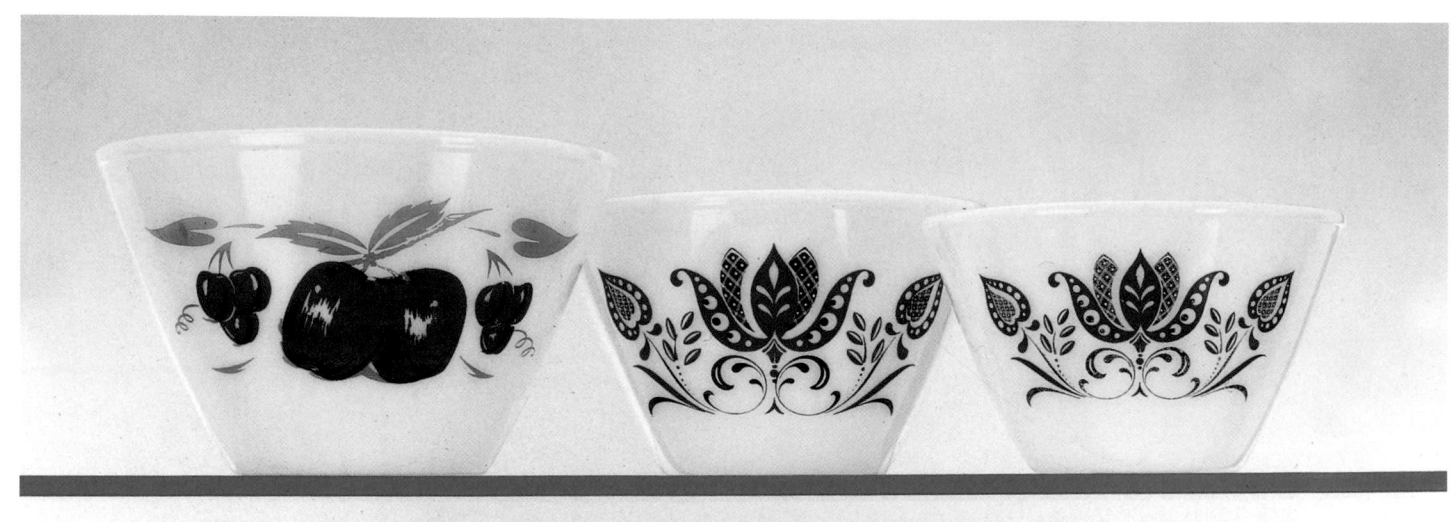

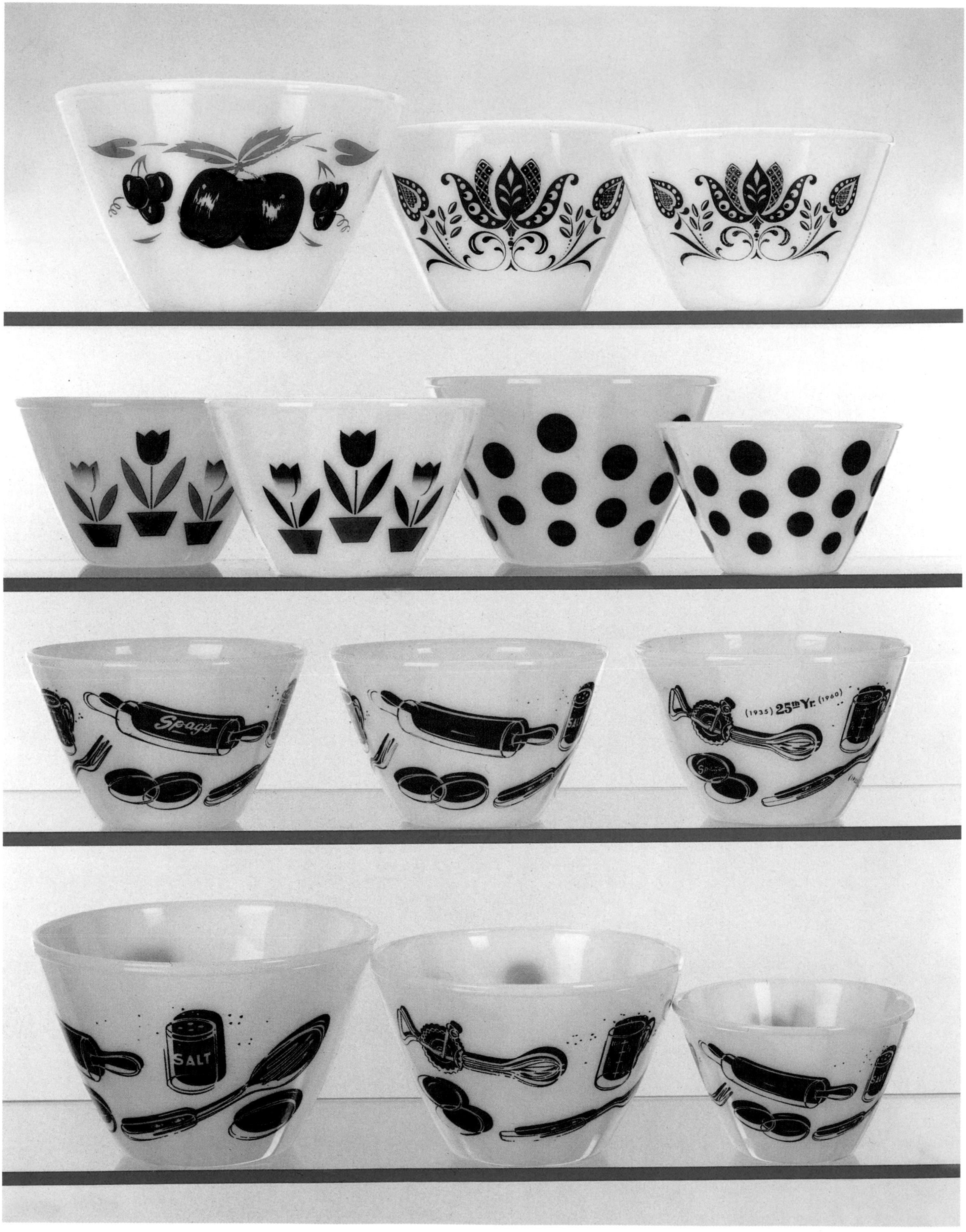
Spag's
(1935) 25th Yr. (1960)
SALT

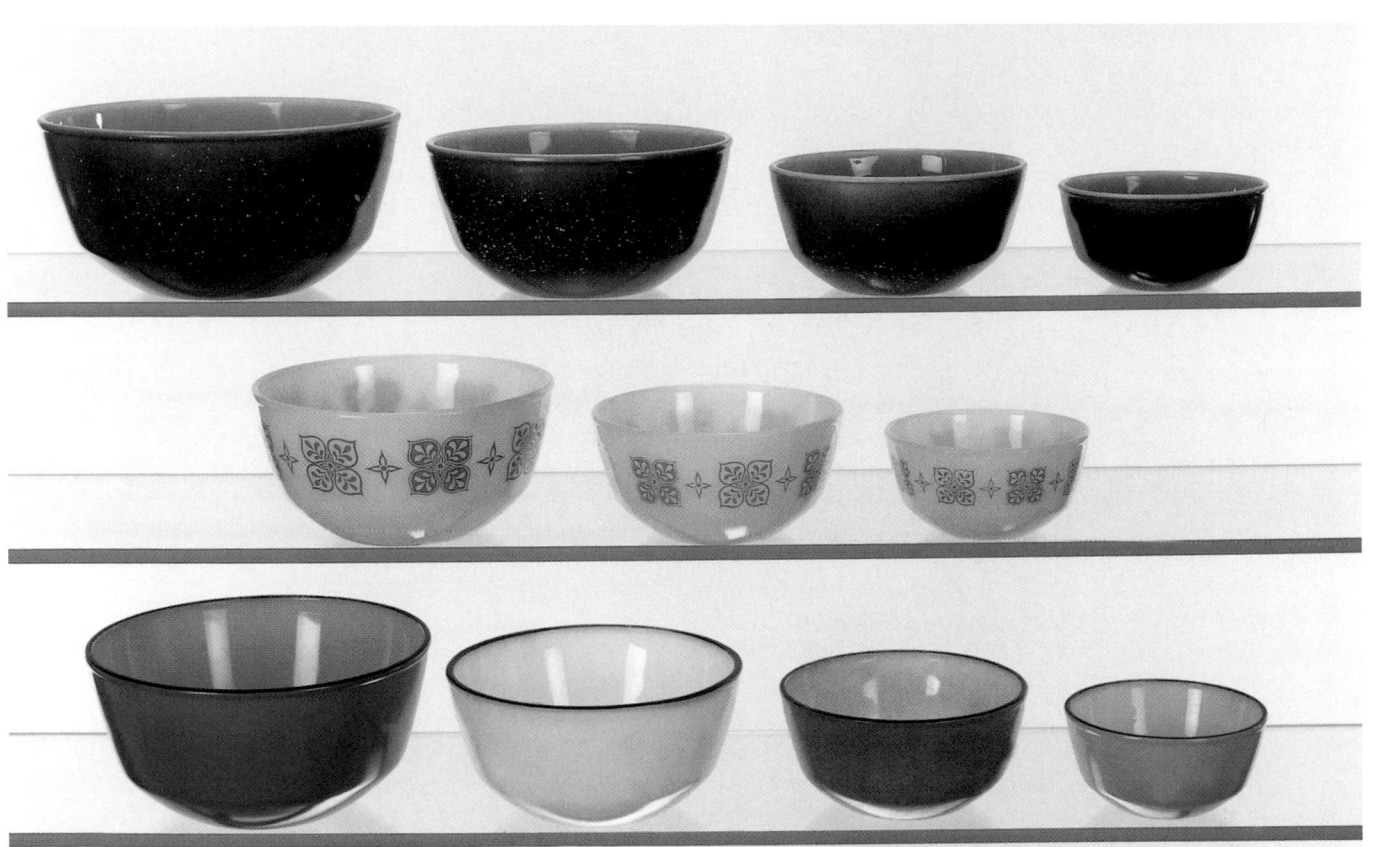

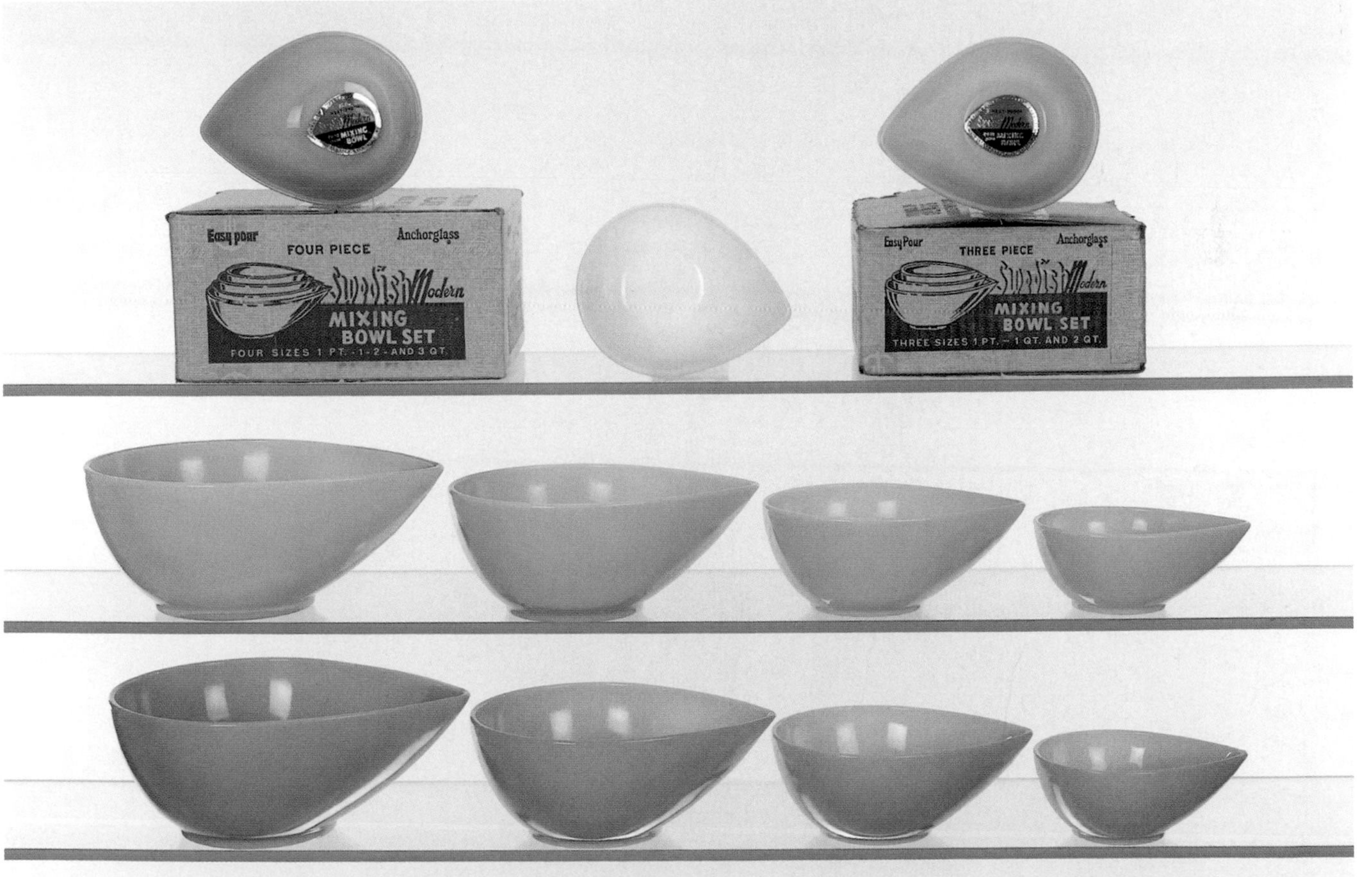
Easy pour
Anchorglass
FOUR PIECE
Swedish Modern
MIXING BOWL SET
FOUR SIZES 1 PT. - 1 - 2 - AND 3 QT.
Easy Pour
Anchorglass
THREE PIECE
Swedish Modern
MIXING BOWL SET
THREE SIZES 1 PT. – 1 QT. AND 2 QT.

Mugs

There are not many Depression glass mug collectors per se; but, I've met a number of collectors of mugs made by Anchor Hocking. Mugs do come in a great variety of colors and shapes, which makes for interesting display concepts. The split pictures were taken at two locations in order to incorporate as many different mugs as possible.

The first mug in Row 1 has the "Fire-King" design on the outside. This is normal for the blue, but very few Jade-ite have the design. It is the design which makes this mug so expensive, since it is very common without the design.

The McKee "Bottoms-Down" mug in Row 4 is very popular, with the Jadite found more often than the Seville yellow. However, I would not pass either by if I found them priced reasonably. I recently bought a pair for $38.00 at an antique show set up in a local mall.

Page 191

Row 1:	#1	Fire-King, Jade-ite (design on outside)	100.00 – 125.00
		no design (not shown)	15.00 – 16.00
	#2	Fire-King, Sapphire blue	25.00 – 30.00
	#3	Hocking, pretzel/beer, green, #636	40.00 – 45.00
	#4	Same, crystal w/trim (wo/trim $12.00 – 15.00)	15.00 – 25.00
	#5	Green, Adam's Rib, Line #900, Diamond Glassware Co.	30.00 – 35.00
	#6	Same, amber	25.00 – 30.00
Row 2:	#1	Cambridge, cobalt blue root beer	75.00 – 80.00
	#2	Yellow root beer	50.00 – 55.00
	#3	Imperial "Chesterfield," Line #600, amber	25.00 – 30.00
	#4	Green Clambroth	50.00 – 55.00
	#5	Barrel shaped, "pinched" handle	50.00 – 55.00
Row 3:	#1	Green root beer	40.00 – 45.00
	#2	Same, pink	40.00 – 45.00
	#3	Amber	35.00 – 40.00
	#4	Black, "Genolite"	40.00 – 45.00
	#5	Fenton green soda fountain type	30.00 – 35.00
	#6	Peacock blue	25.00 – 30.00
Row 4:	#1	McKee "Bottoms-Down" beer mug, Seville yellow	175.00 – 185.00
	#2	Same, Jadite (not shown: crystal, 185.00 – 195.00)	185.00 – 195.00
	#3	Cambridge "Mt. Vernon," emerald green	30.00 – 35.00
	#4	Cambridge "Tally-Ho," red	30.00 – 35.00
	#5	New Martinsville, red	20.00 – 25.00
	#6	Imperial "Chesterfield," Line #600, green	30.00 – 35.00
Row 5:	#1	New Martinsville "Moondrops," cobalt blue	35.00 – 40.00
	#2	Hocking "Colonial," pink	450.00 – 500.00
	#3	Jeannette, #5161, 16 oz., footed, green	40.00 – 45.00
	#4	Same, pink	40.00 - 45.00
	#5	Pink, Adam's Rib, Line #900, Diamond Glassware Co.	35.00 – 40.00

Napkin Holders

Row 1: #1,2   Fan Fold napkin holders (2 shades of green)   150.00 – 175.00

#3   Fan Fold crystal   70.00 – 75.00

#4   Serv-All emerald green   135.00 – 150.00

#5   Serv-All clambroth green   200.00 – 225.00

Row 2: #1   Nar-O-Fold white napkin holder   55.00 – 65.00

#2   Fort Howard Handi-Nap Napkins   55.00 – 65.00

#3   Paramount pink napkin holder (U.S. Glass)

  (see below, right)   400.00 – 450.00

  black amethyst (see below, left and center)   400.00 – 450.00

  green (not shown)   400.00 – 450.00

#4   Paden City crystal   55.00 – 65.00

#5   Paden City green   135.00 – 150.00

Row 3: #1   Frosted crystal   55.00 – 65.00

#2   NAR-O-FOLD, Property of trade Nar-O-Fold mark

  Napkin Company, Chicago, Reg. U.S.A., black   150.00 – 175.00

#3   Same, white   55.00 – 65.00

#4   Emerald green   95.00 –120.00

Row 4: #1   Paden City "Party Line," crystal   55.00 – 65.00

#2   Same, black   150.00 – 175.00

#3   Same, pink   175.00 – 225.00

#4   Same, white   55.00 – 65.00

Row 5: #1   HY-G napkins   175.00 – 195.00

#2   Red/amagrina red   200.00 – 250.00

Kitchen Items

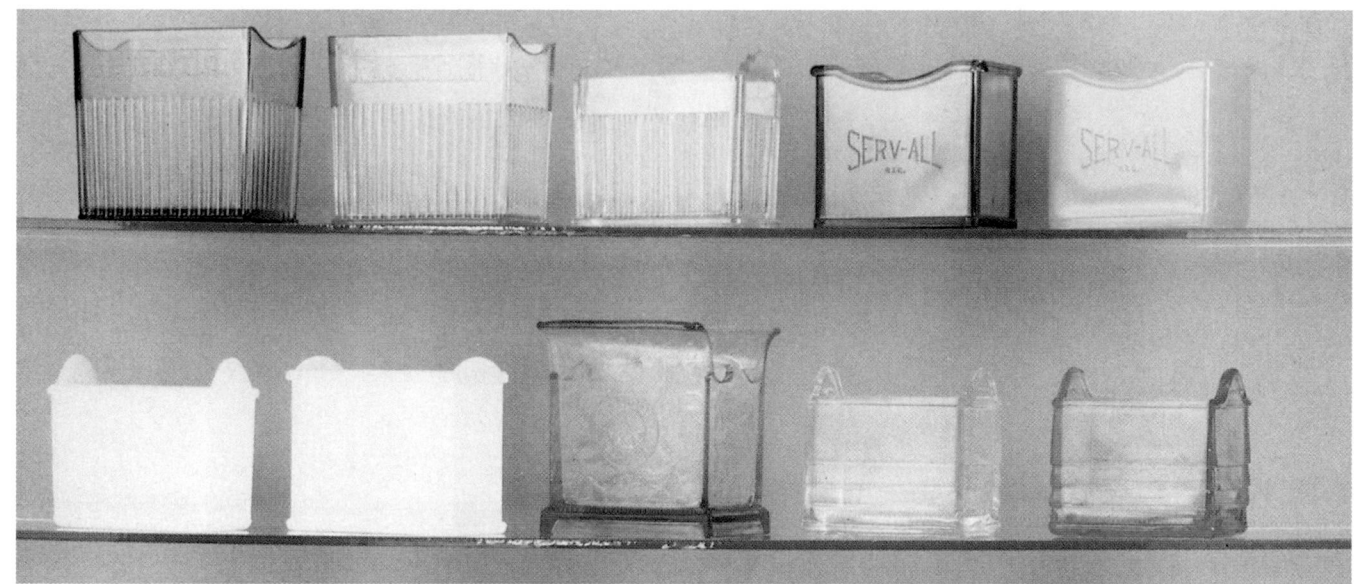

Oil & Vinegar Bottles ≡≡≡

Fostoria and Cambridge oil and vinegar bottles are in demand by collectors who are looking for the better known etched patterns. While plain or unetched varieties do sell, they do not sell nearly as fast as or at as lofty a price. Amber colored bottles are the slowest to sell no matter which company made them or what etching may be on them.

The correct stopper for the pyramid shaped bottle in the bottom row can be seen on page 89. Over the years many bottles had substitute stoppers added. Like lids and cups, many a stopper dropped! Note that colored bottles often have crystal stoppers.

Page 195

Row 1:
#1	Paden City, green	75.00 – 95.00
#2	Same, pink	75.00 – 95.00
#3	Cambridge, etched #520, green	175.00 – 195.00
#4	Same, no etching	100.00 – 125.00
#5	Cambridge, amber w/crystal stopper	45.00 – 55.00
#6	Same, w/amber stopper	55.00 – 65.00
#7	Green set (late 1940s)	65.00 – 75.00

Row 2:
#1	Cambridge "Rosalie" (#731), pink	175.00 – 195.00
#2	Same, green	175.00 – 195.00
#3, 5, 7	Cambridge crystal, ea.	35.00 – 55.00
#4	Cambridge w/sterling stopper	55.00 – 65.00
#6	Hawkes, green	95.00 – 110.00

Row 3:
#1	Heisey, "Flamingo" pink	100.00 – 110.00
#2	Same, crystal ("Mfg. under license granted by T.G. Hawkes & Co.; Fill w/vinegar to line marked Vinegar, w/oil to line marked Oil, salt & pepper, etc., to taste, shake & you have perfect dressing")	55.00 – 65.00
#3	Heisey "Twist," pink	105.00 – 110.00
#4, 9	Fostoria amber, ea.	55.00 – 65.00
#5	Fostoria w/sterling top	35.00 – 45.00
#6, 7	Fostoria, yellow or green	100.00 – 110.00
#8	Fostoria yellow w/crystal top	55.00 – 65.00

Row 4:
#1	Paden City "Party Line," #191, pink	75.00 – 85.00
#2	Unknown "pyramid" style (wrong stopper; see p. 89)	75.00 – 85.00
#3	Cambridge set, 3 pc., pink	110.00 – 120.00
#4, 5	Crackle set (possibly Cambridge), ea.	40.00 – 55.00
#6	Yellow	35.00 – 45.00
#7	Cambridge pink	45.00 – 55.00
#8	Amber	35.00 – 40.00

Range Sets

The grease jar with matching shakers has become highly collectible. Prices have risen and mint condition screw-on lids are being sold for as much as the complete shakers have sold. Mint lithographed scripted **(P)** pepper lids will fetch $10.00 – 12.00 and **(S)** salt, $12.00 – 15.00. Tulip pepper lids bring $12.00 – 15.00, but salt lids easily bring $20.00 – 25.00, if **mint**. Mint is white background and not beige!

Page 197

Row 1: "Blue Circle w/Flowers"

#1,2	Salt or pepper	20.00 – 30.00
#3	Grease jar	35.00 – 50.00
#4,5	Sugar or flour	25.00 – 35.00

Row 2: "Black Circle w/Flowers"

#1,2	Salt or pepper	22.50 – 30.00
#3	Grease jar	40.00 – 55.00
#4,5	Sugar or flour	25.00 – 35.00

Row 3: "Red Circle w/Flowers"

#1,2	Salt or pepper	20.00 – 25.00
#3	Grease jar	35.00 – 40.00
#4,5	Sugar or flour	25.00 - 30.00

Row 4: "Red Tulips"

#1,2	Salt or pepper	17.50 – 25.00
#3	Grease jar	30.00 – 40.00
#4,5	Sugar or flour	22.50 – 35.00

Row 5: "Red Flower Pots"

#1,2	Salt or pepper	15.00 –17.50
#3	Grease jar	30.00 –40.00
#4,5	Sugar or flour	22.50 –35.00

Row 6: "Green Flower Pots"

#1,2	Salt or pepper	40.00 – 45.00
#3	Grease jar	60.00 – 65.00
#4,5	Sugar or flour	45.00 – 50.00

Page 198

Row 1:

#1	Modern Tulips, black	50.00 – 65.00
	Modern Tulips, navy blue (not shown)	70.00 – 75.00
#2	Ivory	16.00 – 18.00
#3	Crystal with etched design	16.00 – 18.00
#4	Gold dots on satinized crystal	30.00 – 45.00

Row 2:

#1	Kitchen Aids	200.00 – 225.00
#2	Crystal	10.00 – 12.00
#3	Crystal with etched design	16.00 – 18.00
#4	Tulips on white	60.00 – 75.00
	Tulips on ivory (not shown)	40.00 – 55.00

Row 3:

#1	Black Dots	50.00 – 65.00
#2	Crystal with cut dots design	16.00 – 18.00
#3	Crystal with etched design	16.00 – 18.00
#4	Red Dots on white	50.00 – 65.00
	Red Dots on ivory (not shown)	40.00 – 55.00

Row 4:

#1	Stripes	50.00 – 65.00
#2	Jade-ite, screw-on lid	75.00 – 85.00
#3	Crystal, screw-on lid	18.00 – 20.00
#4	Ivory, screw-on lid	30.00 – 35.00
#5	Apples	50.00 – 65.00

Page 199

Row 1:

#1	Modern Tulips, navy blue, pr.	60.00 – 75.00
#2	Modern Tulips, black, pr.	45.00 – 50.00
#3,4	Kitchen Aids, pr.	200.00 – 225.00
#5	Tulips, White, pr.	125.00 – 150.00
#6	Tulips, Ivory, pr.	65.00 – 75.00
#7,8	Stripes, pr.	50.00 – 65.00

Row 2:

#1,2	Ivory, pr	14.00 – 16.00
#3	Primrose, pr.	250.00 – 300.00
#4	Red Dots on White, pr.	50.00 – 65.00
	Red Dots on Ivory, pr. (not shown)	45.00 – 50.00
#5,6	White, pr.	25.00 – 30.00

Row 2 (Continued):

#7,8	Black Dots, pr.	60.00 – 75.00

Row 3:

#1-6	Fired-on green, coral or blue, pr.	25.00 – 35.00
#7,8	Jade-ite, pr.	90.00 – 100.00

Row 4:

#1	Box set of Philco give-away shakers	35.00 – 40.00
#2,3	Crystal horizontal ribbed, pr.	10.00 – 12.00
#4,5	Crystal w/red dots, pr.	14.00 – 16.00
#6,7	Soreno, Honey gold, pr.	4.00 – 5.00
#8	Wexford, crystal, pr.	2.50 – 3.00
#9,10	Fired-on red, pr.	25.00 – 28.00

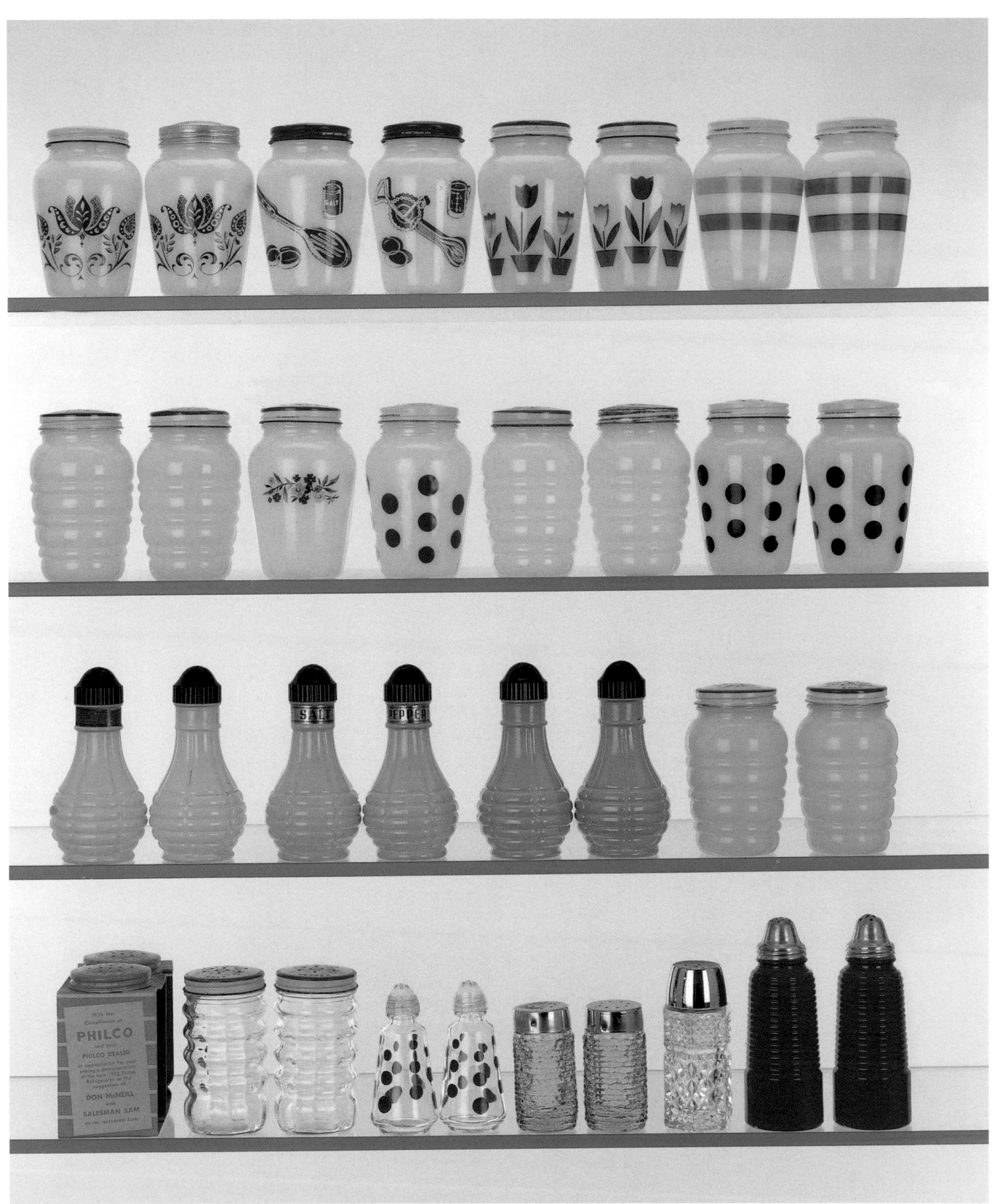

Reamers

These two-part reamers are twice as difficult to find in perfect condition as the one-piece reamers.

The Barnes reamer shown in Row 3 was only the beginning of the repros. Unfortunately, original molds were bought after Westmoreland's demise and used to make some reproductions. The Barnes reamers are all marked with B in a circle, and as such are becoming collectible in their own right. However, Summit Art Glass of Akron, Ohio, used original molds under a private contract without marking the glass in any way! Now those molds are being used at Mosser Glass Co. in Cambridge, Ohio.

Other repros have come from Taiwan. See pages 266 – 270 on reproductions. Items marked with an asterisk have been reproduced. To keep abreast of all the reamer news, I suggest you join the national reamer club. The address is: National Reamer Collectors Association, c/o Debbie Gillham, 47 Midline Court, Gaithersburg, MD 20878.

Page 201

Westmoreland Glass Company (Rows 1-3)

Row 1:	#1	Pink, 2 piece	200.00 – 225.00
	#2	Same, crystal	70.00 – 75.00
	#3	Blue (bottom only $90.00-100.00)	240.00 – 250.00
	#4	Amber, 2 piece	200.00 – 225.00
	#5	Sun-colored-amethyst (bottom only $40.00-45.00)	95.00 – 110.00
	#6	Green, 2 piece	200.00 – 225.00
Row 2 & 3:		**Bottom is worth ⅔ of price except where noted below.**	
*Row 2:	#1	Frosted pink	150.00 – 165.00
	#2	Green (top & bottom about equal in value)	225.00 – 235.00
	#3	Crystal w/decorations	55.00 – 65.00
	#4	Pink (bottom value $20.00-25.00)	200.00 – 225.00
	#5	Frosted blue bottom only	40.00 – 45.00
	#6	Sun-colored-amethyst (SCA)	95.00 – 110.00
*Row 3:	#1	Frosted crystal (decorated add $10.00)	60.00 – 65.00
	#2	Pink decorated	200.00 – 225.00
	#3	Blue (bottom value $40.00-50.00)	240.00 – 250.00
	#4, 5	NEW! RUBINA AND COBALT BLUE MARKED WITH B IN CIRCLE INSIDE CONE OF TOP AND ON BOTTOM OF BASE All BARNES REAMERS MARKED	
		SEE PAGE 266 FOR ADDITIONAL COLORS.	
Row 4:	#1	L.E. Smith (top rare), pink	325.00 – 335.00
	#2	Same, green	325.00 – 335.00
	#3	Same, crystal (in metal add $5.00)	65.00 – 70.00
	#4	Jenkins, green	225.00 – 235.00
	#5	Same, crystal	60.00 – 65.00
	#6	Same, frosted crystal	60.00 – 65.00
Row 5:	#1	Unknown, blue (top $200.00)	450.00 – 465.00
	#2	Unknown, pink (top $100.00)	225.00 – 235.00
	#3	Unknown, crystal (top $10.00)	55.00 – 60.00
	#4	Unknown, frosted crystal, "Baby's Orange"	65.00 – 75.00
	#5	Unknown, crystal	50.00 – 55.00
	#6	Unknown, frosted crystal, decorated "Baby"	85.00 – 95.00
Row 6:	#1	Unknown, crystal	50.00 – 55.00
	#2	Unknown, crystal, called "Button & Bows"	55.00 – 60.00
	#3	Unknown, crystal, probably foreign (emb. sword & hammer)	50.00 – 55.00
	#4	Unknown, crystal, "thumbprint" design	50.00 – 55.00
	#5	Unknown, crystal, notched top	50.00 – 55.00
	#6	Unknown, crystal	50.00 – 55.00
Row 7:	#1	Unknown, decorated crystal, "Orange Juice"	75.00 – 85.00
	#2	Unknown, frosted, decorated crystal	75.00 – 85.00
	#3	Unknown, pink (possibly foreign)	215.00 – 225.00
	#4	Fenton, SCA (sun-colored-amethyst) (bottom $55.00)	95.00 – 110.00
	#5	Fenton, elephant decorated base	110.00 – 125.00

Kitchen Items

The following three pages show the vast price ranges reamer collectors face. Reamers come in all shapes, sizes, and colors. The names in quotes with the Fry reamers are the company names for each color.

The foreign reamers on page 204 represent a separate collecting field in themselves. Not enough information is known about this vast field of reamers. There are many unique shapes and colors to attract a collector to these reamers made outside the United States.

Page 203

Row 1:	#1	Fenton pitcher & reamer set, red	1,000.00 – 1,200.00

(top is ⅓ price; bottom is ⅔ on these)

	#2	Same, black	1,000.00 – 1,200.00
	#3	Same, blue	2,800.00 – 3,000.00
	#4	Same, jade	900.00 – 1,100.00
Row 2:	#1	Same, transparent green, top only	250.00 – 300.00
	#2	Fry, straight side, "Azure," blue	1,800.00 – 2,000.00
	#3	Same, light green	38.00 – 45.00
	#4	Same, "Emerald," green	45.00 – 50.00
Row 3:	#1	Same, "Pearl," opalescent white	35.00 – 40.00

Row 3 (Continued):

		Same, embossed, "Blue Goose"	400.00 – 425.00
	#2	Same, "Canary," vaseline	65.00 – 75.00
	#3	Same, "Rose," pink	65.00 – 75.00
Row 4:	#1	Same, crystal	25.00 – 30.00
	#2	Same, "Amber"	375.00 – 395.00
	#3	Same, "China," white	700.00 – 800.00
Row 5:	#1	Fry, fluted reamer (gelatin mold), "Canary"	350.00 – 375.00
	#2	Same, "Emerald," green	500.00 – 550.00
	#3	Same, "Rose"	225.00 – 250.00
Row 6:	#1	Same, "Pearl"	75.00 – 85.00
	#2, 3	Tufglas, light or dark	100.00 – 125.00

Page 204

Row 1:	#1	Pinkish amber	45.00 – 50.00
	#2	Cobalt blue	110.00 – 120.00
	#3	Smoke	85.00 – 90.00
	#4	Yellowish custard	75.00 – 100.00
	#5	Amber	75.00 – 85.00
Row 2:	#1,5	Pink or light pinkish amber	50.00 – 55.00
	#2,3	Embossed "Foreign," 2 piece, green or pink	125.00 – 135.00
	#4	Yellow	80.00 – 90.00
Row 3:	#1,5	Root Beer & light yellow, ea.	40.00 – 50.00
	#2	Embossed "Tcheco-Scovaquie" on handle, crystal	30.00 – 35.00
	#3	Blue	110.00 – 120.00
	#4	Embossed sword & hammer on handle	20.00 – 25.00
Row 4:	#1,5	Crystal, last has "K" inside shield mark, ea.	20.00 – 25.00
	#2	Light yellow, top only	30.00 – 35.00

Row 4 (Continued):

	#3, 4	Pink or "Coke" bottle green	45.00 – 55.00
Row 5:	#1, 2, 4 & 5	Light green, amber, amethyst or pinkish amber, ea.	45.00 – 55.00
	#3	Crystal	20.00 – 25.00
Row 6:	#1	Light turquoise	65.00 – 75.00
	#2	Green, marked "Argentina"	125.00 – 150.00
	#3,5	Cornflower blue or light green	100.00 – 125.00
	#4	Crystal, embossed fruit	30.00 – 35.00
Row 7:	#1,	Crystal Czechoslovakia	25.00 – 30.00
	#2	Pink	40.00 – 45.00
	#3	Light turquoise	65.00 – 75.00
	#4	Diamond shaped crystal (Rb No 517385)	35.00 – 40.00
	#5	Pink	100.00 – 125.00
	#6	Amber	100.00 – 125.00

Page 205

Rows 1-3 Federal Glass Company

Row 1:	#1	Ribbed, loop handle, pink	40.00 – 45.00
	#2	Same, amber	25.00 – 28.00
	#3	Panelled, loop handle, green	30.00 – 35.00
Row 2:	#1	Same, amber	25.00 – 28.00
	#2	Tab handle, yellowish-amber	300.00 – 325.00
	#3	Same, green	25.00 – 28.00
	#4	Tab handled, ribbed, seed dam, green	25.00 – 28.00
Row 3:	#1	Same, pink	100.00 – 125.00
	#2, 3	Tab handled amber, ea.	20.00 – 25.00
	#4	Green, pointed cone	25.00 – 28.00

Rows 4-6 Indiana Glass Company

Row 4:	#1	Amber, handled, spout opposite	275.00 – 300.00
	#2	Same, crystal	25.00 – 28.00
	#3	Same, pink	85.00 – 95.00
Row 5:	#1	Same, green	40.00 – 45.00
	#2	Crystal, horizontal handle	20.00 – 25.00
	#3	Same, green	35.00 – 40.00
Row 6:	#1	Crystal, emb. ASCO, "Good Morning, Orange Juice"	25.00 – 30.00
	#2	Amber, six sided cone, vertical handle	300.00 – 325.00
	#3	Same, green	70.00 – 75.00
	#4	Same, pink	175.00 – 195.00

Page 207 All Hazel-Atlas Glass Company

Row 1:	#1	Yellow 2 cup pitcher and reamer set	350.00 – 375.00
	#2	Same, cobalt blue	*325.00 – 350.00
	#3	Same, pink	*150.00 – 160.00
	#4	Same, green	*60.00 – 65.00
Row 2:	#1	Crisscross, cobalt blue	300.00 – 325.00
	#2	Same, pink	295.00 – 325.00
	#3	Same, crystal	20.00 – 25.00
	#4	Same, green	35.00 – 40.00
Row 3:	#1	Green, tab handled	25.00 – 28.00
	#2, 3	Decorated 2 cup sets, ea.	55.00 – 65.00
	#4	Fired-on red set	55.00 – 65.00
Row 4:	#1, 3-5	Decorated sets, ea.	55.00 – 65.00
	#2	Tumbler to match #1	12.00 – 15.00
Row 5:	#1	Crisscross, tab handled, pink	300.00 – 355.00
	#2	Same, green	40.00 – 45.00
	#3	Same, crystal	18.00 – 22.00
	#4	Green, tab handled	25.00 – 28.00

* See pages 266 – 270 for reproductions.

Page 208 All Hazel-Atlas Glass Company

Row 1:	#1	Reamer, pitcher, 4 cup marked A&J, green	50.00 – 55.00
	#2	Same, A & J, Pat Applied For, crystal	35.00 – 40.00
	#3	Green, 4 cup, ftd.	45.00 – 55.00
	#4	Green, stippled pitcher	35.00 – 45.00
Row 2:	#1, 2	Tab handle, lemon, pink, light or dark	40.00 – 45.00
	#3	Same, green	25.00 – 28.00
	#4	Same, white w/red trim	30.00 – 38.00
Row 3:	#1-3	White, w/decorated trim, 4 cup	40.00 – 50.00
	#4	White, 4 cup, stippled pitcher	40.00 – 45.00
Row 4:	#1	Small tab handled reamer, pink	40.00 – 45.00
	#2	Same, green	25.00 – 28.00
	#3	Same, cobalt blue	325.00 – 345.00
	#4	Large tab handled reamer, pink	40.00 – 45.00
Row 5:	#1	Same, white	30.00 – 38.00
	#2	Same, cobalt blue	295.00 – 325.00
	#3	Same, crystal	15.00 – 18.00
	#4	Same, green	25.00 – 28.00

Page 209 All Hocking or Anchor Hocking Glass Company

Row 1:	#1	Reamer, pitcher, green	35.00 – 45.00
	#2	"Circle" pitcher w/reamer top, green	45.00 – 50.00
	#3	Ribbed 2-cup pitcher w/top, green	75.00 – 85.00
	#4	Same, pink, pitcher only	60.00 – 70.00
Row 2:	#1	Loop handle orange, "Mayfair" blue	1,000.00 – 1,200.00
	#2	Same, green	30.00 – 35.00
	#3	Same, white, embossed "Vitrock"	28.00 – 35.00
		Same, unembossed	15.00 – 20.00
	#4	Tab handle, green Clambroth	175.00 – 195.00
Row 3:	#1	Loop handle orange, ribbed, green	30.00 – 35.00
	#2	Same, "Coke" bottle green	30.00 – 35.00
	#3	Same, flashed black	30.00 – 35.00
	#4	Tab handle, green	25.00 – 28.00
Row 4:	#1	2-cup pitcher w/reamer top, green	55.00 – 65.00
	#2	Same, "Mayfair" blue	1,600.00 – 1,800.00
	#3	Same, "Vitrock" white	40.00 – 45.00
	#4	Indiana green	30.00 – 35.00
Row 5:	#1	Indiana amber	300.00 – 350.00
	#2	Same, pink	175.00 – 195.00
	#3	Same, green	70.00 – 75.00

The reamers shown on page 211 are found mainly on the West Coast. I am astonished at the diversity of tints of opaque red found on Fleur-de-Lis reamers. A fleur-de-lis emblem is embossed on the side of most of these. (If not, it is listed as unembossed.) The opalescent red shades are quite stunning, particularly when they are exhibited in an illuminated cabinet.

Price differences are controlled by color variations, whether or not there are emblems, and whether or not the reamers have rims.

Page 211

Row 1:	#1	"VALENCIA," white (embossed word)	120.00 – 150.00
	#2	Same, crystal	150.00 – 200.00
	#3	Same, green	250.00 – 275.00
Row 2:	#1	Plain, no embossing, "VALENCIA"	125.00 – 150.00
	#2	Same, opalescent white	60.00 – 70.00
	#3	Same, pink	150.00 – 175.00
	#4	Same, pinkish amber	325.00 – 350.00
Row 3:	#1,4	"Fleur-de-Lis," red/orange slag	375.00 – 400.00
	#2	Same, amberina/opalescent	550.00 – 600.00
	#3	Same, mustard/slag	375.00 – 400.00

Row 4:	#1	Embossed white "Fleur-de-Lis"	65.00 – 75.00
	#2	Same, red/orange slag	375.00 – 400.00
	#3	Same, red	400.00 – 425.00
	#4	Same, root beer	475.00 – 500.00
Row 5:	#1	Same, crystal	100.00 – 125.00
	#2	Unembossed, grayish custard	300.00 – 350.00
	#3	Same, custard w/"rim edge"	125.00 – 135.00
	#4	Same, white w/"rim edge"	65.00 – 75.00
Row 6:	#1	"LINDSAY," pink	450.00 – 500.00
	#2	"LINDSEY," pink	450.00 – 500.00
	#3	"LINDSAY," green	450.00 – 500.00

Page 212

Row 1:	#1	Large crystal (called "monster")	40.00 – 45.00
	#2	Light turquoise, OJ extractor	100.00 – 125.00
	#3	Foreign, pink	50.00 – 55.00
	#4	Crystal, Glasbake, McKee on handle	65.00 – 75.00
Row 2:	#1	Hazel-Atlas old reamer (recently iridized)	75.00 – 95.00
	#2	Green "log" handle	100.00 – 125.00
	#3	Crystal	15.00 – 20.00
	#4	"Colony" like, twin spout	*15.00 – 20.00
		Same, white	150.00 – 200.00
	#5	Foreign, amber	45.00 – 55.00
Row 3:	#1	"Clambroth," "British make," embossed	200.00 – 225.00
	#2	"MacBeth-Evans Glass Co., Charleroi, Pa."	175.00 – 200.00
	#3	"Clambroth," boat-shaped	200.00 – 225.00
Row 4:	#1	Black, "Orange Juice Extractor"	425.00 – 450.00

Row 4 (Continued):			
	#2	Same, green	55.00 – 65.00
	#3	Same, pink	125.00 – 145.00
	#4	Same, "Clambroth"	75.00 – 85.00
Row 5:	#1	Green, like #2, but unembossed	175.00 – 200.00
	#2	Crystal, embossed "Sunkist Oranges & Lemons" or "Los Angeles Fruit Growers Exchange," ea.	30.00 – 35.00
	#3	Pink, unembossed	200.00 – 225.00
Row 6:	#1	Crystal, square, marked Italy	20.00 – 25.00
	#2	"Easley's," (called "chisel cone")	65.00 – 75.00
	#3	"Easley's," square opalescent white	200.00 – 225.00
	#4	"Read," some embossed, some not	100.00 – 125.00
	#5	Unusual six-sided top	45.00 – 50.00

Page 213

Row 1:	#1	"Hex Optic" bucket reamer, green	45.00 – 50.00
	#2	Same, pink	45.00 – 50.00
Row 2:	#1	2-cup pitcher w/sunflower in bottom, green	125.00 – 135.00
	#2	Same, dark Jadite	85.00 – 95.00
	#3	Same, light Jadite	85.00 – 95.00
	#4	Large, loop handle, crystal	20.00 – 25.00
Row 3:	#1	Same, yellowish Jadite	150.00 – 175.00
	#2	Same, light Jadite	50.00 – 53.00
	#3	Same, dark Jadite	50.00 – 55.00
	#4	Same, green	30.00 – 35.00

Row 4:	#1	"Jennyware," pink	125.00 – 135.00
	#2	Same, ultra-marine	125.00 – 135.00
	#3	Small loop handle, light Jadite	50.00 – 55.00
	#4	Same, Delphite blue	125.00 – 135.00
Row 5:	#1	Large, 5⅞", tab handle, pink	35.00 – 40.00
	#2	Same, green	25.00 – 28.00
	#3	Small, 5" tab handle, pink	40.00 – 45.00
	#4	Same, green	25.00 – 28.00

* See pages 266 – 270 for reproductions.

McKee Glass Company made most of the Sunkist reamers, though not all. **According to records uncovered at the Fenton factory, the very first Sunkist reamers were made by Indiana Glass Company.**

The McKee symbol is an "McK" with a circle around it, and this insignia adds interest to a reamer. Collectors of reamers concern themselves with color, type (lemon, orange, grapefruit), handles, spouts, seed dams or not, footed or flat bottomed, embossing, size and shape of the reaming section, etc. As usual, scarcity and demand determine price for reamers, many of which are not cheap!

Page 215

Row 1:	#1	Cambridge green	200.00 – 225.00
	#2, 3	Same, light pink	200.00 – 225.00
Row 2:	#1	Same, amber	500.00 – 550.00
	#2	Same, green w/silver Rockwell decoration	225.00 – 250.00
	#3	Cambridge, crystal	25.00 – 28.00
		Same, Cobalt blue (shown page 54)	2,750.00 – 3,000.00
Row 3:	#1	Cambridge, small tab, crystal	18.00 – 20.00
	#2	Same, cobalt blue	375.00 – 395.00
	#3	Cambridge, small, ftd., green	550.00 – 600.00
		Same, crystal, (not shown)	22.00 – 25.00

Row 3 (Continued):			
		Same, pink, (not shown)	550.00 – 600.00
		Same, cobalt blue, (not shown)	1,000.00 – 1,200.00
All grapefruits are McKee.			
	#4	Grapefruit, ultra-marine	800.00 – 850.00
Row 4:	#1	Same, Seville yellow	225.00 – 250.00
	#2	Same, flat yellow	225.00 – 250.00
	#3	Same, custard	600.00 – 650.00
Row 5:	#1	Same, "Caramel"	700.00 – 750.00
	#2	Same, black	1,000.00 – 1,200.00
	#3	Same, white	200.00 – 250.00
Row 6:	#1	Same, Jadite	225.00 – 250.00
	#2	Same, Chalaine blue	900.00 – 950.00
	#3	Same, pink	800.00 – 850.00

Page 216 Sunkist

Row 1:	#1	Black	600.00 – 650.00
	#2	Chocolate	750.00 – 850.00
	#3	Crown Tuscan	375.00 – 395.00
	#4	Butterscotch	375.00 – 395.00
Row 2:	#1	Caramel	375.00 – 395.00
	#2	Caramel fry (meaning opalescence)	500.00 – 700.00
	#3	White "BLOCKED" (refers to lettering of Sunkist)	90.00 – 100.00
	#4	Chalaine blue, dark	125.00 – 155.00
Row 3:	#1,2	Chalaine blue, light/dark	200.00 – 225.00
	#3	Turquoise blue	395.00 – 450.00
	#4	Jadite, dark, embossed	75.00 – 95.00

Row 4:	#1	Jadite, dark, unembossed	100.00 – 125.00
	#2	Jadite, light	75.00 – 85.00
	#3	Forest green	650.00 – 700.00
	#4	Apple green	55.00 – 65.00
Row 5:	#1	Seville yellow	55.00 – 60.00
	#2	French ivory	45.00 – 55.00
	#3	Custard, dark	40.00 – 45.00
	#4	Custard, light	40.00 – 45.00
Row 6:	#1	Opalescent white ("Fry")	150.00 – 195.00
	#2	White w/caramel swirl	375.00 – 400.00
	#3	Pink	60.00 – 70.00
	#4	White (embossed Thatcher Mfg. Co.)	25.00 – 30.00

Page 217 "SUNKIST" Rows 1-3

Row 1:	#1	Ivory	85.00 – 100.00
	#2	Gray	100.00 – 175.00
	#3	Opal white (value determined by opalescence)	65.00 – 175.00
	#4	White	10.00 – 20.00
Row 2:	#1	"Blocked" letters in "SUNKIST," white	90.00 – 100.00
	#2	Opal Crown Tuscan	375.00 – 395.00
	#3	Crown Tuscan milk glass	375.00 – 395.00
	#4	Caramel variation	375.00 – 395.00
Row 3:	#1	Caramel, light	375.00 – 395.00
	#2	Caramel, medium	375.00 – 395.00
	#3	Caramel, butterscotch	375.00 – 395.00
	#4	Mustard	500.00 – 550.00

Row 4:	#1	Skokie Green, pointed cone, 5 1/4"	75.00 – 85.00
	#2	Same, Custard	45.00 – 50.00
	#3	Jadite, unembossed, smaller foot than embossed in Row 6	55.00 – 65.00
Row 5:	#1	White, "McK" embossed	25.00 – 30.00
	#2	Same, Custard	35.00 – 40.00
	#3	Same, Jadite	65.00 – 75.00
	#4	Same, Delphite	375.00 – 400.00
Row 6:	#1	White, 6", "McK" embossed	30.00 – 35.00
	#2	Same, Custard w/red trim	35.00 – 40.00
	#3	Same, Jadite	55.00 – 65.00
	#4	Same, Delphite	700.00 – 750.00

You can find numerous cocktail shaker bottoms missing their metal reamer tops. That metal top is a hard to find item, so don't buy too many topless cocktail shakers expecting to find a top. To my knowledge, there are no replacements for these available. See **Reproduction Section pages 266 – 270** for items with asterisks.

There are *several different* inserts for the U.S. Glass reamers. The pitcher in Row 1, #1 and the tubs in Row 2 on Page 220 each have a 4¹/₂" diameter reamer top. A 4¹/₈" top fits the other pitchers on Page 220 *and* the slick handled, horizontal ribbed two cup pitchers on that page. That 4¹/₈" top fits all the loop handled two cup pitchers on Page 221, but the insert for the four cup pitchers is 5¹/₈" in diameter.

Kitchen Items

Page 219

Row 1:	#1	Pink cocktail shaker/ reamer, "Party Line" #191	70.00 – 75.00
	#2	Same, amber	55.00 – 65.00
	#3	Green, cocktail shaker/ reamer, "Speakeasy"	55.00 – 65.00
	#4	Pink pitcher & reamer top	275.00 – 295.00
		Same, crystal pitcher w/black handle & top (shown page 44)	300.00 – 350.00
	#5	Green, 4 cup pitcher & top, "Party Line"	135.00 – 145.00
Row 2:	#1	Same, pink	135.00 – 145.00
	#2	Same, crystal, complete	75.00 – 85.00
		Same, turquoise blue complete (top shown)	400.00 – 450.00
		Same, black (not shown)	600.00 – 650.00

Row 2 (Continued):			
	#3	Westmoreland, green, 2 piece, embossed orange/lemon	*175.00 – 195.00
	#4	Same, pink	*175.00 – 195.00
Row 3:	#1	Same, crystal	*175.00 – 195.00
	#2, 3	Westmoreland, crystal de- corated oranges or lemons, flattened loop handle, ea.	*50.00 – 55.00
Row 4:	#1	Same, dark green	*110.00 – 125.00
	#2	Same, light green	*110.00 – 125.00
	#3	Same, bluish green	*125.00 – 140.00
Row 5:	#1	Same, white	*225.00 – 265.00
	#2	Same, pink	*110.00 – 125.00
	#3	Same, amber	*325.00 – 350.00

Page 220 All U.S. Glass Company

Row 1:	#1, 4	Reamer pitcher set, 3 piece, pink, ea.	275.00 – 295.00
	#2	Reamer pitcher set, green	275.00 – 295.00
		Same, yellow, shown on page 121	650.00 – 750.00
	#3	Tumbler for set	14.00 – 15.00
Row 2:	#1	Tub, w/reamer top, pink	200.00 – 225.00
	#2	Same, green	200.00 – 225.00
	#3	"Vidrio Products No. J-50"	120.00 – 135.00
	#4	Slick handle, 2 piece, horizontal ribs, (each rib is ¹/₂ cup) amber	350.00 – 375.00
Row 3:	#1	Slick handle, green, insert near top of cup (graduated measurements on side)	55.00 – 65.00

Row 3 (Continued):			
	#2	Same, pink	60.00 – 70.00
	#3	Same as Row 2, #4, pink	60.00 – 70.00
	#4	Same, frosted pink	60.00 – 70.00
Row 4:	#1	Same, green	55.00 – 65.00
	#2	Same, turquoise blue	100.00 – 125.00
	#3	Same, crystal	35.00 – 40.00
	#4	Same, frosted green	55.00 – 65.00
Row 5:	#1	Slick handle, barred or vertical ribs	65.00 – 75.00
	#2	"Handy Andy," green (note reamer cone differs)	55.00 – 65.00
	#3	Crystal, same as #1	35.00 – 40.00

Page 221 All U.S. Glass Company

Row 1:	#1	4 cup pitcher set, amber	550.00 – 600.00
	#2	Same, green	140.00 – 150.00
	#3	Same, pink	325.00 – 350.00
Row 2:	#1	2 cup, pitcher set, light pink	60.00 – 65.00
	#2	Same, dark pink	60.00 – 65.00
	#3	Same, white	100.00 – 125.00
	#4	Same, amber	350.00 – 375.00
Row 3:	#1	Same, yellow (light honey amber)	350.00 – 375.00
	#2	Same, blue complete	750.00 – 795.00
		Same, crystal, complete	35.00 – 45.00
	#3, 5	Same, crystal, decorated, ea.	45.00 – 55.00

Row 3 (Continued):			
	#4	Tumbler, matching reamer	10.00 – 15.00
Row 4:	#1	Same, frosted green	55.00 – 65.00
	#2	Same, bluish green (turquoise)	115.00 – 125.00
	#3	Same, dark green	55.00 – 65.00
	#4	Same, light green	55.00 – 65.00
Row 5:	#1	Slick handle, light pink	130.00 – 150.00
	#2	Same, dark pink	130.00 – 150.00
	#3	Same, amber	350.00 – 395.00
Row 6:	#1	Same, white	85.00 – 95.00
	#2	Same, green	100.00 – 125.00
	#3	Slick handle, grapefruit	400.00 – 450.00

This remains the "catch-all" section on reamers with those not fitting the previous categories gathered here. Many of the glass reamer manufacturers are unknown, although I am sure that McKee made the Saunders and most likely the Radnt. However, to my knowledge, no valid catalog information has ever surfaced to prove that.

I shall repeat the RE-GO reamer story as shown in Rows 3 and 5 on page 223. I find it unbelievable that these ever survived being used. It is a mechanical, glass, two part reamer. The only thing separating the glass from crunching together is a small wooden peg that allows the insert to be turned by hand to extract the juice.

The name RE-GO comes from a reamer that originally said "pu**RE-GO**ld." (The small letters in pure gold were placed there for emphasis by me.) The PURE-GOLD reamer itself may never have been marketed; the first name was altered by removing the letters "p, u, l, d" to leave the name RE-GO. The old letters can still be seen on these reamers, albeit slightly (shown close up on page 225).

The green insert shown in Row 3 #1 is called "EASY SQUEEZE" and is used on a base similar to that of the RE-GO.

Page 223

Row 1:	#1	Jadite, embossed SAUNDERS	1,600.00 – 1,700.00
	#2	"Sanitary Bess Mixer," (embossed **"4"** inside a large **"1"**)	175.00 – 200.00
	#3	"Ideal," Pat'd Jan 31, 1888	175.00 – 195.00
	#4	Black, same as #1	1,500.00 – 1,600.00
Row 2:	#1	"Tricia," black	1,400.00 – 1,500.00
	#2	Same, pink, complete (bottom shown)	950.00 – 1,000.00
		Same, crystal, complete (top shown)	450.00 – 500.00
	#3	Same, green	950.00 – 1,000.00
Row 3:	#1	"EASY SQUEEZE," green top only	200.00 – 250.00
		Same, complete (not shown)	600.00 – 650.00
	#2	Green RE-GO	600.00 – 650.00
	#3	RE-GO, crystal top only	125.00 – 150.00
		Same, complete (not shown)	350.00 – 450.00
Row 4:	#1	"RADNT," crystal	125.00 – 135.00
	#2	Same, green	400.00 – 450.00
	#3	Same, pink	400.00 – 450.00
Row 5:	#1	RE-GO, opalescent white	700.00 – 750.00
	#2	Same, blue	1,250.00 – 1,350.00
	#3	Same, black (top shown)	1,150.00 – 1,250.00

Page 224

Row 1:	#1	Metal insert	175.00 – 195.00
	#2	Glass insert, probably Hocking	295.00 – 325.00
	#3	Mount Joy	275.00 – 295.00
Row 2:	#1	"Mayfair" blue glass insert, probably Hocking	700.00 – 750.00
	#2	Sunkist bowl, pink	275.00 – 295.00

Page 225

Row 1:	#1	Saunders with metal top	1,600.00 – 1,700.00
	#2,3	RE-GO (2 views)	1,250.00 – 1,350.00

Refrigerator Containers

Page 227

Row 1:	#1	Pyrex, 4¼" x 6¾", blue & white (12.00 – 15.00); blue	18.00 – 25.00
	#2	Same, 3½" x 4¾", blue & white (10.00 – 12.00); blue	18.00 – 22.00
	#3	Same, red (10.00 – 12.00); crystal "Crosley Shelvador"	10.00 – 12.00
	#4	Green, 5" x 5", leaf design, U.S. Glass Co.	30.00 – 35.00
Row 2:	#1	Federal, pink 4" x 4" (30.00 – 35.00); 4" x 8" (40.00 – 45.00); 8" x 8"	50.00 – 55.00
	#2	Same, 4½" #2528, pink (30.00 – 35.00); white 5½" round	18.00 – 20.00
	#3	Same, 4½" #2528, amber (20.00 – 25.00); 8" x 8"	30.00 – 35.00
		4" x 4"	15.00 – 18.00

Hazel-Atlas Glass Company

Row 3:	#1	5¾" round, flat knob, green (30.00 – 35.00); cobalt blue	65.00 – 75.00
	#2	5¾" round, pointed knob, decorated	30.00 – 35.00
	#3	Same as #1, white	25.00 – 30.00
	#4	5" round, white w/green leaf	20.00 – 25.00
Row 4:	#1	"Crisscross," blue, 4" x 4" (42.00 – 48.00); 4" x 8" (115.00 – 125.00); 8" x 8"	135.00 – 145.00
	#2	Same, 3½" x 5¾", crystal (25.00 – 30.00); blue (135.00 – 145.00); green	70.00 – 75.00
	#3	Same, 5½" round, pink or green	185.00 – 195.00
	#4	4½" x 5" pink or yellow	40.00 – 45.00
		green (30.00 – 35.00); blue	60.00 – 70.00

Page 228

Row 1:	#1	Fry, 4½" x 8"	40.00 – 45.00
	#2	Glasbake, 4¼" square, light blue	12.00 – 15.00
	#3	Same, 4½" x 5", crystal	12.00 – 15.00
	#4	Green Clambroth, 3⅝" square	30.00 – 35.00
Row 2:	#1	McKee, 4" x 5" red "Dots" (35.00 – 38.00); Delphite	50.00 – 55.00
		blue "Dots," 5" x 8"	45.00 – 55.00
	#2	5" x 8" Chalaine blue (75.00 – 85.00) 4" x 5" Custard or Seville	30.00 – 35.00
	#3	5" x 8" Seville yellow (35.00 – 45.00); 4" x 5" Jadite	35.00 – 40.00
		4" x 5" Chalaine	55.00 – 65.00
Row 3:	#1	Seville yellow, 7¼" square	45.00 – 50.00
	#2	Crystal, 3½" x 5½"	15.00 – 20.00
	#3	Jadite, 4¼" beater bowl	65.00 – 95.00
	#4	Jadite, 10 oz. canister	45.00 – 55.00

Hocking Glass Company

Row 4:	#1	4¼" x 4¾", 2 styles, green, ea.	30.00 – 35.00
	#2	Same, green Clambroth	40.00 – 45.00
	#3	6" square, green, U.S. Glass	35.00 – 40.00
	#4	"Fire-King," 4" x 4⅛"	12.50 – 15.00
Row 5:	#1	8" x 8", Vitrock (55.00 – 65.00); 4" x 4", Vitrock	25.00 – 30.00
		4" x 4", green, ea.; plain top (22.00 – 28.00); indent handle	30.00 – 35.00
	#2	"Fire-King," Jade-ite, 4½" x 5¼" (35.00 – 40.00); 5" x 9"	75.00 – 80.00
	#3	Same, blue, 4½" x 5"	15.00 – 18.00
	#4	Oval, 8" green (50.00 – 55.00); 7" fired-on blue	30.00 – 35.00
		6" green Clambroth	35.00 – 40.00

Page 229

Row 1:	#1	"Jennyware" 16 oz. round	55.00 – 65.00
	#2	Glasbake, 5½" square w/lid	20.00 – 25.00
	#3, 4	McKee Hall's, 4" x 5" or 4" x 6" ea.	35.00 – 45.00

Jeannette Glass Company

Row 2:	#1	Floral, 5" x 5", Jadite (65.00 – 75.00); 5" x 10"	75.00 – 95.00
	#2	4" x 4" Jadite (30.00 – 35.00); Delphite	45.00 – 55.00
	#3	4" x 8" Jadite (55.00 – 65.00); Delphite	65.00 – 75.00
Row 3:	#1	Floral, 5" x 5", green	65.00 – 75.00
	#2, 3	Round dish, 32 oz., Jadite or Delphite	75.00 – 85.00
	#4	Round crock, 40 oz., Jadite	85.00 – 95.00
Row 4:	#1	"Kompakt," green, 4" x 4" (25.00 – 30.00); 4" x 8" (not shown)	45.00 – 50.00
		Same, SCA, 4" x 8"	20.00 – 22.00
	#2	Jennyware, 4½" square pink (30.00 – 35.00); ultra-marine	30.00 – 35.00
	#3	Same, 4½" x 9", pink (45.00 – 55.00); ultra-marine	45.00 – 55.00
Row 5:	#1	"Hex Optic," 6" round base (18.00 – 20.00); lid (20.00 – 25.00); 3 piece	75.00 – 85.00
	#2	Same, 4½" x 5", green, base (15.00); lid (20.00); 3 piece	45.00 – 50.00
	#3	Radnt jar, 5" lid & 5½" tall	30.00 – 35.00
	#4	Ultra-marine 4" x 4" (35.00 – 40.00); 4" x 8"	50.00 – 55.00

Rolling Pins

Rolling pin reproductions have caused my mail box to fill up for about two years. A word of warning to those of you who may have found a colored rolling pin with a screw-on metal lid. No "old" rolling pins with screw-on metal lids have ever been found in any transparent color other than crystal. If you have pink, cobalt blue, red, or an odd shade of green, then you have a "recent vintage" rolling pin!

The abundance of crystal rolling pins has not noticeably diminished. These sell in the $10.00 – 12.00 range. Dealers who sell primitives or crafts are filling these with marbles, beans, and other colorful things to sell them. I saw one around Easter with jelly beans priced at $25.00!

Jadite rolling pins have been reproduced. I have not seen one to compare to old, but beware unless buying from a reputable dealer. One dealer told me hers had an "off" color and was easily distinguished from true Jadite.

Page 231 McKee Glass Company except for last row.

Row 1: Note circular band opposite shaker top end.

	#1	Jadite*	800.00 – 900.00
	#2	Custard	350.00 – 400.00

Row 2 & 3: Note smooth end opposite shaker top end on these rows.

	#1	Seville yellow	350.00 – 450.00
	#2	Delphite blue	1,800.00 – 2,000.00
Row 3:	#1	Chalaine blue	1,800.00 – 2,000.00
	#2	Jadite*	800.00 – 900.00
Row 4:	#1	Crystal w/screw-on cobalt handles	300.00 – 350.00

*Reproductions on market, especially through the Internet.

Wooden Handles
Page 232

Row 1:		Peacock blue (handles attached to metal rod inside pin)	275.00 – 295.00
Row 2:	#1	Green transparent (handles attached to wood dowel pin)	450.00 – 500.00
	#2	Pink (screw-on wooden handles)	450.00 – 500.00
Row 3:	#1	White (comes w/wood or metal screw-on handles), ea. marked "Imperial Mfg. Co., Cambridge, Ohio"	90.00 – 110.00
		Same, Custard color (not shown)	165.00 – 175.00
	#2	Cobalt blue (handles attached to metal rod inside pin)	450.00 – 500.00
Row 4:		Clambroth white (screw-on wood handles)	125.00 – 135.00

Blown Rolling Pins
Page 233

Row 1:	#1	Amethyst	120.00 – 135.00
	#2	Cobalt blue	180.00 – 200.00
Row 2:	#1	Amber, light	100.00 – 120.00
	#2	Forest green	150.00 – 175.00
Row 3:	#1	Peacock blue, dark	200.00 – 225.00
	#2	Crystal, "Kardov Flour, Famous Self Rising"	85.00 – 95.00
Row 4:	#1	Chalaine blue	500.00 – 600.00
	#2	Blue, light	175.00 – 225.00

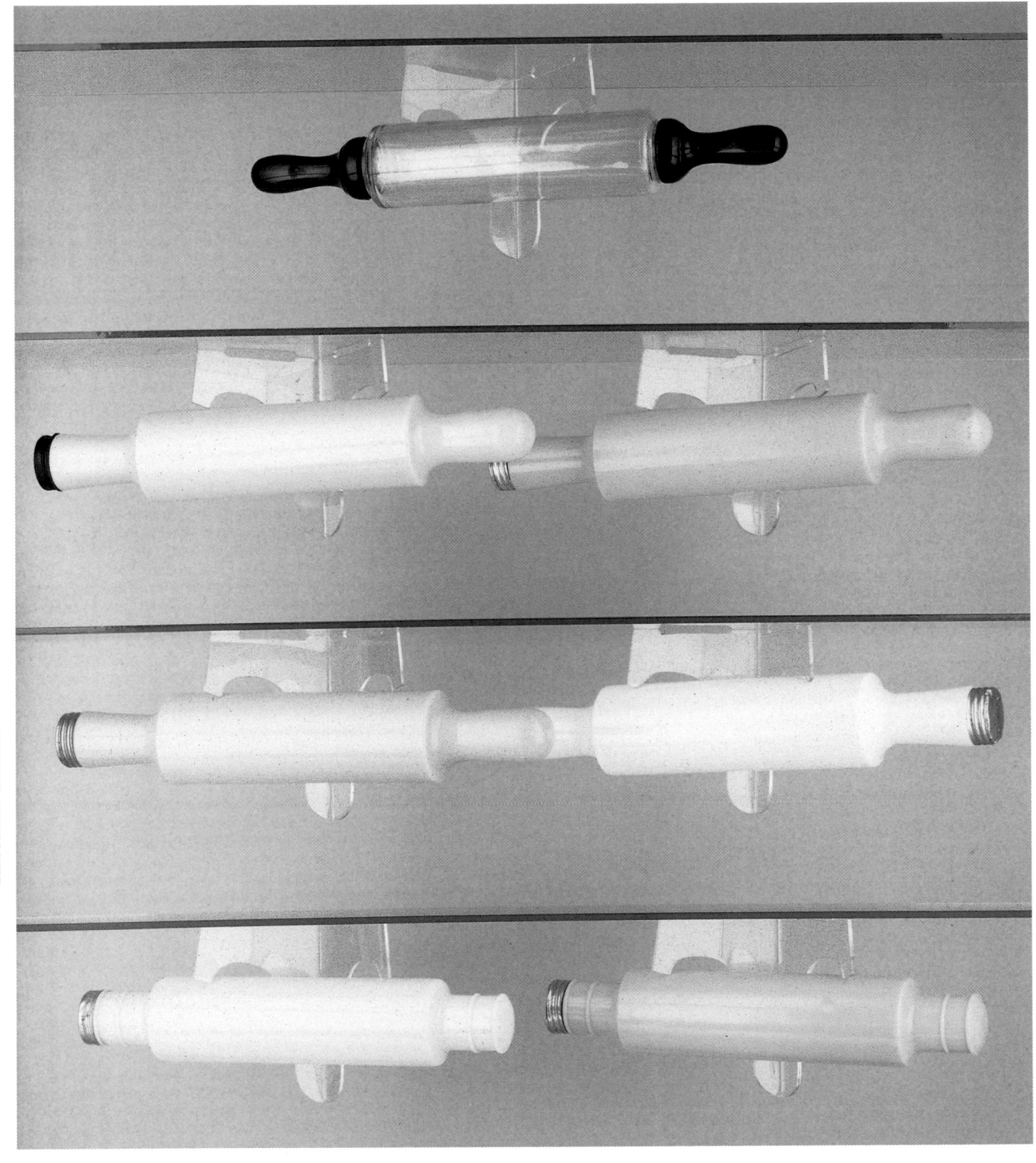

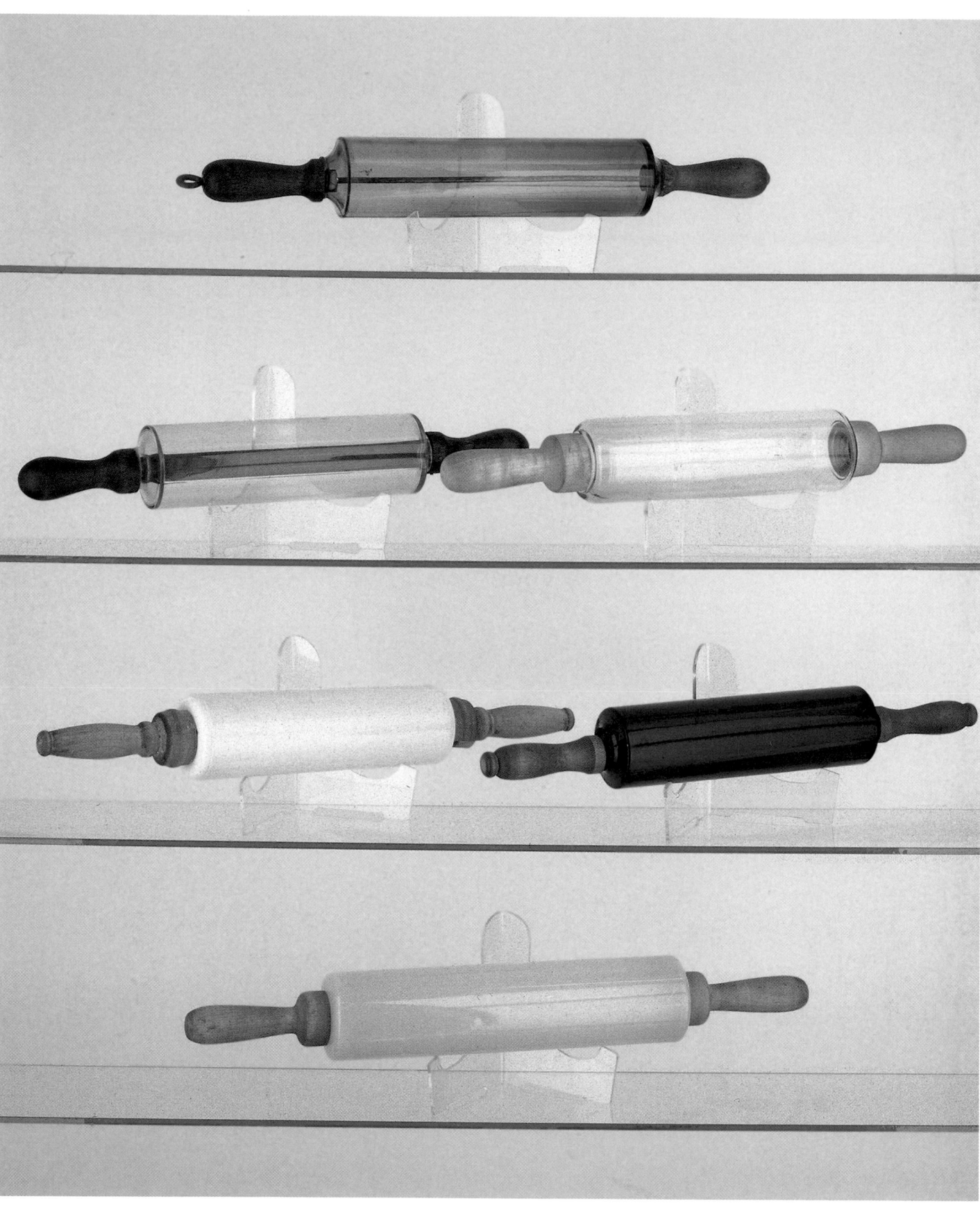

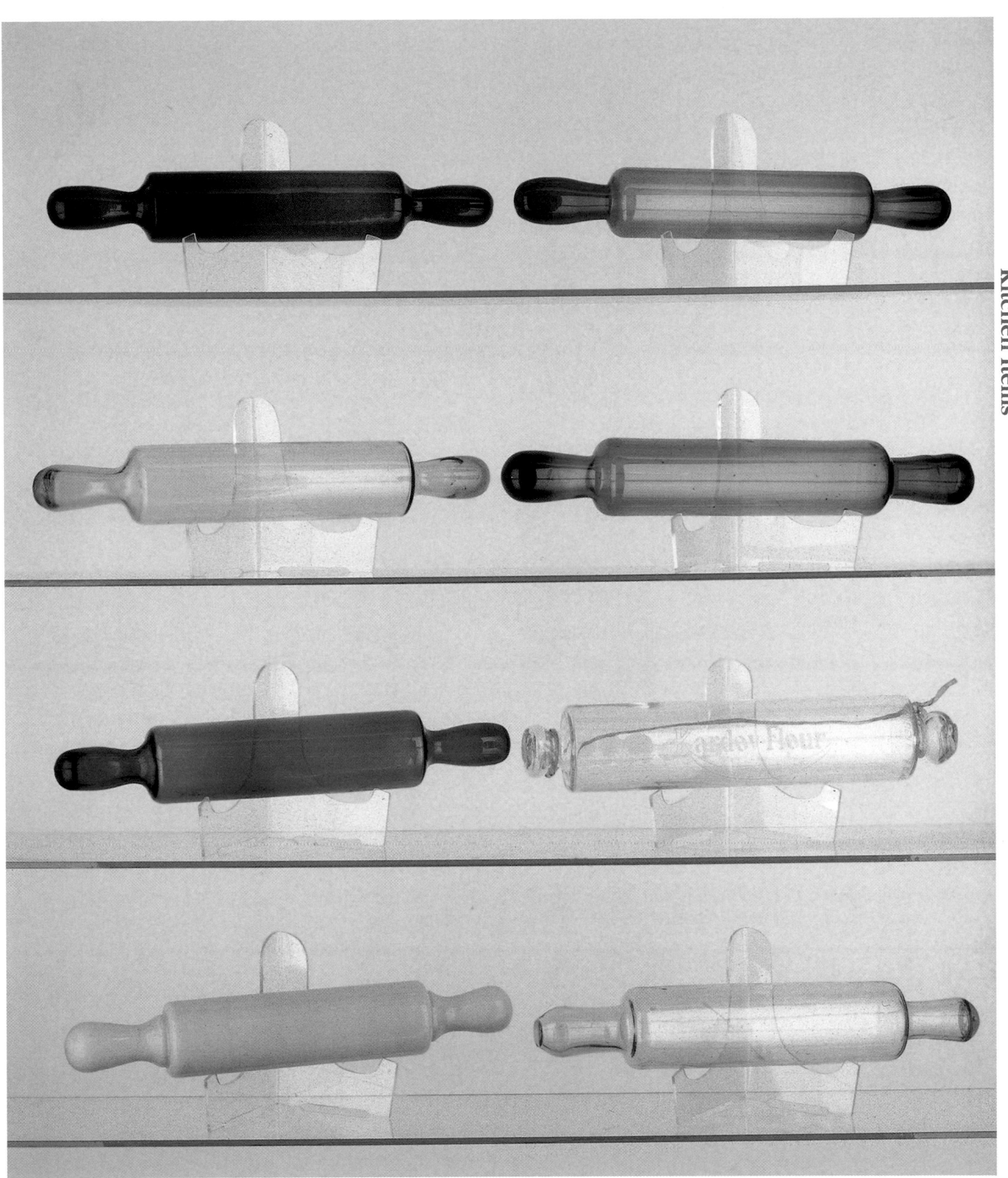

Kitchen Items

Page 235

Row 1:	#1	Cobalt blue, blown (common)	180.00 – 200.00
	#2	Dark, amber, blown	100.00 – 120.00
	#3	Amethyst, blown	120.00 – 135.00
	#4	Light amber, molded	100.00 – 120.00
	#5	Peacock blue, blown	200.00 – 225.00
Row 2:	#1-3	White, marked Imperial Mfg. Co., Cambridge, Ohio, ea.	90.00 – 110.00
Row 3:	#1	Jadite, molded, plain	800.00 – 900.00
	#2	Seville yellow, plain or shaker top, ea.	350.00 – 450.00
	#3	Jadite w/circular band	800.00 – 900.00
	#4	Custard, plain or shaker top, ea.	350.00 – 400.00
Row 4:	#1	Cobalt blue, wood handles	450.00 – 500.00
	#2	Chalaine blue, blown	500.00 – 600.00
	#3	Coke bottle blue, molded	85.00 – 100.00
	#4	Crystal, screw-on black wood handles	65.00 – 75.00
Row 5:	#1	Delphite blue, fired-on	100.00 – 125.00
	#2	Crystal, Kardov Flour Famous Self Rising	85.00 – 95.00
	#3	Crystal, Jewel Tea Co. paper insert	25.00 – 35.00
	#4	Crystal, ringed like Manhattan	25.00 – 35.00
Row 6:	#1	White, blown	75.00 – 85.00
	#2	Clambroth, wood handles	125.00 – 135.00
	#3	White, screw-on metal handles	110.00 – 125.00
	#4	Crystal, with cork end	22.00 – 35.00

Two styles of McKee.

Comparison of Delphite blue (bottom pin above) to Chalaine blue (at left).

McKee, white, 300.00 – 325.00

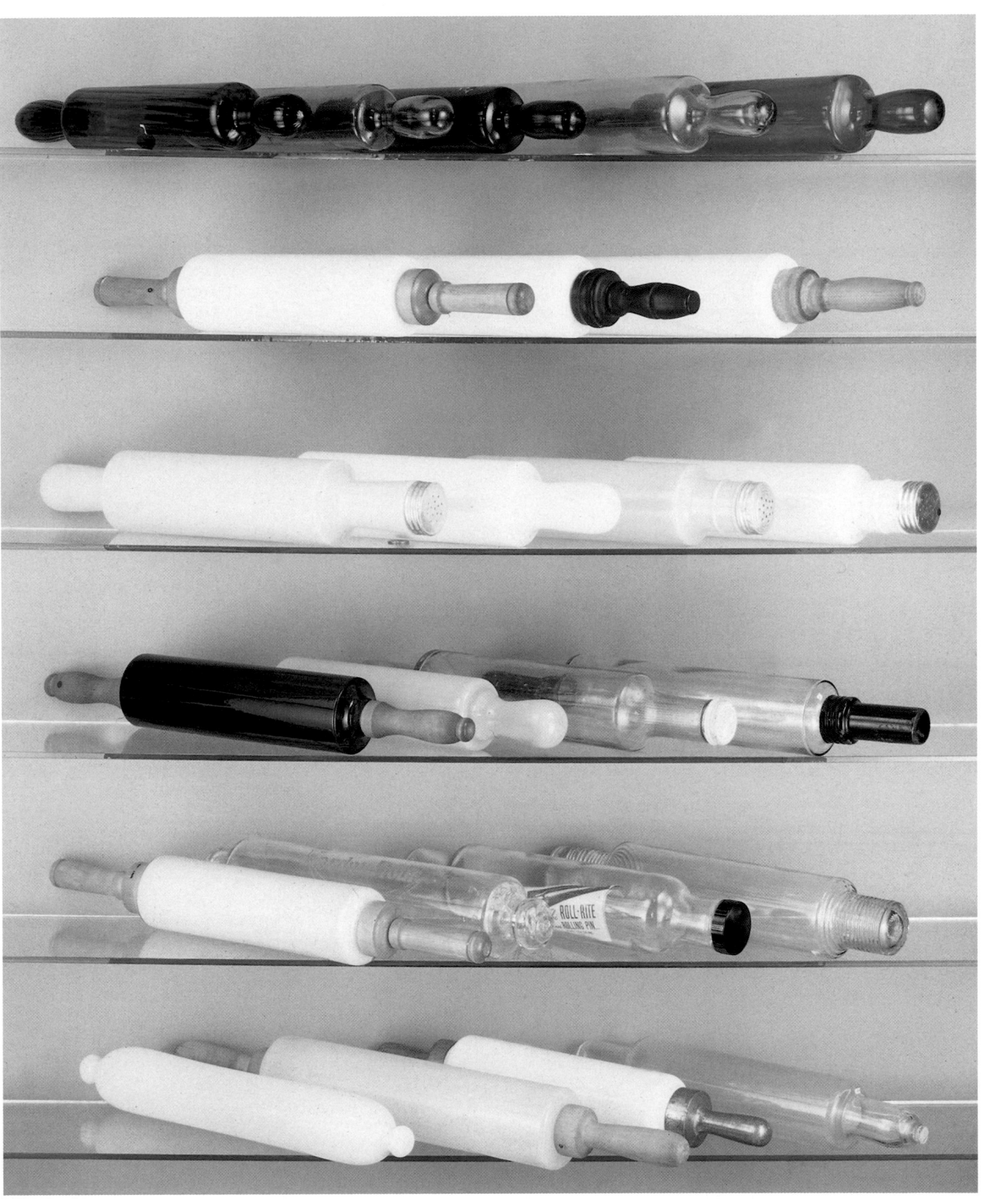

Salad Sets

Prices of the colored salad sets have soared, especially those from the Cambridge, Imperial, or Heisey companies. Items made by major glass companies of that time are always more collectible than unidentified glassware.

The inclusion of salad sets in the Kitchen book opened a new collecting field for some buyers who were not aware of the variety available before then. Many of these sets were of foreign manufacture — mainly Czechoslovakia.

Forks and spoons sell for around the same price, but there seems to be a small premium ($1.00 – 5.00) for a set.

Page 237

Row 1:	#1	Blue, large pointed handle set	85.00 – 95.00
	#2	Amber set	55.00 – 65.00
	#3	Yellow, small pointed handle set	65.00 – 75.00
		Same, pink (not shown) marked "TCHECOBLOV"	85.00 – 95.00
	#4, 5	Green set	85.00 – 95.00
	#6-9	Same, peacock or cobalt blue set	85.00 – 95.00
	#10	Same, red set	95.00 – 110.00
	#11, 12	Boxed forks, green or pink, ea.	30.00 – 35.00
Row 2:	#1, 2	Long crystal handled amber set	45.00 – 55.00
	#3, 4	Red teardrop handle set	95.00 – 110.00
		Same, cobalt blue (not shown)	95.00 – 110.00
		Same, amethyst (not shown)	95.00 – 110.00
	#5	Green top and bottom set	75.00 – 95.00
	#6	Blue spoon	42.50 – 47.50
	#7, 8	Green set	85.00 – 95.00
	#9	Amber flattened striped handle set	50.00 – 65.00
Row 3:	#1, 2	Forest green set	85.00 – 95.00
	#3, 4	Black handled set	95.00 – 110.00
	#5, 6	All amber set, found with Czechoslovakia labels	100.00 – 125.00
	#7	White set, serrated and waffle back	85.00 – 95.00
	#8	Canary yellow or vaseline, set	125.00 – 145.00

Page 238

Row 1:	#1, 2	Cobalt blue, rounded, ribbed handle set	75.00 – 85.00
	#3, 4	Same, green	75.00 – 85.00
	#5, 6	Same, light blue	75.00 – 85.00
	#7, 8	Same, amber	45.00 – 55.00
	#9	Same, crystal	35.00 – 50.00
		Same, pink (not shown)	75.00 – 85.00
Row 2:	#1	Blue top w/crystal handle, set	75.00 – 90.00
	#2, 3	Forest green flattened handle set	75.00 – 90.00
	#4, 5	Pink set, edge down sides	75.00 – 85.00
	#6, 7	Same, cobalt blue	75.00 – 85.00
	#8, 9	Same, amber	45.00 – 55.00
Row 3:	#1	Blue pointed fork, set	75.00 – 90.00
	#2, 3	Amber flattened handle set	45.00 – 55.00
	#4	Same, pink	75.00 – 90.00
	#5, 6	Same, green	75.00 – 90.00
	#7, 8	Amber set	45.00 – 55.00
	#9-11	Amber 2 piece set	45.00 – 55.00
		Same, cake server only	55.00 – 75.00

Page 239

Row 1:	**All Cambridge Glass Company**		
	#1, 2	Crystal set w/label	55.00 – 75.00
	#3-6	Black or light blue	150.00 – 195.00
	#7, 8	Amber	85.00 – 110.00
	#9	Green set	140.00 – 175.00
	#10	Red set	225.00 – 250.00
Row 2:	#1, 2	Light blue set, **Imperial** (box shown $5.00)	120.00 – 135.00
	#3, 4	Same, amber	75.00 – 95.00
	#5, 6	Same, green	115.00 – 125.00
	#7, 8	Pink set, possibly Imperial	115.00 – 125.00
	#9, 10	Same, blue	125.00 – 145.00
Row 3:	#1	Green fork	65.00 – 75.00
	#2	Cobalt blue, set	275.00 – 300.00

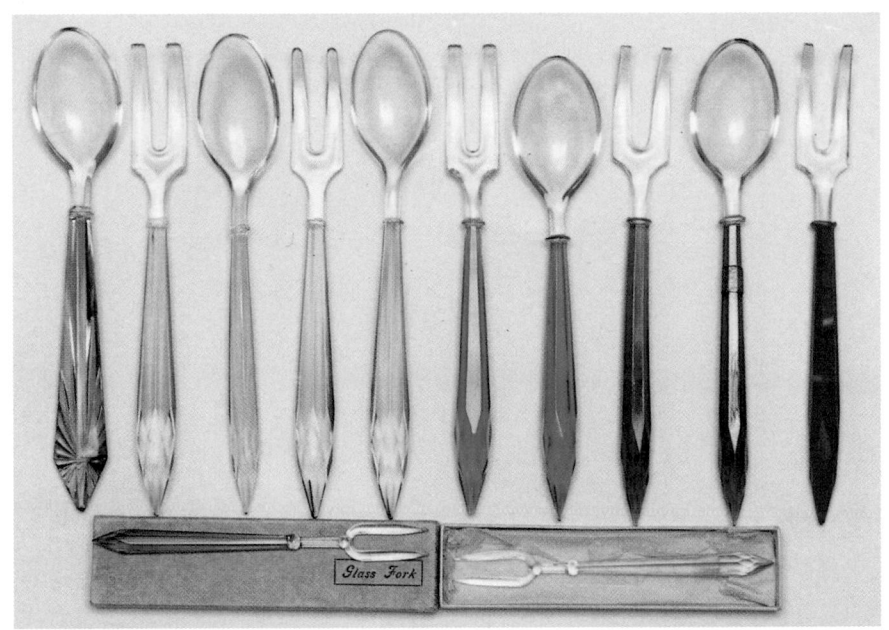

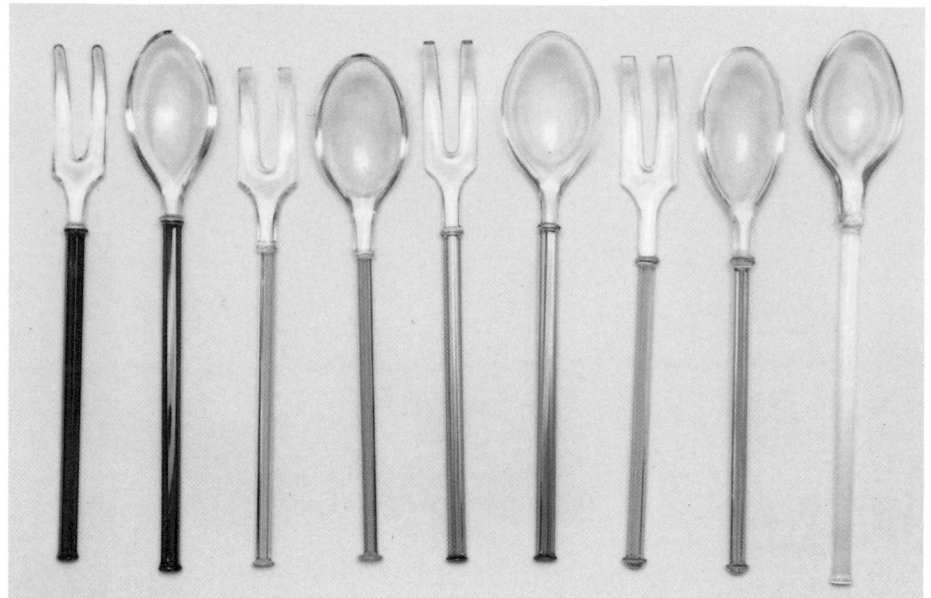

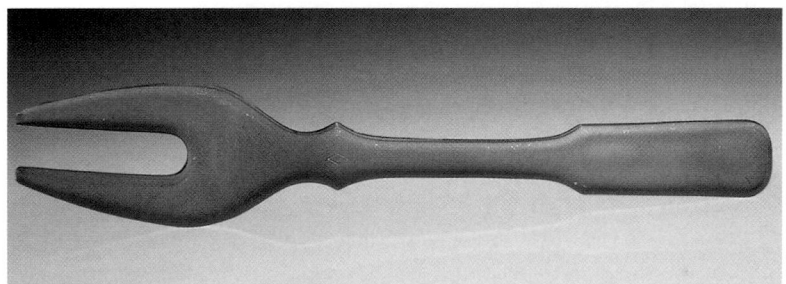

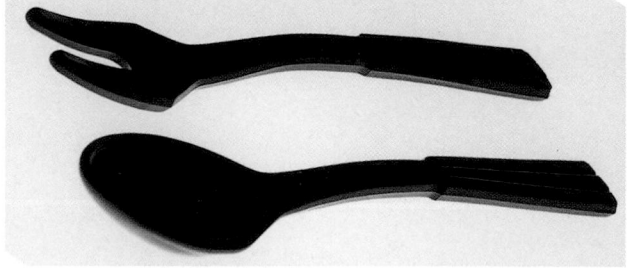

Salt Boxes

Salt boxes are another of the items that few collectors buy per se, but many are bought by collectors of color or by collectors of sets. The "Zipper" or the "Sneath" canister sets are not complete without the salts shown here. There is considerable demand for these latter types, and they sell very quickly on the market.

Crystal salt boxes are gathered by collectors looking to complete "Hoosier" or comparable kitchen cabinet spice and canister sets. I have seen some very high prices on these in shops that sell "primitive" antiques. What I wonder is, do they actually sell for those prices?

Page 241

Row 1:	#1	Crystal w/glass lid, embossed SALT, Flintext	100.00 – 125.00
	#2	Jadite, McKee	165.00 – 195.00
	#3	Same, Chalaine blue	225.00 – 235.00
Row 2:	#1	Green "Zipper" w/lid	175.00 – 195.00
		Same, wo/lid (shown below)	125.00 – 135.00
	#2	Peacock blue	145.00 – 155.00
	#3	Green, "Sneath"	250.00 – 275.00
Row 3:	#1	Jadite w/lid, Jeannette	350.00 – 375.00
	#2	White, embossed SALT box	150.00 – 165.00
	#3	White, round embossed SALT box	150.00 – 165.00
Row 4:	#1	Crystal, "Sneath"	30.00 – 35.00
	#2	Amber, "Sneath"	185.00 – 195.00
	#3	Crystal, embossed SALT	25.00 – 30.00
	#4	Crystal, "Zipper"	25.00 – 30.00
Row 5:	#1	Green Jeannette round, embossed SALT on lid,	250.00 – 275.00
		pink (not shown)	275.00 – 295.00
	#2	Crystal salt w/lid	25.00 – 30.00
	#3	Crystal, ribbed, embossed SALT	25.00 – 30.00
	#4	Crystal, ribbed	20.00 – 25.00

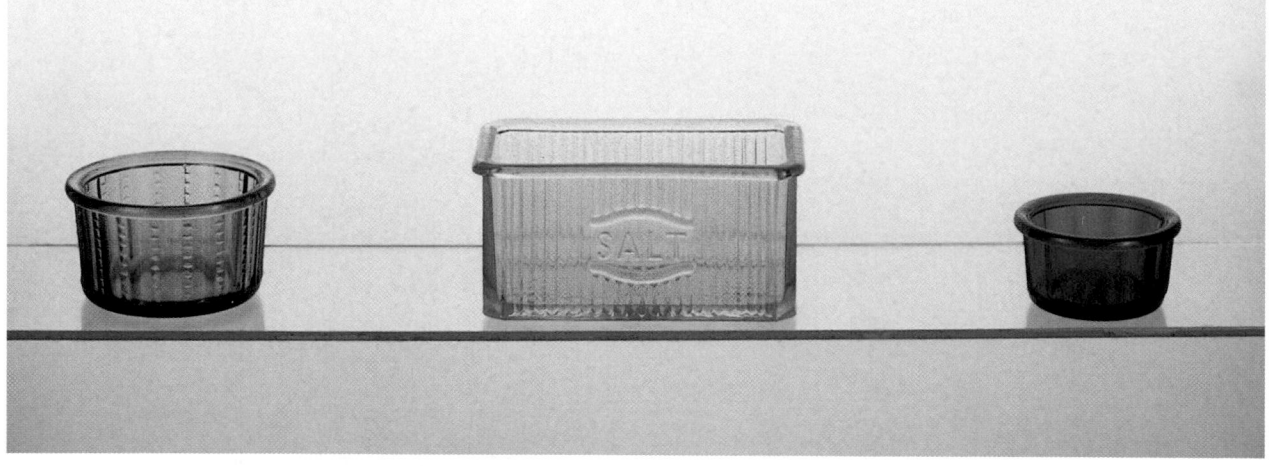

Page 240

Left to right:	Green "Zipper"	125.00 – 135.00
	Green Sneath	250.00 – 275.00
	Peacock blue	145.00 – 155.00

SALT
SALT
SALT

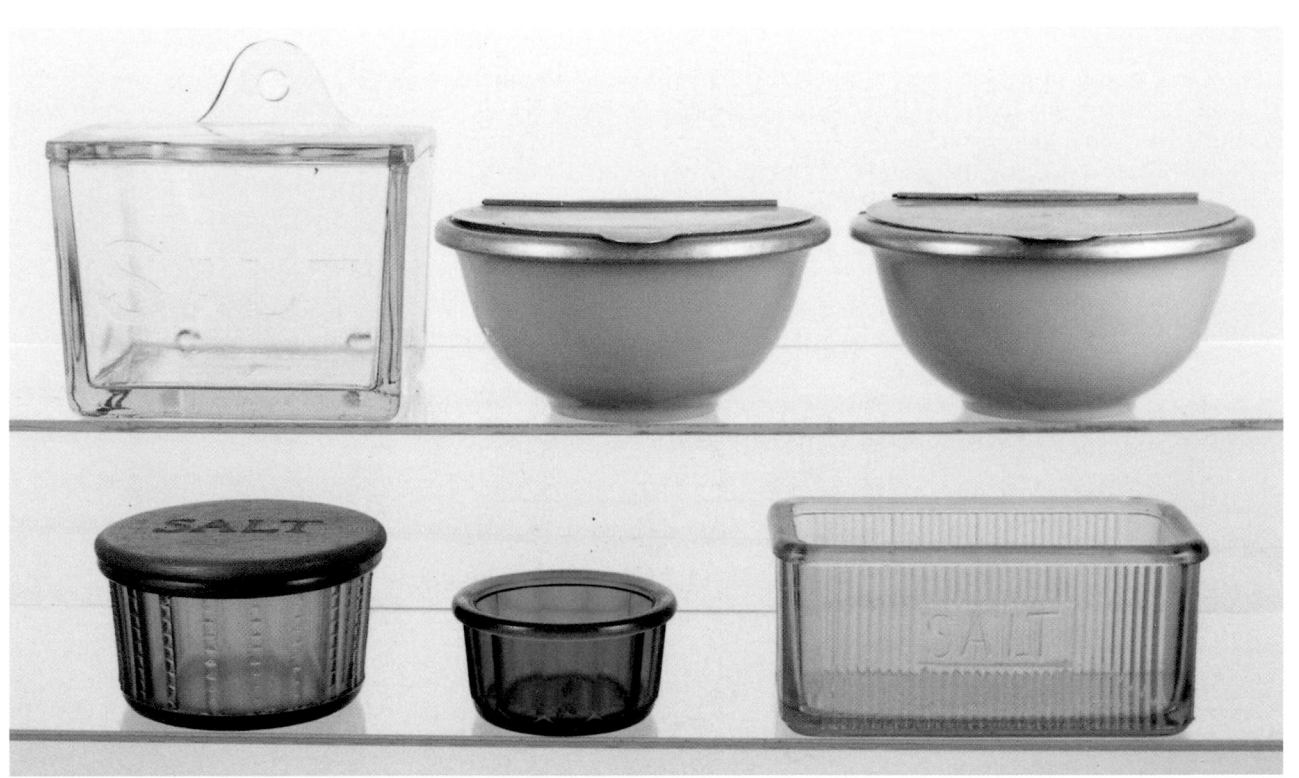

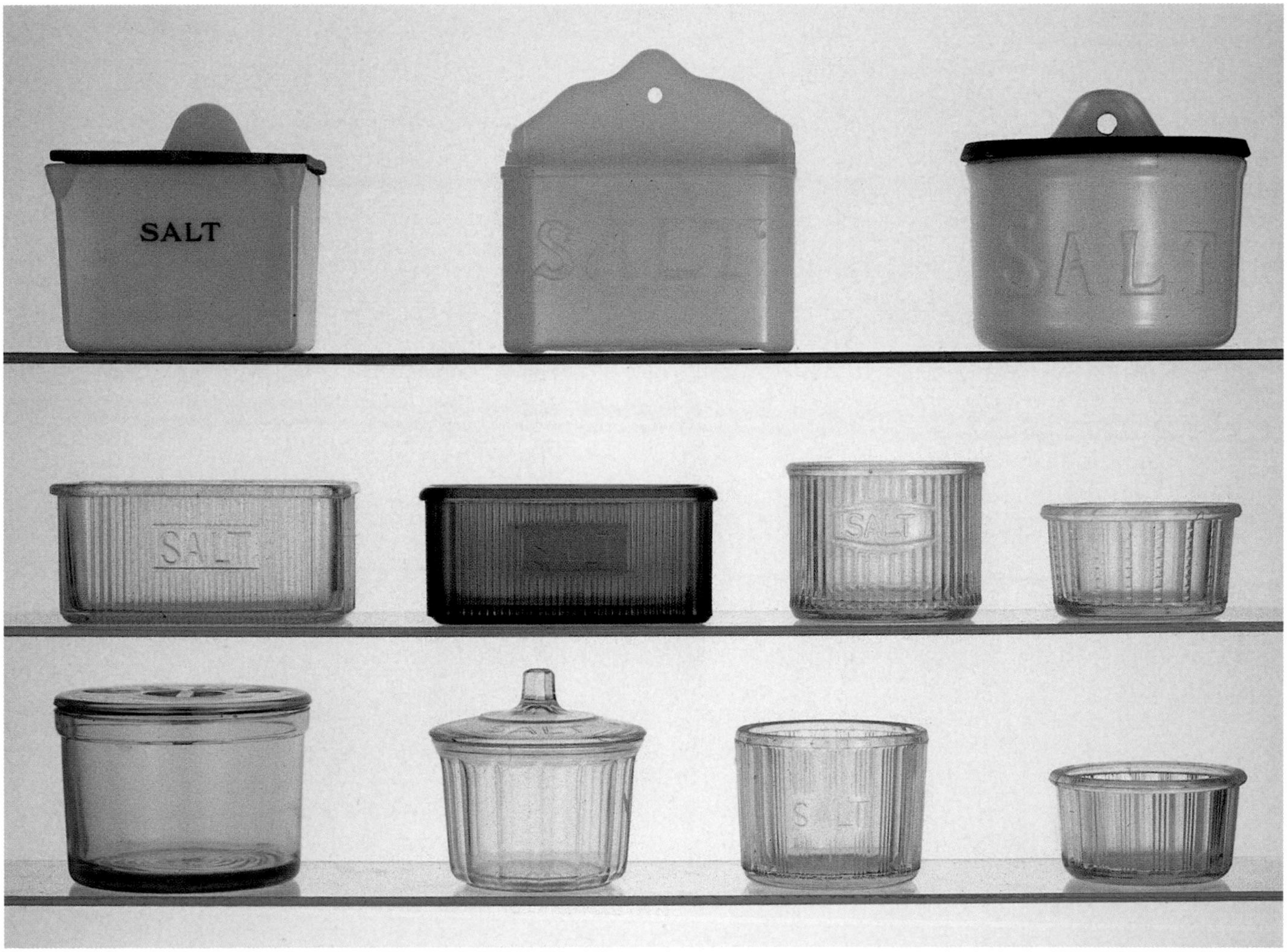
SALT
SALT
SALT
SALT
SALT
SALT

Shakers

Please note that the previously listed "kitchen cabinet shakers" shown on page 245 Row 4, #5 and #6 were strictly vacuum cleaner attachments used for blowing moth crystals into your closet. Two readers have definitely confirmed this with vacuum advertising! Live and learn!

See Reproduction Section pages 266 – 270 for items marked with asterisks.

Kitchen Items

Page 243

Row 1:	#1	Black lettering pepper or salt, ea.	20.00 – 25.00
	#2	Bicentennial Martha & George, pr.	75.00 – 100.00
Row 2:	#1	Red pepper	25.00 – 30.00
	#2,5	Flour or sugar	85.00 – 95.00
	#3,4	Pepper or salt	65.00 – 75.00

Row 3:	#1,3	Lincoln shakers, pr.	60.00 – 65.00
	#2	Lincoln 1 lb. butter	70.00 – 75.00
	#3,4	Bachelor Bros. salt & pepper, pr.	75.00 – 100.00

Page 244 Hocking Glass Company (Rows 1-3)

Row 1:	#1,2	Salt or pepper, opaque yellow, ea.	25.00 – 30.00
	#3,4	Flour or sugar, opaque yellow, ea.	40.00 – 50.00
	#5,6,8,9	Fired-on yellow or blue, salt or pepper, ea.	20.00 – 25.00
	#7,10	Fired-on yellow or blue flour or sugar, ea.	30.00 – 35.00
Row 2:	#1	Fired-on green	30.00 – 35.00
	#2,3	Panelled fired-on blue, ea.	15.00 – 18.00
	#4-6	Green Clambroth, panelled, ea.	22.00 – 25.00
	#7,8	Transparent green, ea.	20.00 – 22.00
	#9,10	Vitrock, ea.	15.00 – 18.00
Row 3:	#1	Crystal w/raised dots	8.00 – 10.00
	#2	Clambroth	15.00 – 18.00
	#3	Green, plain	15.00 – 18.00
	#4	Tulip (lid is valued at half shaker price)	32.50 – 37.50
	#5,7	White salt or pepper	17.50 – 20.00
	#6	Green Jade-ite	40.00 – 45.00
	#8	White sugar	20.00 – 25.00
	#9	Green, round	35.00 – 40.00
Row 4:	#1,2	Hazel-Atlas embossed pink salt or pepper	*60.00 – 65.00

Row 4 (Continued):			
	#3	Same, crystal	25.00 – 30.00
	#4 5	Same, green salt or pepper	*55.00 – 60.00
	#6,7	Same, flour or sugar	80.00 – 90.00
	#8	Dutch salt	15.00 – 18.00
	#9,10	White w/green, ea.	15.00 – 18.00
Row 5:	#1,2	White w/black, salt or pepper	15.00 – 18.00
	#3,4	White w/black sugar or flour	22.00 – 25.00
	#5	Black fired-on, pepper	15.00 – 18.00
	#6	Black flour	22.00 – 28.00
	#7	Owens-Illinois ovoid shape (good lettering)	20.00 – 25.00
	#8,9	Same, square shapes	12.00 – 15.00
	#10,11	Sneath, amber, ea.	25.00 – 28.00
Row 6:	#1	Crystal, embossed celery	10.00 – 12.00
	#2	Crystal, embossed salt	10.00 – 12.00
	#3	Crystal, embossed sugar	12.00 – 15.00
	#4	Green, embossed flour	35.00 – 40.00
	#5	Green	30.00 – 35.00
	#6	"Clambroth"	18.00 – 22.00
	#7	"Clambroth"	15.00 – 18.00
	#8	Black, round	30.00 – 32.00
	#9	Black, pepper	30.00 – 35.00
	#10	Black, ribbed	30.00 – 35.00

Page 245

Row 1:	#1,2	Lady salt or pepper	50.00 – 55.00
	#3,4	Same, flour or sugar	65.00 – 70.00
	#5	Jadite, sugar	75.00 – 85.00
	#6	Jadite, pepper	60.00 – 65.00
	#7,8	"Art Deco," pr.	80.00 – 100.00
	#9,10	Blue, pr.	22.00 – 28.00
	#11,12	Fired-on blue, pr.	12.00 – 15.00
Row 2:	#1	Fired-on Dutch set	100.00 – 120.00
	#2	Dutch white set	20.00 – 25.00
	#3	Lady watering spice set	120.00 – 150.00
Row 3:	#1	Singing birds set	120.00 – 140.00

Row 3 (Continued):			
	#2,3	Scotty dogs, ea.	20.00 – 25.00
	#4	Rooster set	30.00 – 35.00
	#5,6	"Sombrero Sam" set	45.00 – 55.00
	#7,8	White set w/salt dehumidifier	12.50 – 15.00
Row 4:	#1, 2	Black set (w/good lettering)	60.00 – 70.00
	#3,4	Uncle Sam's hat set	40.00 – 45.00
	#5,6	Vacuum cleaner attachments for blowing moth crystals, ea.	12.00 – 15.00
	#7-9	Floral or cherry, ea.	15.00 – 20.00

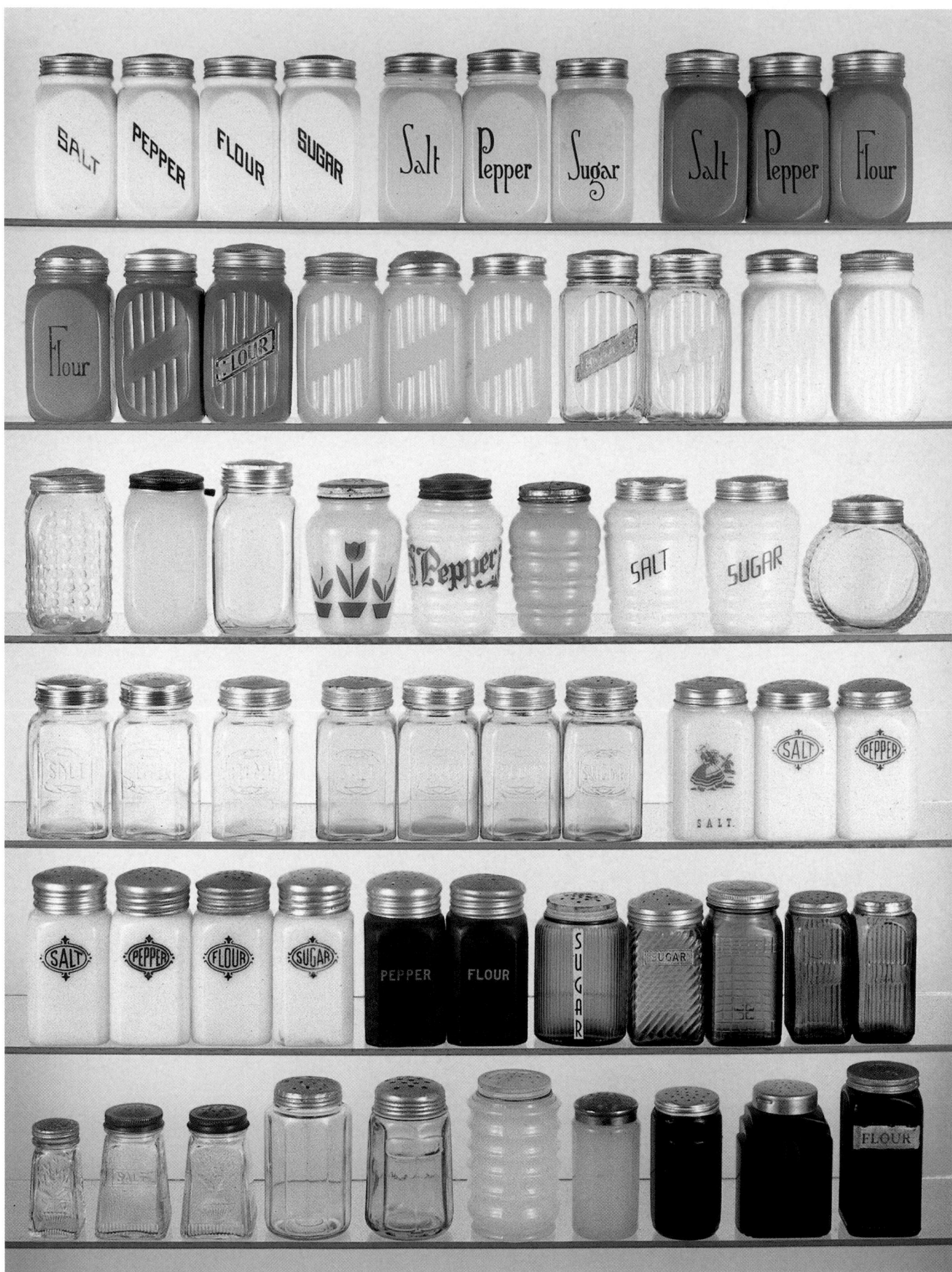

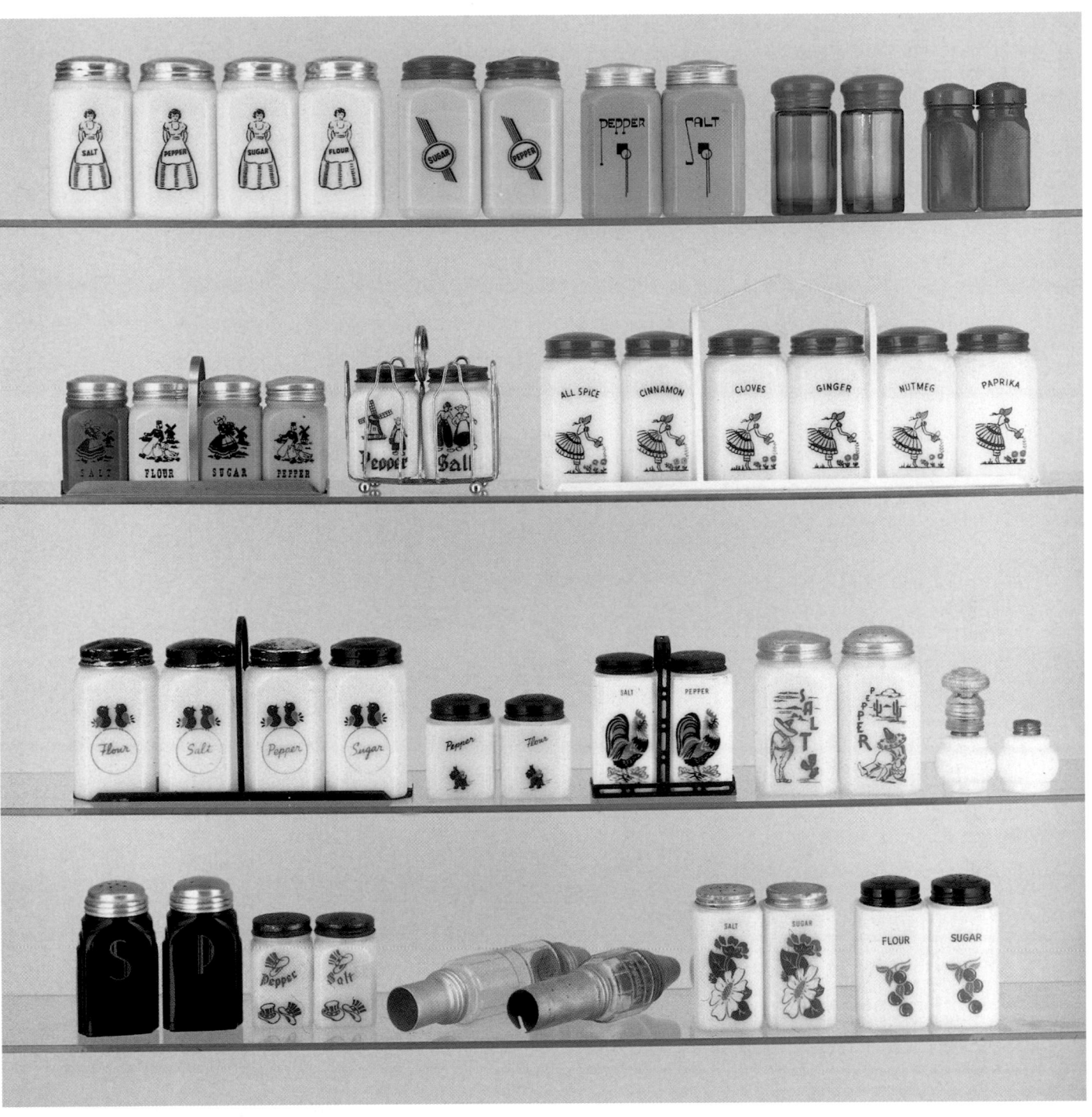

All blue shakers are in demand, but there has also been an increase in demand for white and the later issued Fire-King sets. New collectors start with the inexpensive sets and graduate to higher priced sets. Generally speaking, it would be better to buy the more expensive sets first! That is, if you can find them to buy!

Availability of all shakers has decreased in recent years. There are more salt and peppers found than other shakers, but one major problem with these heavily used items is worn lettering. Mint lettering on salt shakers is a premium! There were fewer flour, sugar, and spice sets made than salt and pepper sets. Possibly extra shakers came with grease sets and likely, ladies just did not buy shakers for flour and sugar!

Jeannette Glass Company (first 4½ rows)
Page 247

Row 1:	#1,2	Delphite blue, 8 oz., salt	50.00 – 55.00
		pepper	50.00 – 55.00
	#3	Same, sugar	130.00 – 140.00
	#4	Same, paprika	135.00 – 145.00
	#5,6	Jadite, decorated salt/pepper, ea.	30.00 – 40.00
	#7,8	Same, mouth wash or bicarbonate soda	145.00 – 175.00
	#9,10	Jadite, 6 oz. wo/label, ea.	15.00 – 20.00
Row 2:	#1,2	Jadite light, salt or pepper	30.00 – 40.00
	#3,4	Same, flour or sugar	50.00 – 60.00
	#5	Jadite dark, pepper	30.00 – 40.00
	#6	Same, flour	50.00 – 60.00
	#7,8	Delphite blue, square, salt or pepper	120.00 – 135.00
	#9	Same, flour or sugar	135.00 – 150.00
Row 3:	#1,2	Jadite dark, square, salt or pepper	35.00 – 45.00
	#3,4	Same, flour or sugar	55.00 – 65.00
	#5,6	Jadite light, square, salt or pepper	35.00 – 45.00

Row 3 (Continued):			
	#7,8	Same, flour or sugar	55.00 – 65.00
	#9	"Jennyware" pink	30.00 – 35.00
Row 4:	#1-4	"Jennyware" ultra-marine (subtract $1.00 missing label), ea.	30.00 – 35.00
	#5-8	Same, crystal	20.00 – 25.00
Row 5:	#1-4	"Jennyware" flat shaker, pink, ea.	35.00 – 45.00
	#5	Same, crystal	20.00 – 25.00
	#6	Green, sold as sugar shaker	40.00 – 45.00
	#7	Unknown manufacturer, green "Zipper"	40.00 – 45.00
	#8	Crystal, "Zipper"	18.00 – 20.00
Row 6:	#1	Green, embossed flour	65.00 – 75.00
	#2	Crystal, embossed salt	20.00 – 27.00
	#3	Crystal, embossed allspice	25.00 – 28.00
	#4	Crystal, embossed cinnamon	25.00 – 28.00
	#5	Crystal, ribbed	10.00 – 12.00
	#6-11	Sneath green, ea.	55.00 – 65.00

Page 248 McKee "Roman Arch" Shakers

Row 1:	#1,2	Skokie green, salt or pepper	55.00 – 65.00
	#3,4	Same, flour or sugar	85.00 – 100.00
	#5	Same, cinnamon	135.00 – 150.00
	#6,7	Delphite blue, salt or pepper	125.00 – 150.00
	#8	Fired-on red salt	18.00 – 20.00
	#9,10	Fired-on flour or sugar	22.00 – 28.00
Row 2:	#1,2,5-8	"Dots," salt or pepper	35.00 – 45.00
	#3,4,9	Same, flour or sugar	50.00 – 60.00
	#10	Custard w/green pepper	25.00 – 35.00
Row 3:	#1,2	Custard salt or pepper	20.00 – 25.00
	#3,4	Same, flour or sugar	30.00 – 35.00
	#5,6	"Diamond Check" on white, ea.	35.00 – 40.00
	#7,8	"Dots" on white, ea.	25.00 – 35.00
	#9,10	Fired-on red, ea.	18.00 – 22.00

Row 4:	#1,2	White w/black, salt or pepper, ea.	20.00 – 25.00
	#3,4	Same, flour or sugar, ea.	30.00 – 35.00
	#5	White w/red salt.	25.00 – 30.00
	#6,7	Same, flour, sugar, ea.	35.00 – 40.00
	#8, 9	Crystal, frosted, salt or pepper, ea.	12.00 – 15.00
Row 5:	#1-11	Black, pepper, salt, flour, sugar, ea.	30.00- 35.00
		all others w/good lettering	45.00 – 50.00
		Black wo/lettering	15.00 – 18.00
Row 6:	#1-4	Fired-on colored set	40.00 – 45.00
	#5	"Bow," red on white	18.00 – 20.00
	#6,7	"Ships," salt or pepper	25.00 – 27.50
	#8,9	Same, flour or sugar	35.00 – 38.00

Page 249 McKee "Square" Shakers

Row 1:	#1	Large, pepper, 16 oz.	60.00 – 70.00
	#2,3	Same, flour or sugar, ea.	70.00 – 80.00
	#4,5	Small, 8 oz., ea.	22.00 – 25.00
	#6,7	Same, flour or sugar, ea.	30.00 – 35.00
	#8,9	Skokie green, ea.	40.00 – 50.00
Row 2:	#1,2	Embossed dark jade salt or pepper	85.00 – 95.00
	#3,4	Same, flour or sugar	95.00 – 120.00
	#5	Embossed Chalaine blue, ea.	250.00 – 300.00
	#6,7	Chalaine blue, salt or pepper	125.00 – 135.00
	#8,9	Chalaine blue, flour or sugar	135.00 – 150.00
Row 3:	#1	White, salt, ea.	18.00 – 22.00
	#2,3	Flour or sugar, ea.	22.00 – 28.00
	#4,5	"HOTPOINT" or "ELECTROCHEF" embossed white, ea.	18.00 – 22.00
	#6,7,8	Flour or sugar	22.00 – 28.00
	#9,10	White, flour or sugar	22.00 – 28.00
Row 4:	#1,2,5,6	Skokie, green salt or pepper	40.00 – 50.00

Row 4 (Continued):			
	#3,4,7	Same, flour or sugar	65.00 – 75.00
	#8	Same, "Cinnamon"	95.00 – 100.00
	#9	Black salt	22.00 – 28.00
	#10	Black sugar	35.00 – 40.00
Row 5:	#1,2	Custard, ea., salt or pepper	18.00 – 22.00
	#3,4	Flour or sugar	40.00 – 45.00
	#5-7	Same, ginger, cinnamon, nutmeg w/good lettering, ea.	95.00 – 100.00
	#8	Seville yellow, salt or pepper	20.00 – 25.00
	#9,10	Same, flour or sugar	30.00 – 35.00
Row 6:	#1,2	Seville yellow, salt or pepper	18.00 – 22.00
	#3,4	Same, flour or sugar	30.00 – 35.00
	#5,6	Skokie green, dark, salt or pepper, ea.	35.00 – 45.00
	#7,8	Same, flour or sugar, ea.	55.00 – 65.00

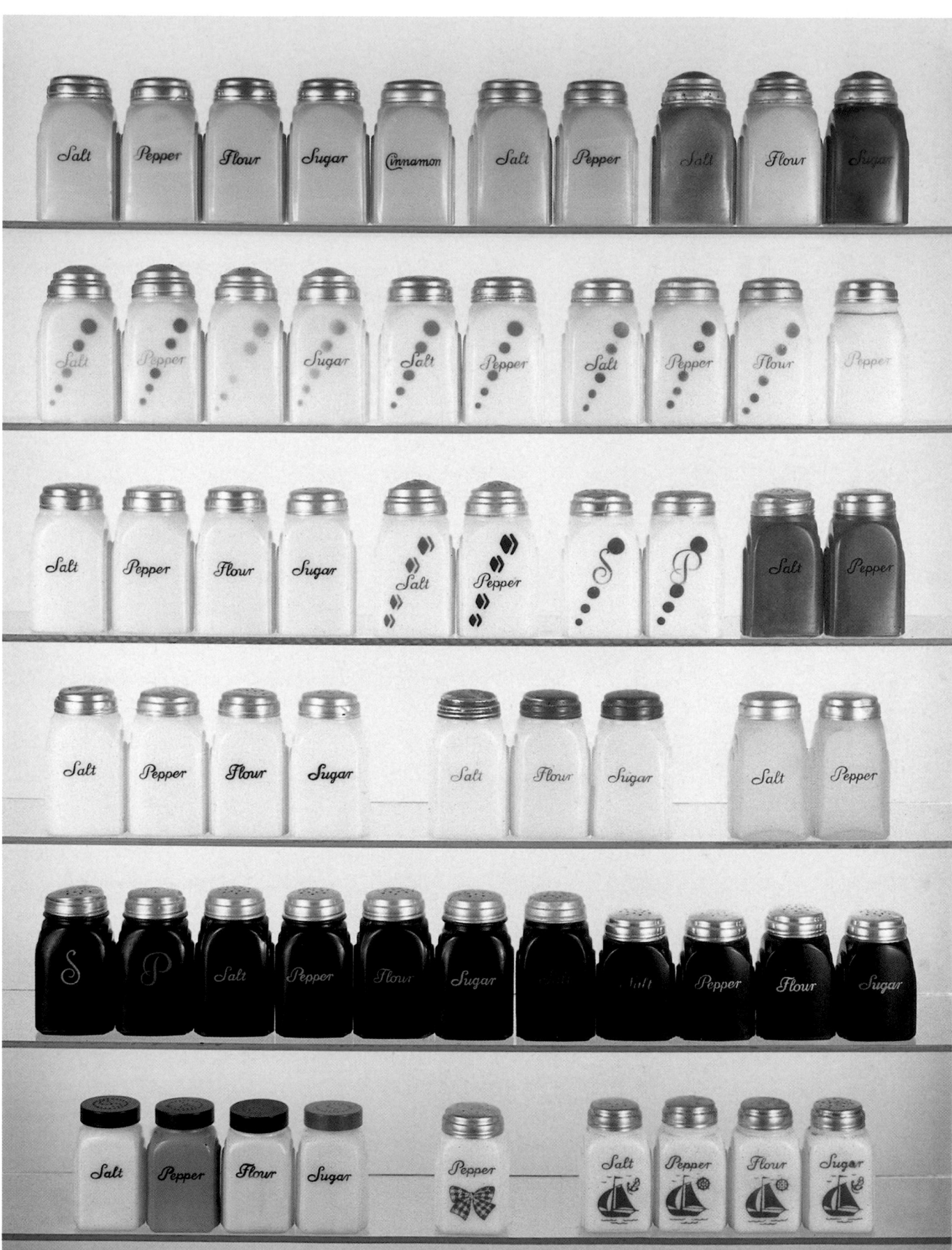

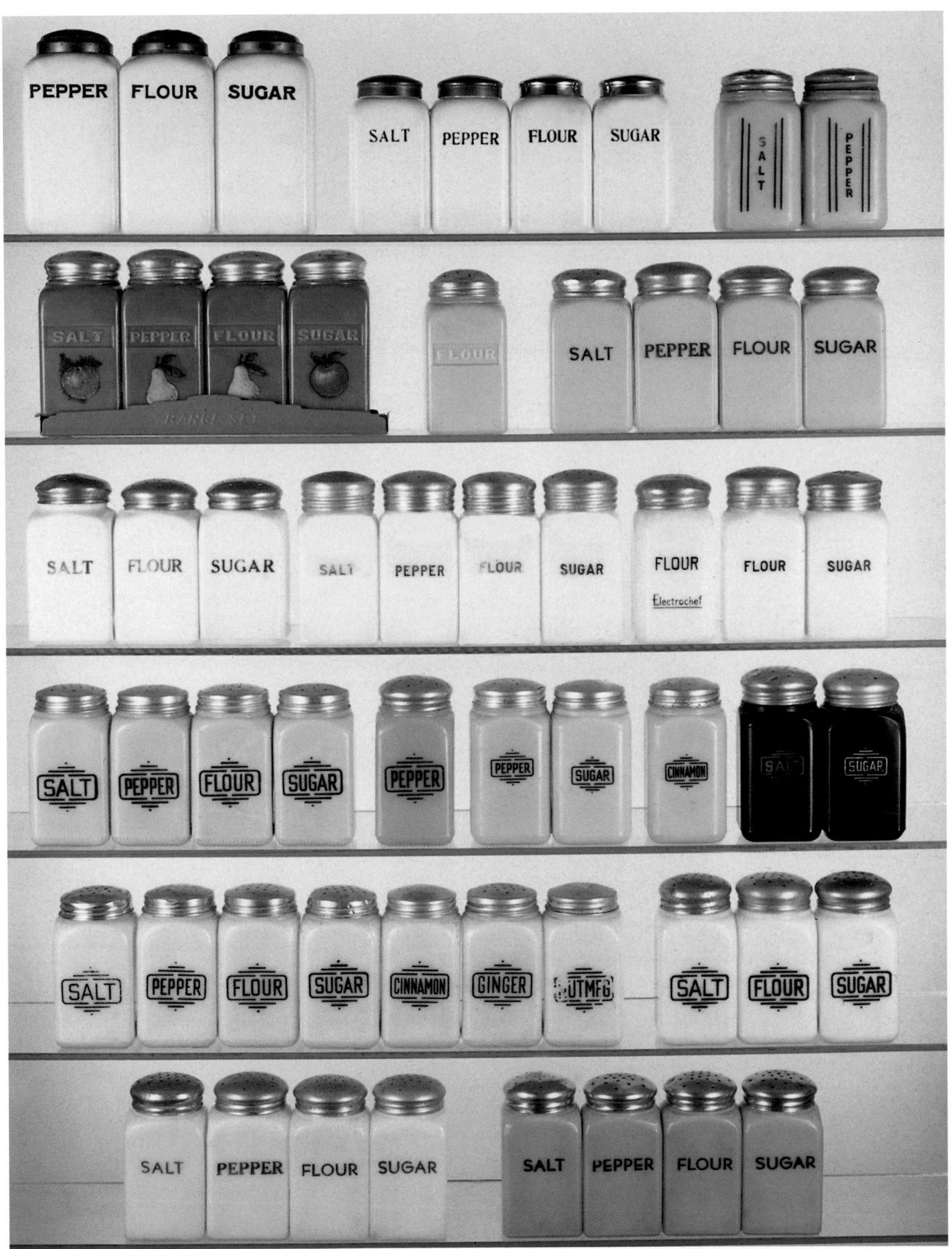

Straw Holders

Unfortunately, the biggest news on straw holders regards reproductions. Beware of any odd colored jars with a diamond design around the base. This design is similar to that on page 253, Row 1, #2. These are being made in pink, an odd shade of green, and cobalt blue at the present. By the time you read this, there may be additional colors. When you see a new metal insert — **beware** — it could be a newly made jar! As with any purchase, know from whom you are buying; if the price seems **too good to be true**, it usually is.

Page 251

Row 1:	#1	Black	725.00 – 750.00
	#2	Green, tall	425.00 – 450.00
	#3	Green, short w/fancy metal base	450.00 – 500.00
	#4,5	Green, short, ea.	400.00 – 425.00
Row 2:	#1-4	Green, short, ea.	400.00 – 425.00
		(Some dealers ask a premium for jointed straw lifters)	
	#5	Pink, Imperial vase (used as straw jar, but is vase)	95.00 – 105.00

Page 252

Row 1:	#1	Cobalt blue, 12" (vase or straw jar?)	225.00 – 275.00
	#2, 3	Crystal Heisey w/top	300.00 – 325.00
	#4	Crystal Heisey "Greek Key" wo/lid (metal lid	175.00 – 195.00
		belongs page 253, Row 1, #2) w/glass lid	350.00 – 425.00
	#5	Pink, Imperial vase (used as straw jar, but is vase)	95.00 – 105.00
Row 2:	#1	Crystal, w/metal base	180.00 – 200.00
	#2	Crystal	110.00 – 125.00
	#3	Green, short	400.00 – 425.00
	#4	Green, short w/fancy metal	450.00 – 500.00
	#5	Crystal, tall	110.00 – 125.00

Page 253

Row 1:	#1	Crystal, "Pattern Glass," zipper design, w/lid	225.00 – 275.00
	#2	Crystal, w/metal base and lid (lid put on Greek	
		Key jar on page 252 by mistake)	180.00 – 200.00
	#3	Emerald Green "Coca Cola"	1,200.00 – 1,500.00
	#4	Crystal knobbed lid (Candlewick collectors notice	
		this first)	145.00 – 165.00
	#5	Crystal, "Pattern Glass," w/lid	250.00 – 275.00
Row 2:	#1	Red, later made, possibly late 1950s/early 1960s	135.00 – 150.00
	#2	Crystal, jointed straw lifter	110.00 – 125.00
	#3	Crystal, named "Manhattan"	190.00 – 200.00
	#4	Crystal, cut design on jar	120.00 – 145.00
	#5	Crystal, zippered design, missing lid	115.00 – 125.00
	#6	Amber, "English Hobnail," vase or straw jar	70.00 – 85.00

Page 250

#1	Cobalt blue	225.00 – 250.00
#2,3	Red, peacock blue	135.00 – 150.00
#4	Blue	175.00 – 200.00
	Amber (not shown)	135.00 – 175.00
#5	Crystal w/painted	
	flowers	100.00 – 125.00
#6	Fostoria American	
	w/lid	265.00 – 295.00

Sugar Shakers

The bullet-shaped sugar shakers with indented dots near the top have been found in McKee catalogs.

Row 3 (Continued):

Kitchen Items

Page 255

Row 1: #1,2 Cambridge, #732, pink   175.00 – 185.00
     (ewer creamer 50.00 – 60.00)
   #3,4 Cambridge #732, green   175.00 – 185.00
     (tall ewer cream 50.00 – 60.00)
   #5 Cambridge, blue   225.00 – 250.00
   #6,7 Cambridge, amber   125.00 – 135.00
     (syrup w/cover 60.00 – 65.00)

Row 2: #1,2 Cambridge, pink   125.00 – 135.00
     (ewer cream 35.00 – 45.00)
   #3 Cambridge, amber, crystal foot
     & glass top   125.00 – 135.00
   #4,5 Same, pink   145.00 – 155.00
     (ewer cream 35.00 – 45.00)
   #6,7 Heisey "Yeoman," pink   95.00 – 125.00
     (cream 30.00 – 35.00);
     (add 10.00 – 15.00 w/glass top)
   #8 Cobalt blue   325.00 – 350.00
   #9 Green, w/green screw-in top 255.00 – 275.00

Row 3: #1,2 Green or pink, footed
     ("Tilt-a-spoon")   350.00 – 375.00
   #3,4 Green, 2 shades, possibly
     Paden City   200.00 – 220.00
   #5 Same, cobalt blue   900.00 – 1,000.00

Row 3 (Continued):
   #6 Same, amber   295.00 – 320.00
   #7 Paden City, pinched in,
     amber   295.00 – 320.00
   #8 Same, green   200.00 – 220.00

Row 4: #1 Green, Hocking   200.00 – 220.00
   #2 Green, Hocking   200.00 – 220.00
   #3 Unknown   145.00 – 165.00
   #4 Green, "Hex Optic"   200.00 – 220.00
   #5 Amber   125.00 – 135.00
   #6 Unknown, pink   175.00 – 195.00
   #7 Pink, w/red top   240.00 – 265.00
   #8 Paden City "Party
     Line," pink   155.00 – 165.00

Row 5: #1 Crystal, Paden City,
     2-part dispenser   20.00 – 25.00
   #2 Crystal, L.E. Smith   65.00 – 75.00
   #3 Crystal, "West Sanitary
     Automatic Sugar"   30.00 – 35.00
   #4,5 Crystal, Hazel-Atlas &
     unknown, ea.   20.00 – 25.00
   #6 Crystal, faintly marked
     "Czechoslovakia"   20.00 – 25.00

Page 256

Row 1: #1 Lancaster Glass Co., "Beehive,"
     green   220.00 – 240.00
   #2-7 "Bullet" shape made by both
     Jeannette & Paden City
   #2,3 Green   220.00 – 240.00
   #4 Yellow   375.00 – 395.00
   #5 Pink   295.00 – 320.00
   #6 Crystal   55.00 – 65.00
   #7 Pink   295.00 – 320.00

Row 2: #1 Blue, "Monroe Mfg. Co., Elgin,
     Ill., Pat Pend." (liquid)   275.00 – 295.00
   #2 Same, pink   200.00 – 225.00
   #3,5 Green   200.00 – 220.00
   #4 Pink   275.00 – 295.00

Row 3: #1,4 Jeannette, light or
     yellowish Jadite   165.00 – 175.00
   #2,5,6 Pink decorated, or pink   125.00 – 135.00
   #3,7,8 Jeannette, green   125.00 – 135.00

Row 4: #1 White "Clambroth"   55.00 – 65.00
   #2,3 Green or pink   50.00 – 55.00
   #4,5 Orange or forest green   125.00 – 135.00
   #6 Red   175.00 – 200.00
   #7 Amber, horseshoe pattern   40.00 – 45.00
   #8 Green, older style   65.00 – 75.00
   #9 Crystal, marked sugar &
     cinnamon   25.00 – 28.00

Page 257

Row 1: #1 "Bullet," ultra-marine   275.00 – 300.00
   #2 Same, crystal   55.00 – 65.00
   #3 Same, emerald green   220.00 – 240.00
   #4 Green   200.00 – 220.00
   #5 Crystal, "Beehive"   65.00 – 75.00
   #6 Crystal, cone   55.00 – 65.00

Row 2: #1 Pink, footed   275.00 – 295.00
   #2 Same, green   200.00 – 220.00
   #3 Same, crystal   30.00 – 35.00
   #4 Same, black   425.00 – 450.00
   #5 Same, SCA   65.00 – 75.00
   #6 Same, amber   275.00 – 295.00

Row 3: #1 Jeannette, dark jade   165.00 – 175.00
   #2 Same, pink   135.00 – 150.00
   #3 Jeannette "Hex Optic," green 200.00 – 220.00
     Same, pink, #300   225.00 – 245.00
   #5 Paden City "Rena," Line 154,
     green   220.00 – 240.00

Row 3 (Continued)
   #6 Same, pink   275.00 – 295.00

Row 4: #1,2 Heisey, pink or green   220.00 – 240.00
   #3 Same, crystal   75.00 – 85.00
   #4 Pink measured teaspoon   250.00 – 295.00
   #5 Crystal   30.00 – 35.00
   #6 Red fired-on   28.00 – 35.00
   #7 Blue   250.00 – 275.00

Row 5: #1 Paden City, "Rena," Line 154,
     individual sugar, crystal   25.00 – 30.00
   #2 Amber, individual sugar   135.00 – 150.00
   #3 Owens-Illinois, forest
     green   25.00 – 30.00
   #4 Green   125.00 – 135.00
   #5 Green, handled (possibly
     Pattern Glass syrup)   150.00 – 160.00
   #6 Crystal, decorated w/flowers 15.00 – 20.00
   #7 Blue, marked "Made in
     Japan" (New!)   10.00 – 15.00

Kitchen Items

Syrup Pitchers

I've often remarked on the fact that many Depression Glass collectors are "item" collectors; however, the number of people I'm encountering in my travels who collect only syrup pitchers is amazing even to me. Somewhere in the course of their conversation, they generally speak of what attractive displays the pieces make in their homes and how fascinating they find the various shapes. I particularly remember one man, a farmer, who seemed rather shy and hesitant until he began speaking of his interest in syrup pitchers. His weathered face, eyes, and voice suddenly were transformed into the soft, glowing enthusiasm of a connoisseur. Depression glass...the stuff dreams are made of?

Kitchen Items

Page 259

Row 1:	#1	Hazel-Atlas, pink	65.00 – 75.00
		Same, green (not shown)	50.00 – 60.00
	#2	Pink	65.00 – 75.00
	#3	Federal, crystal	18.00 – 22.00
	#4	Crystal, flat, flip-up lid	18.00 – 22.00
	#5,6	Imperial, slotted lids, pink	75.00 – 85.00
		Crystal	40.00 – 45.00
Row 2:	#1	Cambridge "Tally Ho" amber	55.00 – 65.00
	#2	Cambridge etched, w/underplate, pink	75.00 – 80.00
	#3	Cambridge amber	60.00 – 65.00
	#4	Crystal	35.00 – 40.00
	#5, 6	Fostoria yellow, Mayfair	65.00 – 70.00
		Same, green	65.00 – 75.00
Row 3:	#1-6	All Paden City, green	50.00 – 55.00
		Same, pink	65.00 – 75.00
		"Party Line," green	50.00 – 55.00
		Same, amber	50.00 – 55.00
		Same, pink	50.00 – 55.00
		Amber, w/underplate	55.00 – 60.00
	#7	Green	50.00 – 55.00
Row 4:	#1	Paden City, green w/underplate	65.00 – 75.00
	#2	Paden City, green	50.00 – 55.00
	#3	Paden City, pink	65.00 – 75.00
	#4	Green	50.00 – 55.00
	#5	Crystal	25.00 – 28.00
	#6	Pink	65.00 – 70.00
	#7	Green swirl design	50.00 – 55.00
Row 5:	#1	All Heisey row: Crystal, ea.	50.00 – 55.00
	#2	Yellow (Sahara)	75.00 – 85.00
	#3	Green (Moongleam)	75.00 – 85.00
	#4	Crystal	50.00 – 55.00
	#5	Pink (Flamingo)	75.00 – 85.00
	#6,7	Crystal, ea.	35.00 – 40.00
Row 6:	#1	Crystal	20.00 – 22.00
	#2	Crystal, Bakelite handle	15.00 – 18.00
	#3-5	Crystal, ea.	25.00 – 28.00
	#6	Crystal, Bakelite handle	15.00 – 18.00
	#7	Crystal, Ball jar, Bakelite handle	15.00 – 18.00

259

As with many of the other item collections, the major glass companies' syrup pitchers are noticed first.

Kitchen Items

Page 261

Row 1:	#1	Cambridge, w/cover, amber	60.00 – 65.00
	#2	Same, green	70.00 – 75.00
	#3	Paden City, green	50.00 – 55.00
	#4	Imperial, w/slotted lid, pink	75.00 – 85.00
	#5	Same, amber	70.00 – 75.00
Row 2:	#1	Amber/yellow combination w/glass lid	60.00 – 65.00
	#2	Pink w/green knob, handle & pink underliner	85.00 – 95.00
	#3	Duncan & Miller "Caribbean," blue	225.00 – 250.00
	#4	Same, crystal	95.00 – 100.00
	#5	Cambridge, amber	55.00 – 60.00
Row 3:	#1, 2	Fostoria "Mayfair," green or pink w/underliner	65.00 – 75.00
	#3	Fostoria "Chintz"	400.00 – 450.00
	#4	Fostoria, "Mayfair," yellow w/underliner	65.00 – 75.00
	#5	Same, amber	60.00 – 65.00
Row 4:	#1	Pink	50.00 – 55.00
	#2	Green w/liner	55.00 – 60.00
	#3	Imperial, pink	55.00 – 60.00
	#4	Imperial, pink w/floral cutting	55.00 – 60.00
	#5	Same, green, plain	55.00 – 60.00
Row 5:	#1	Paden City #198, 8 oz., amber	50.00 – 55.00
	#2	Same, green	50.00 – 55.00
	#3	Same, pink	50.00 – 55.00
	#4	Paden City "Party Line," green	50.00 – 55.00
	#5	Same, pink	50.00 – 55.00
	#6	Paden City #198, 12 oz. green w/liner	60.00 – 65.00

Water Bottles

There are many types of water containers shown throughout this book. People tend to think of plastic jugs as water containers today. Water bottles have gone the way of ice boxes which is where most of these were originally used.

Page 263

Row 1:	#1	"Water Falls"	25.00 – 30.00
	#2	"Water"	18.00 – 20.00
	#3	"G.E." shows old refrigerator	25.00 – 30.00
	#4	"Well," amber	65.00 – 75.00
	#5	"Ships"	25.00 – 30.00
Row 2:	#1	Owens-Illinois "Juice" on one side & "Water" on other	12.00 – 18.00
	#2	Forest green "Penguin"	30.00 – 35.00
	#3	Lattice design w/lid	50.00 – 60.00
	#4	Hocking "Royal Ruby"	225.00 – 250.00
	#5	"G.E." round	15.00 – 18.00
Row 3:	#1	"Crisscross," crystal, 32 oz.	35.00 – 40.00
	#2	"The Well Informed Choose Ice Refrigeration"	15.00 – 18.00
	#3	"Beveragette," Pat. 1919	20.00 – 25.00
	#4	Cobalt blue, 64 oz., 10" tall	60.00 – 75.00
	#5	Same, 32 oz.	60.00 – 75.00

Page 264

Row 1:	#1	L.E. Smith cobalt blue water dispenser	400.00 – 450.00
	#2	Same, light blue; crystal (not shown, 150.00 – 175.00)	400.00 – 450.00
	#3	McKee white dispenser	150.00 – 165.00
Row 2:	#1	McKee Jade Green dispenser, 5¼" tall, gal., "Deluxe"	325.00 – 350.00
	#2	McKee Jade Green dispenser	225.00 – 250.00
	#3	McKee custard dispenser	165.00 – 195.00
Row 3:	#1	McKee w/Jade Green top	225.00 – 250.00
	#2	Sneath Glass Co. green clambroth w/crystal top	145.00 – 165.00
	#3	Water dispenser, Jade Green top	95.00 – 125.00

Page 265

Row 1:	#1	Cambridge cobalt blue Thermos	400.00 – 425.00
	#2	Same, amethyst	375.00 – 400.00
	#3	Thermos	15.00 – 20.00
	#4,	Ice box water bottle	18.00 – 20.00
Row 2:	#1	Georgian ice bucket	40.00 – 45.00
	#2	Ice bucket w/metal drainer	45.00 – 50.00
	#3	Pink flared rim ice bucket	50.00 – 55.00
	#4	Pink elephant ice bucket	35.00 – 40.00
	#5	Frosted and striped ice bucket	35.00 – 40.00
Row 3:	#1	Metallic finish ice bucket	18.00 – 20.00
	#2	Cambridge cobalt blue ice bucket	150.00 – 165.00
	#3,5	Hocking Royal Ruby ribbed or plain water w/lid, ea.	225.00 – 250.00
	#4	Black amethyst ice bucket	60.00 – 65.00

Kitchen Items

Reproductions

REPRODUCTIONS — BARNES REAMERS

The picture on page 267 and the lists below show the colors of Barnes marked reamers that were issued as of March 2001. THESE ARE LIMITED EDITION REAMERS. They are becoming collectible in their own right. Some colors are sold out and are selling above the issue price. Additional colors have been made, but are not pictured. They are pink carnival, milk blue, opal blue, opal pink, amethyst, opal crystal, emerald (dark green), white (pink rosebuds on stem), rose, Jadite, Delphite, and red carnival.

Page 267

Rows 1-3: See pages 200 – 201 for original colors. Both the top (inside cone) and the bottom (on the base) are marked with a **B** in a circle. A few of the cobalt blue are marked with an N and not a B, so be aware of that. These will be listed in the order they were made. (Some are satinized or frosted.)

#1 Cobalt	Row 1, #1	#12 Pink carnival (not shown)
#2 Rubina	Row 2, #3	#13 Milk blue (not shown)
#3 Vaseline & frosted	Row 1, #2, 3	#14 Opal blue (not shown)
#4 Black	Row 3, #1	#15 Opal pink (not shown)
#5 Apple green & frosted	Row 2, #1, 2	#16 Amethyst (not shown)
#6 Cranberry Ice & frosted	Row 1, #4, 5	#17 Opal crystal (not shown)
#7 Gold & frosted	Row 2, #4, 5	#18 Emerald (dark green) (not shown)
#8 Blue Bell & frosted	Row 3, #2, 3	#19 White (pink rosebuds on stem) (not shown)
#9 White Milk & painted blue & painted pink flowers also	Row 3, #4, 5	#19 Rose (not shown)
#10 Aqua & frosted (not shown)		#20 Jadite (not shown)
#11 Red (not shown)		#21 Delphite (not shown)
		#22 Red carnival (not shown)

Rows 4-7: Show Barnes reamers which are called 5" and 2½", but really measure 4¾" and 2¼". There is a **B** in a circle on the tab handle of both sizes. Some of these have also been frosted.

Row 4: Heatherbloom, Custard, Green Carnival, Forest Green
Row 5: Cobalt, Sapphire, Harvest Swirl
Row 6: Cranberry Ice, Gold, Pink Rosemarie
Row 7: Red Glow, Depression Green, Chocolate
Not shown: Milk Blue, Jadite

Pictured here are samples of Jadite items being reproduced in China. These are sold in Cracker Barrel and other stores and through various catalogs.

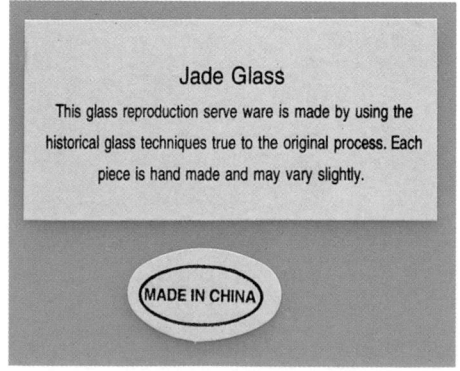

Jade Glass

This glass reproduction serve ware is made by using the historical glass techniques true to the original process. Each piece is hand made and may vary slightly.

MADE IN CHINA

The original measuring pitchers in white or green are shown on page 169. Any other colors including cobalt blue pictured are new. Note the bold stippling on the white and very light stippling on the cobalt blue. Measurements on the cobalt blue are inaccurate; note how the marking is on the very first line on pitcher.

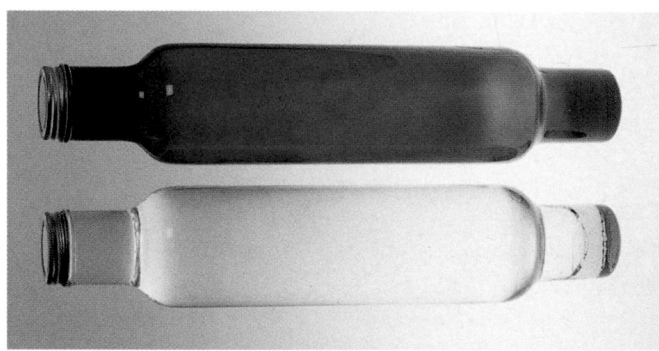

Transparent screw-on rolling pins originally were not made in color.

Both ¼ pound and pound Crisscross butters have been made in cobalt blue. Be aware that these are almost exact reproductions. Differences are minute. You need to know the dealer from whom you are purchasing them. If there is no wear on the bottom or other places, **BUYER BEWARE!**

See descriptions for this pitcher on page 269, Row 1, #4 and #5.

When I wrote the earlier editions of *Kitchen Glassware,* there were only a few kitchenware items to report as reproductions. With the demise of Westmoreland Glass Company and the sale of their glass moulds, a whole new world of reproductions appeared. I will approach each item shown on pages 269 and 270 separately. These are all new! If you wish to purchase any of these, you need to realize that the price for newly made items is determined by seller demand and what the buyer is willing to pay. There is little structured market price, especially on the "foreign" made "rip-offs."

Do not be surprised at any color appearing in these items whether it is pictured or not! Know your dealer if you do not know the merchandise! Subscribe to a national trade paper to keep abreast of the latest happenings. See reproductions on www.glassshow.com

Row 1: #1-3 – Westmoreland reamer pitchers w/oranges and lemons were made by Summit Art Glass in colors of black, "Moonlight" blue, cobalt blue, and "vaseline." Original moulds were used **(only pink, green, and crystal were made originally)**. See page 219. Today other colors are being made by Mosser Glass Co. Additional colors are red, red carnival, French opal, chocolate, chocolate carnival, Delphite, Jadite, and crown tuscan.

Row 1: #4, 5 – Hazel-Atlas 2 cup reamer being made in the Far East (Taiwan) in green, cobalt blue, and pink. THIS IS A MAJOR PROBLEM! Even reamer collectors are having difficulty with this one. The green is easily seen by the horrible color; the pink and blue are fairly true to the originals. **They are good copies!** The repros all have an oily slick feel and are slightly heavier than the older ones. The repros are grainy and lettering on the sides is slightly different. The spouts on the new ones protrude sharply. However, it is impossible to tell you **one** sure way to distinguish the old from the new in words so you can feel safe in buying these. I can only emphasize that you know who you are dealing with, and if the price seems too reasonable for an expensive piece, then there might be a good reason to refrain from buying. **BUYER BEWARE!**

Row 2: #1-4 – Easley pat. July 10 1888, Sept 10, 1888. Never made in color originally. Original crystal sells $12.00 – 15.00.

Row 2: #5 – Hazel-Atlas cobalt blue three spout, one cup measuring cup made in Taiwan. Spouts are not smoothly made, but it is a good copy. Measurements on the side are inaccurate.

Row 2: #6 – Hazel-Atlas "Kellogg's" embossed cup was made in green and pink in Taiwan. Major difference is on the number 4 in 4 oz. measurement on side. In old, line forming 4 crosses in **middle** of 4 while on new, the perpendicular line crosses ¾ of the way down the 4. Measurements on the side are inaccurate.

Row 1: #1-5 – Gillespie cup w/reamer top made by Summit Art Glass and now being made at Mosser Glass Co. Cup was never made in color and originally had a measure top instead of reamer top.

Row 1: #6, 7 – Dry measure w/reamer top made by Summit Art Glass but heretofore unknown.

Row 2: #1, 2 – Hazel-Atlas shakers (salt and pepper) made in Taiwan. Not made originally in cobalt blue. Pink quality varies greatly as do designs. Stippling effect behind embossed salt or pepper is very pronounced on new. New tops are punched in circular pattern.

Row 2: #3 – Fostoria "Colony-like" two spout reamer made only in white and crystal originally.

Row 2: #4-7 – Duboe Pat. July 24, 1917, made by Summit and copied without markings in Taiwan. Never made in color originally and sells $40.00 – 50.00 in crystal.

Row 3: #1-4 – Made by Summit Art Glass and now by Mosser Glass Co. from Westmoreland mould. Original colors are shown on page 219 in Rows 3-5 – All additional colors are NEW!

Row 4: #1, 3 – Same as dry measures in *Row 1,* #6, 7 but spout pulled to make measure cup.

Row 4: #2 – Possible Westmoreland cup, footed and spouted, and made by Summit in black.

Row 4: #4 – Same as Row 1 without reamer top.

Row 4: #5, 6 – Cobalt blue and black made for Barnes by Imperial in 1981. (Marked IG 81)

OTHER BOOKS BY GENE FLORENCE

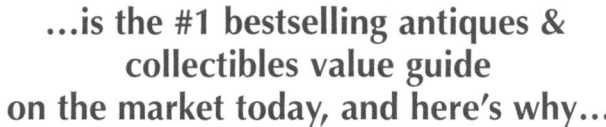